?

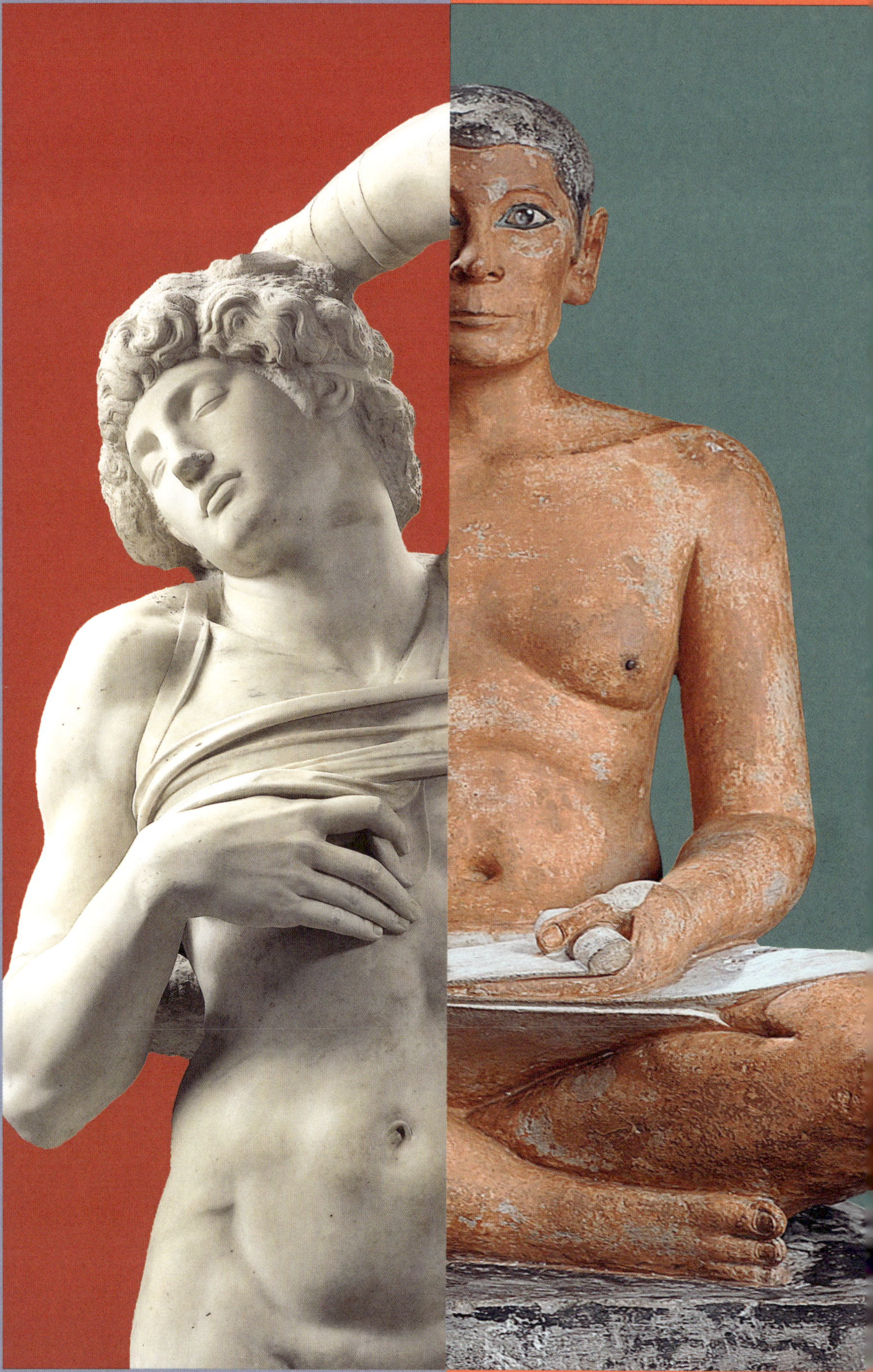

Why Is It Famous?

The Incredible Journey
of the Louvre's Icons

Vincent Brocvielle

LOUVRE

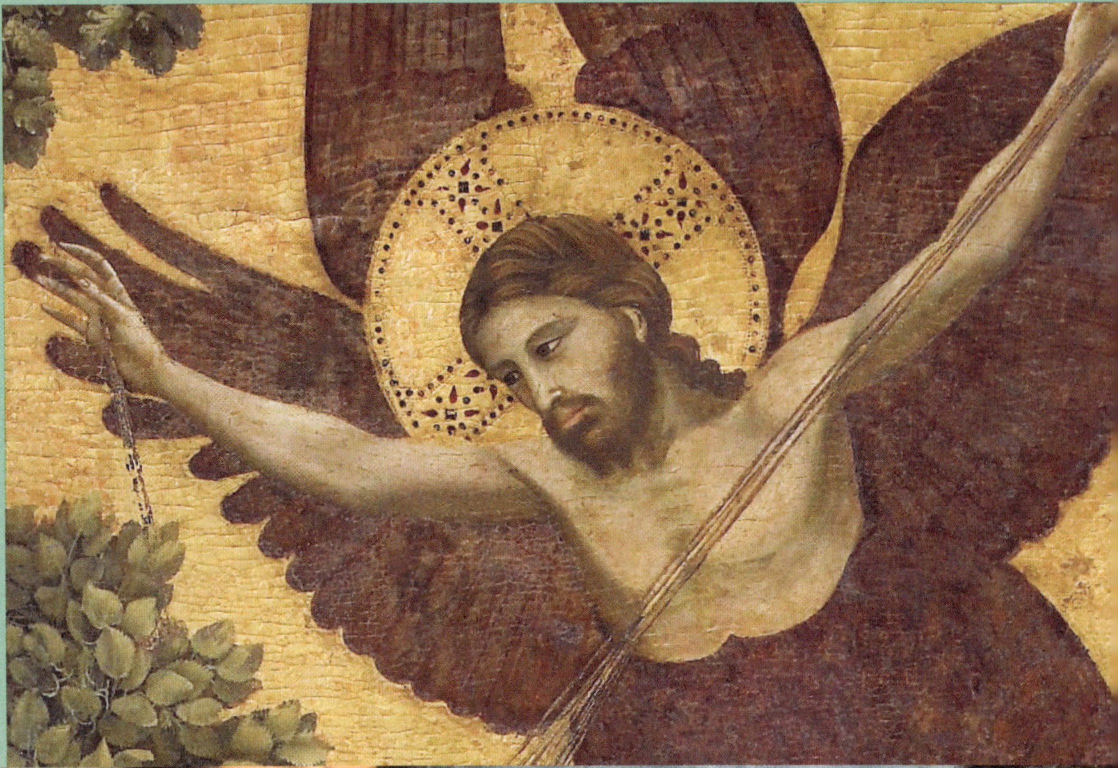

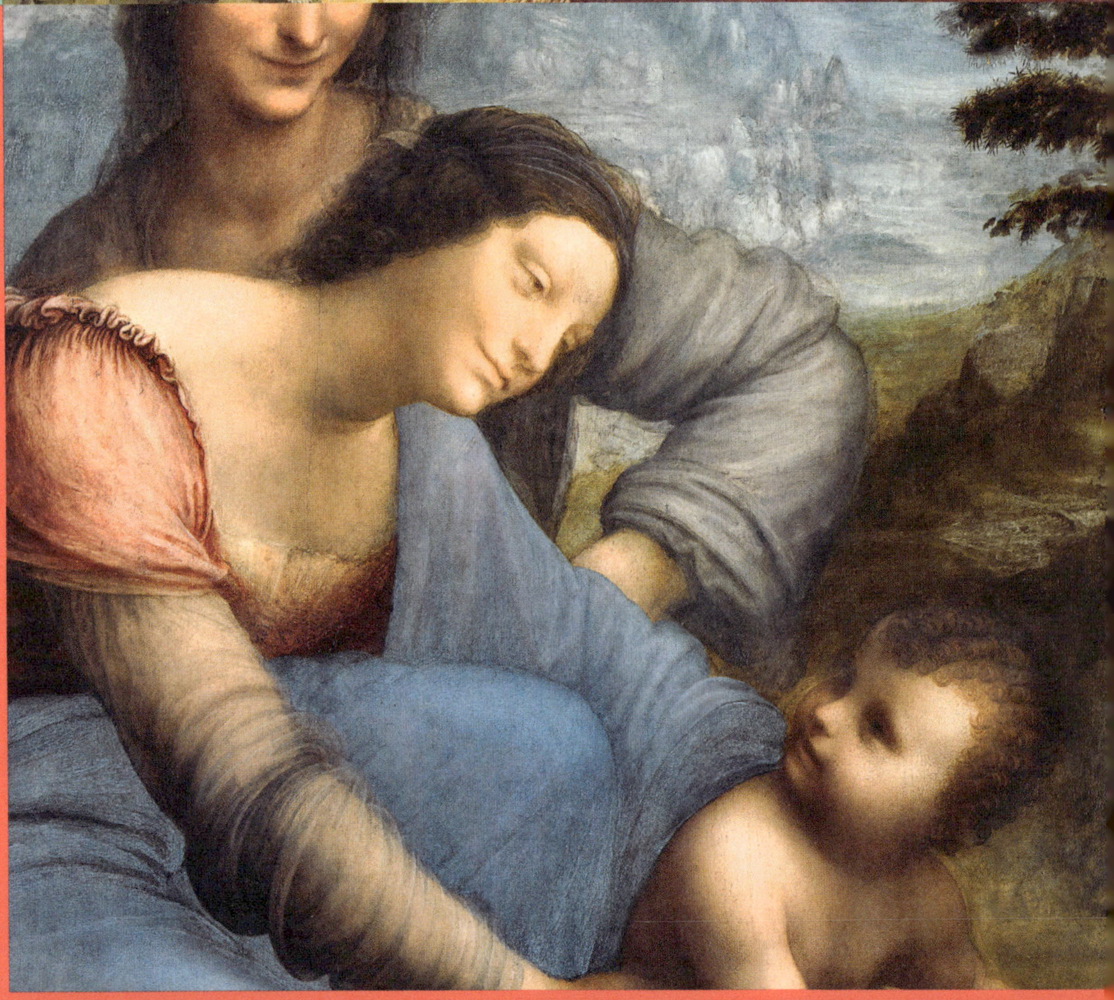

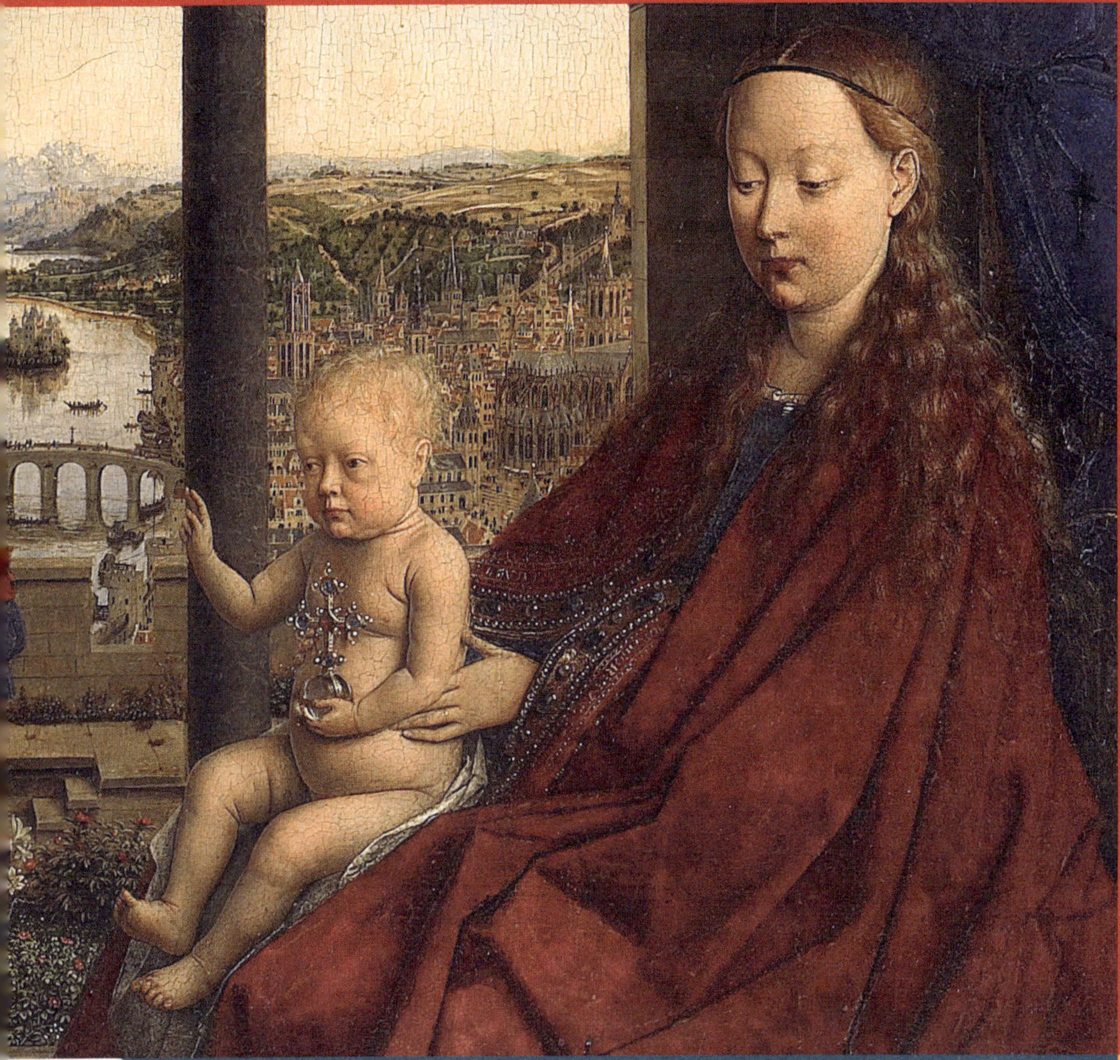
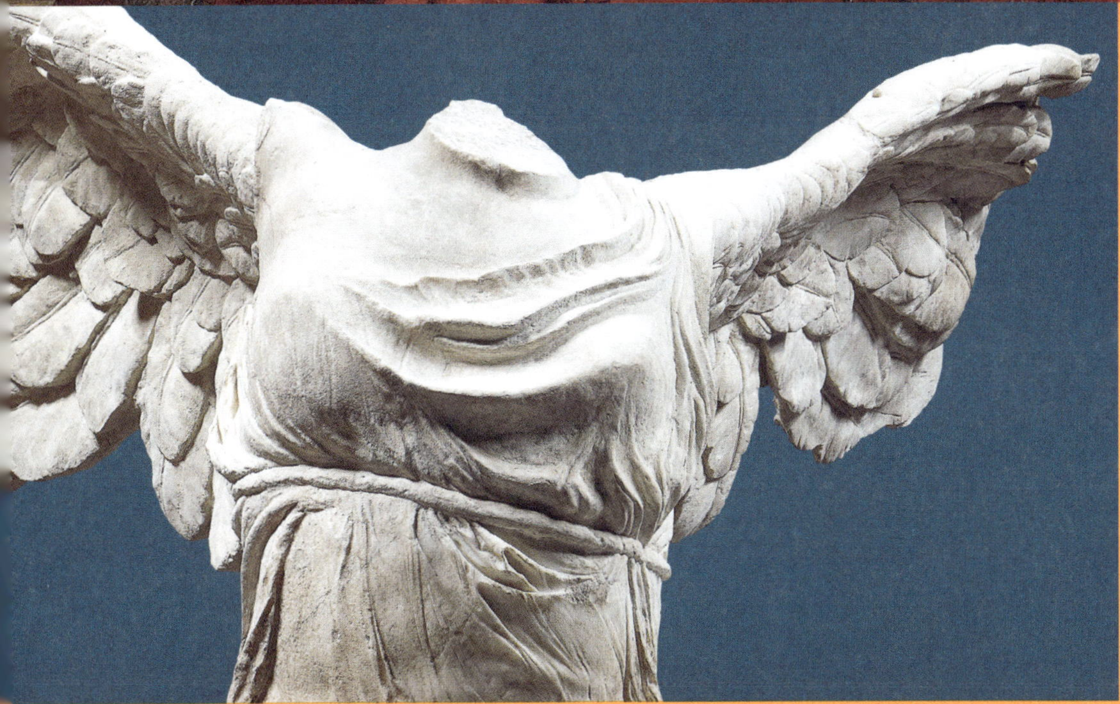

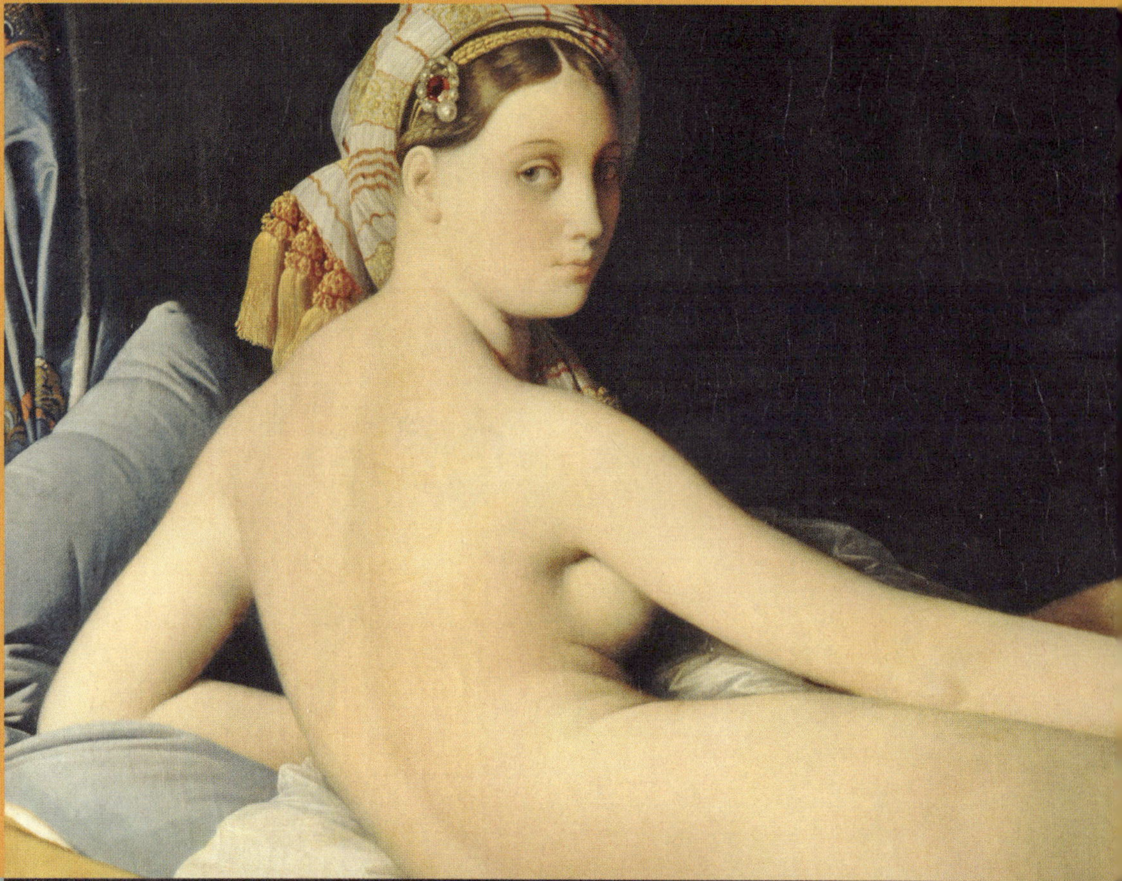

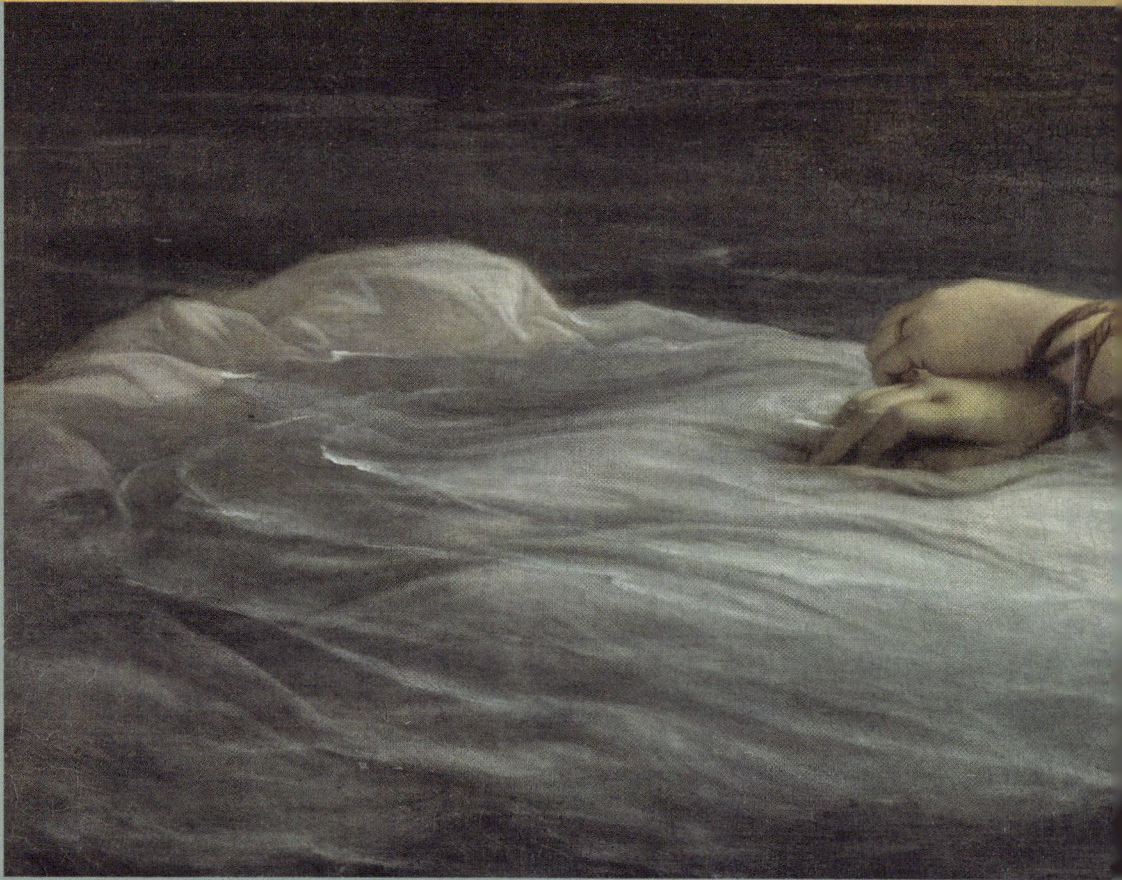

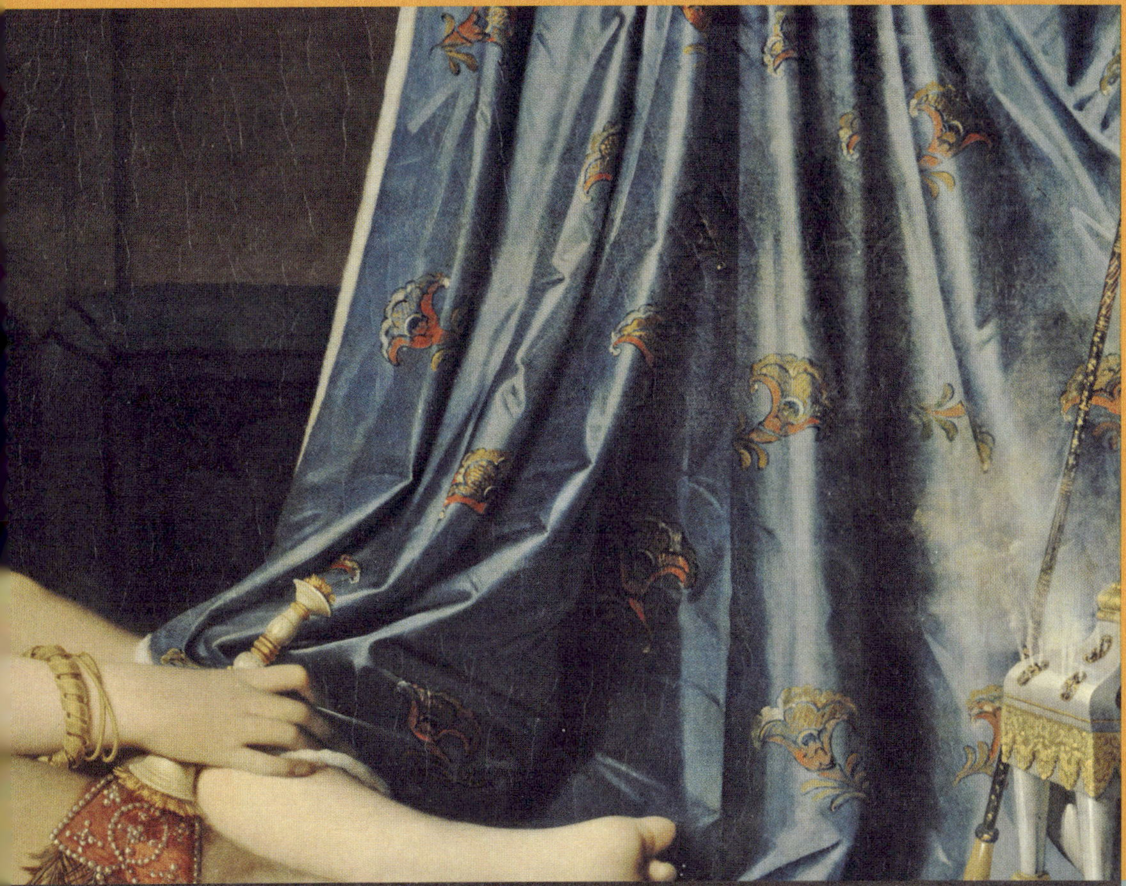

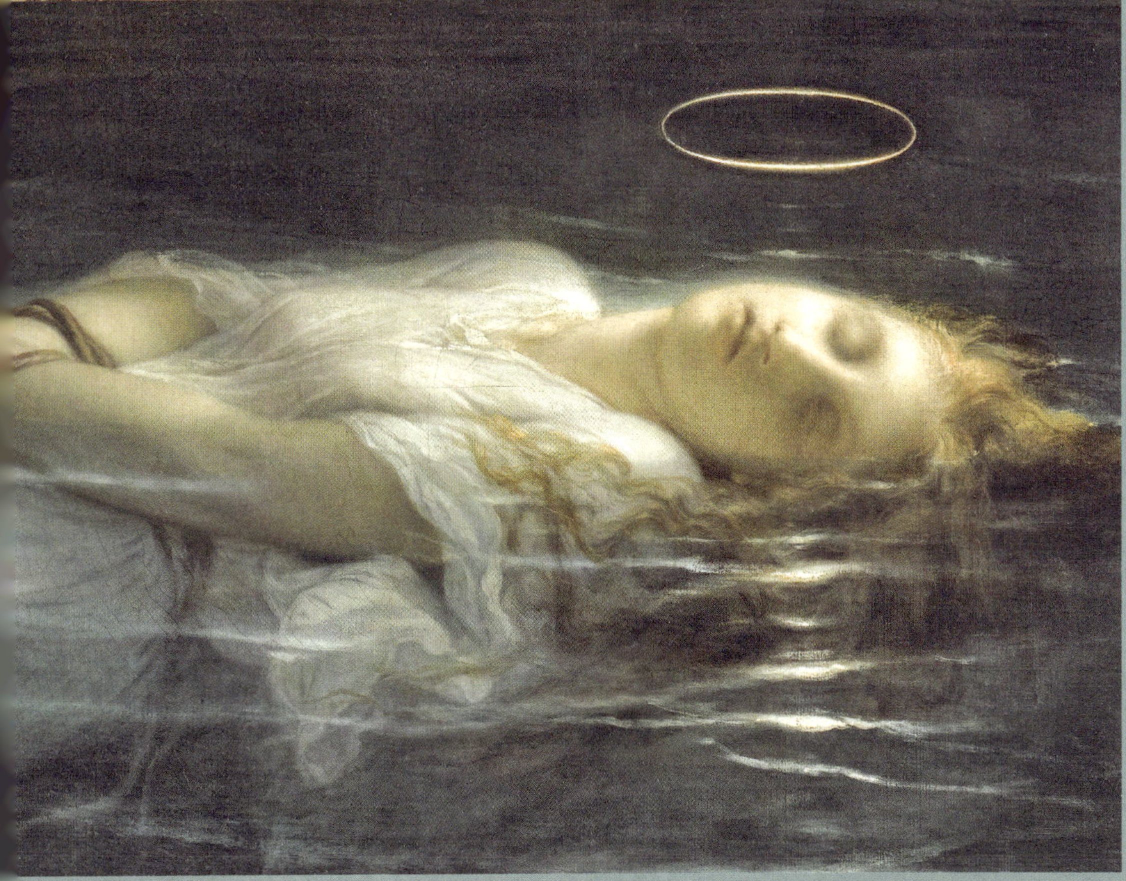

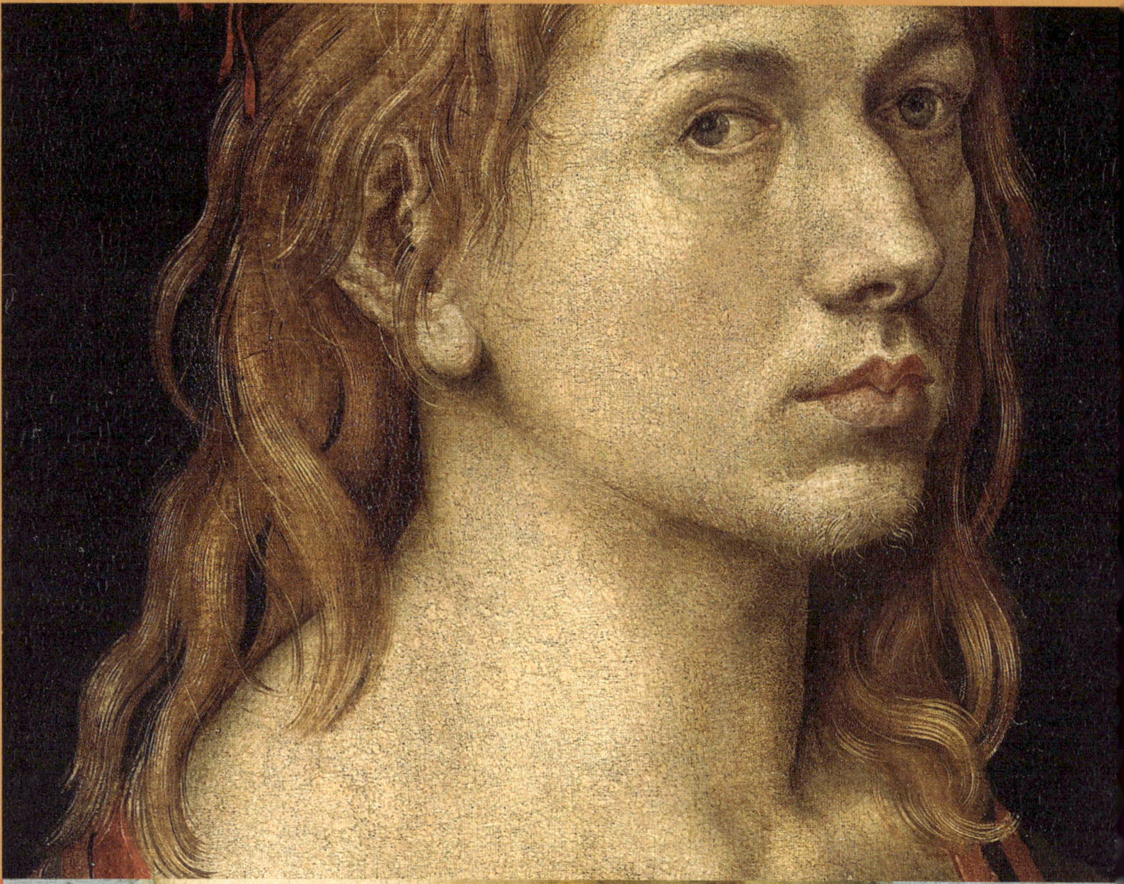

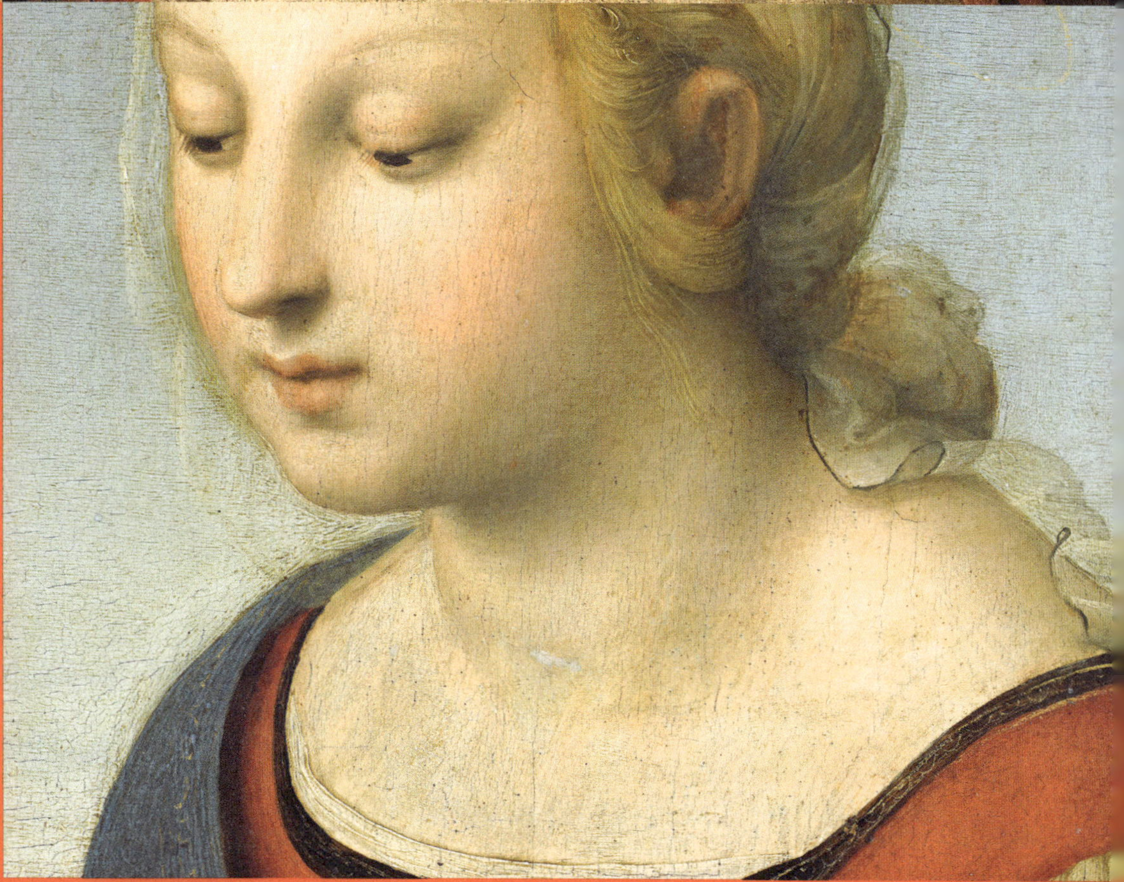

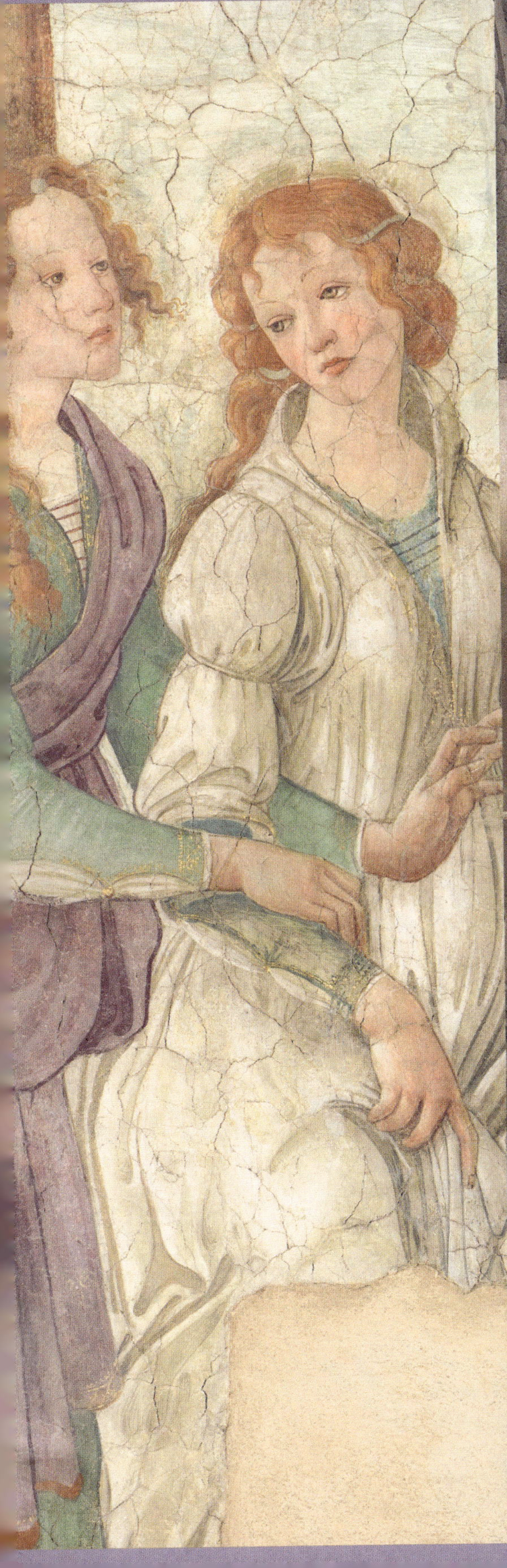
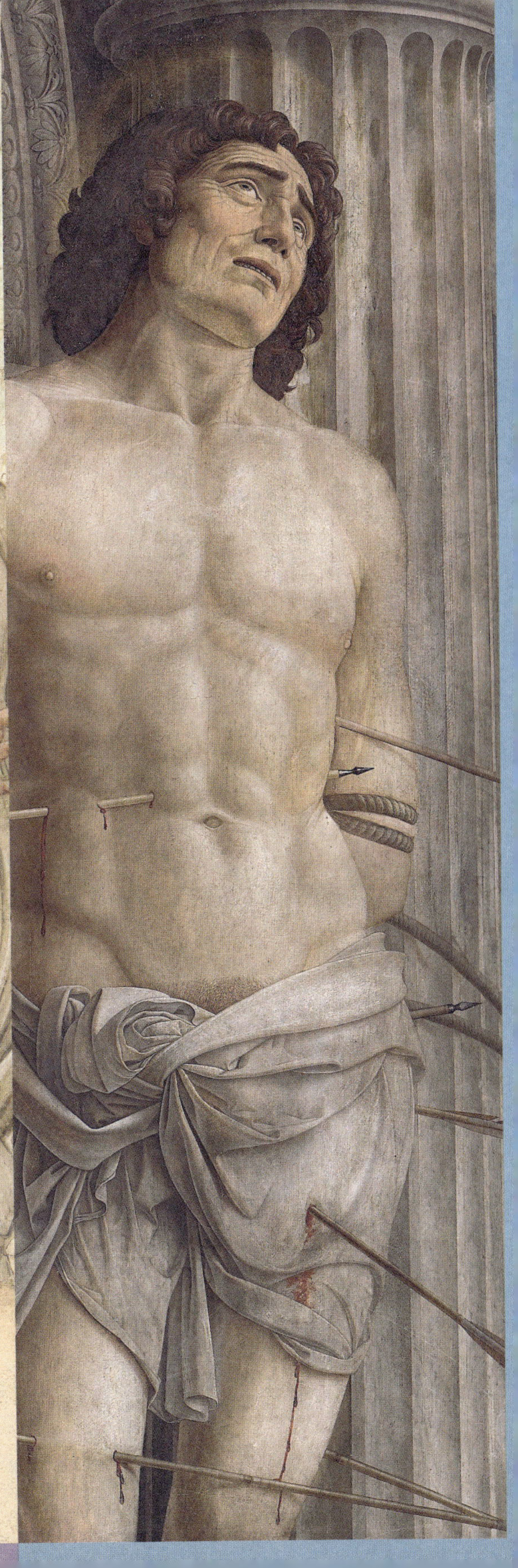

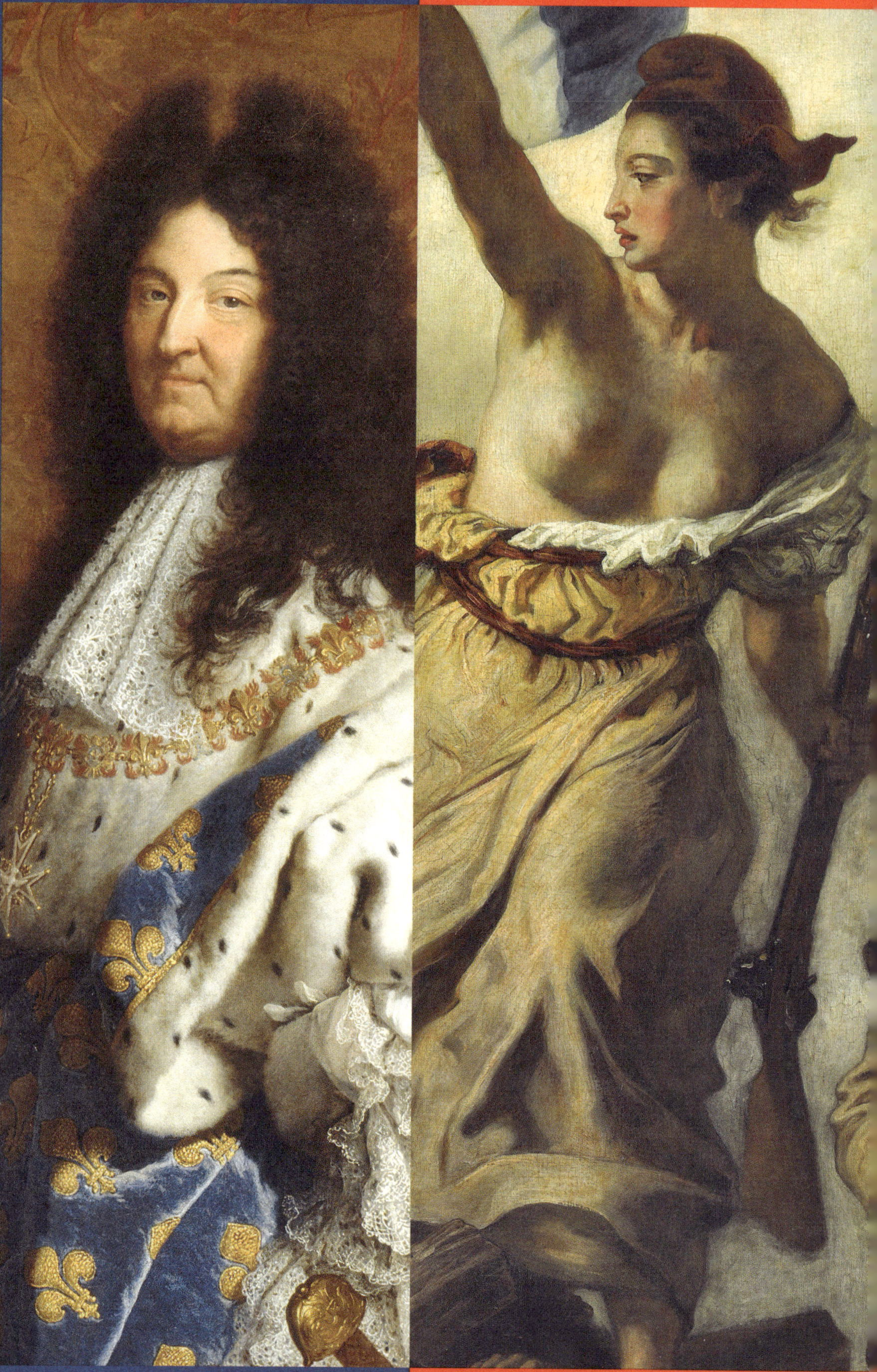

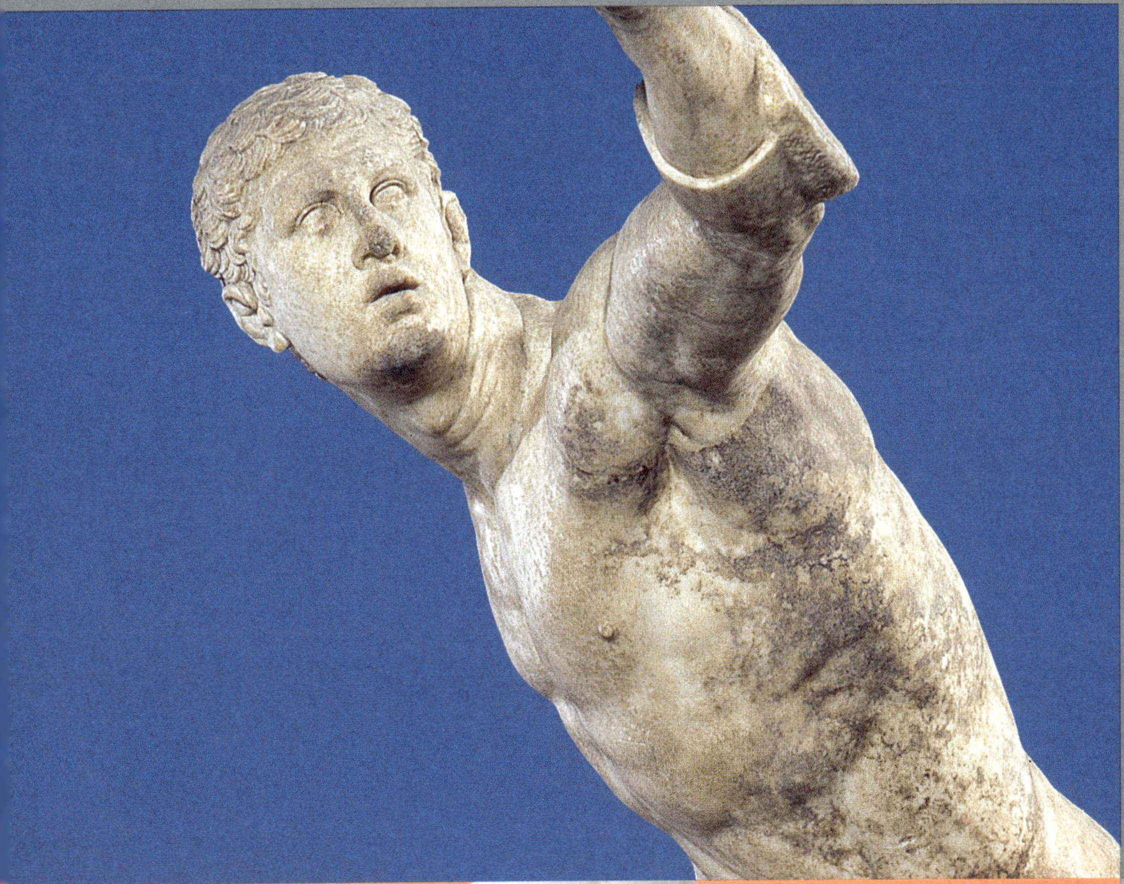
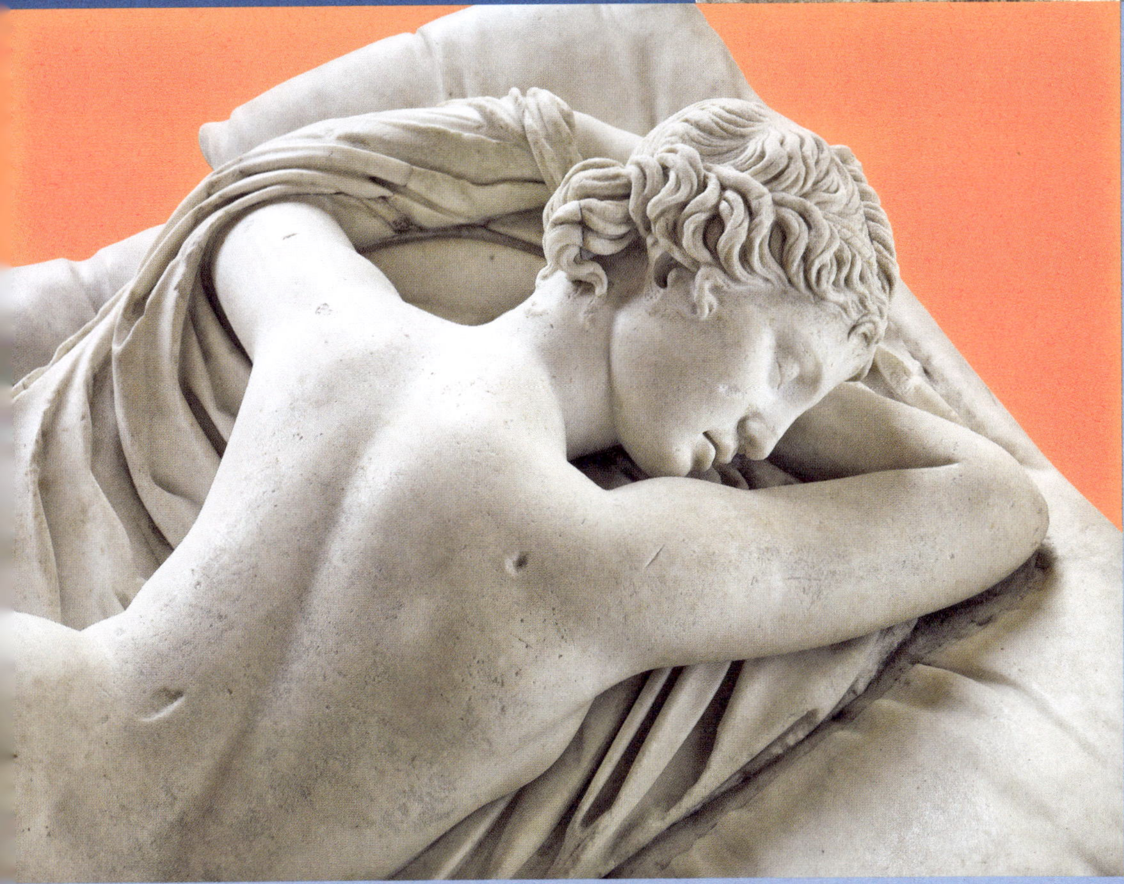

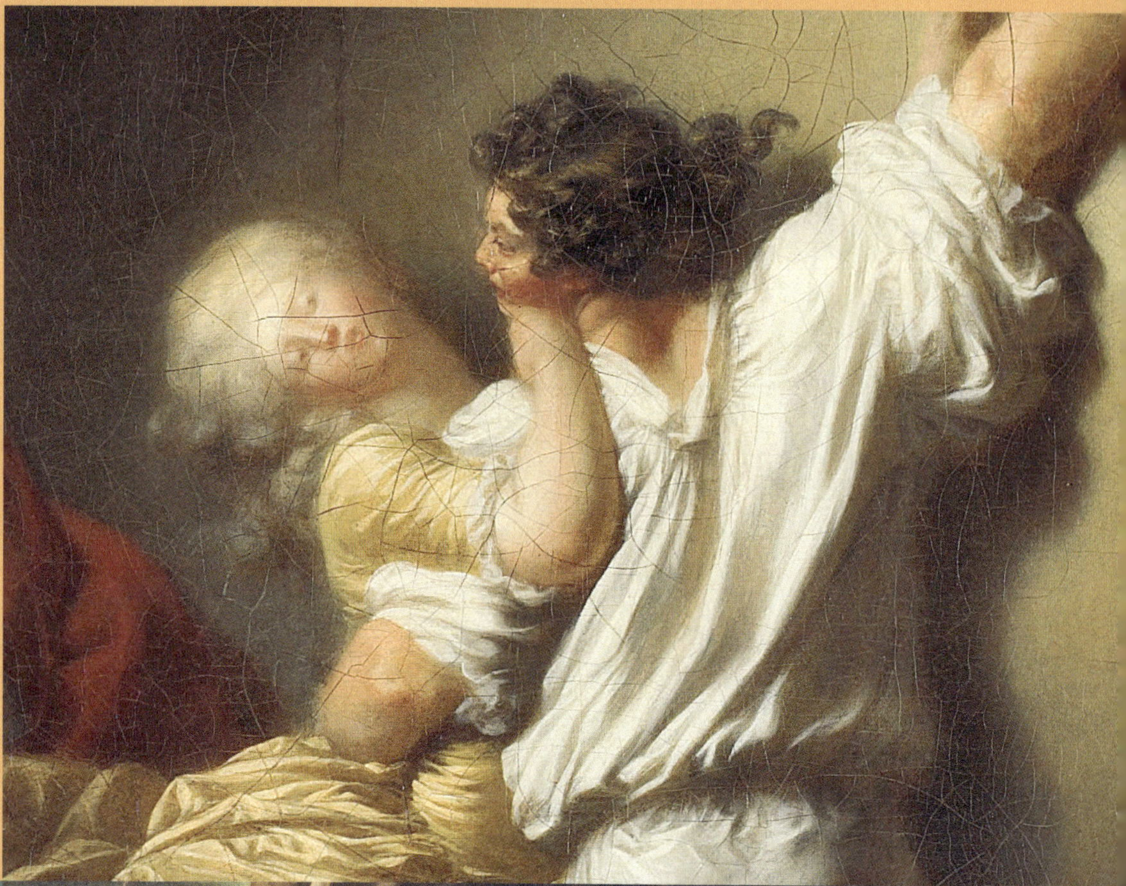

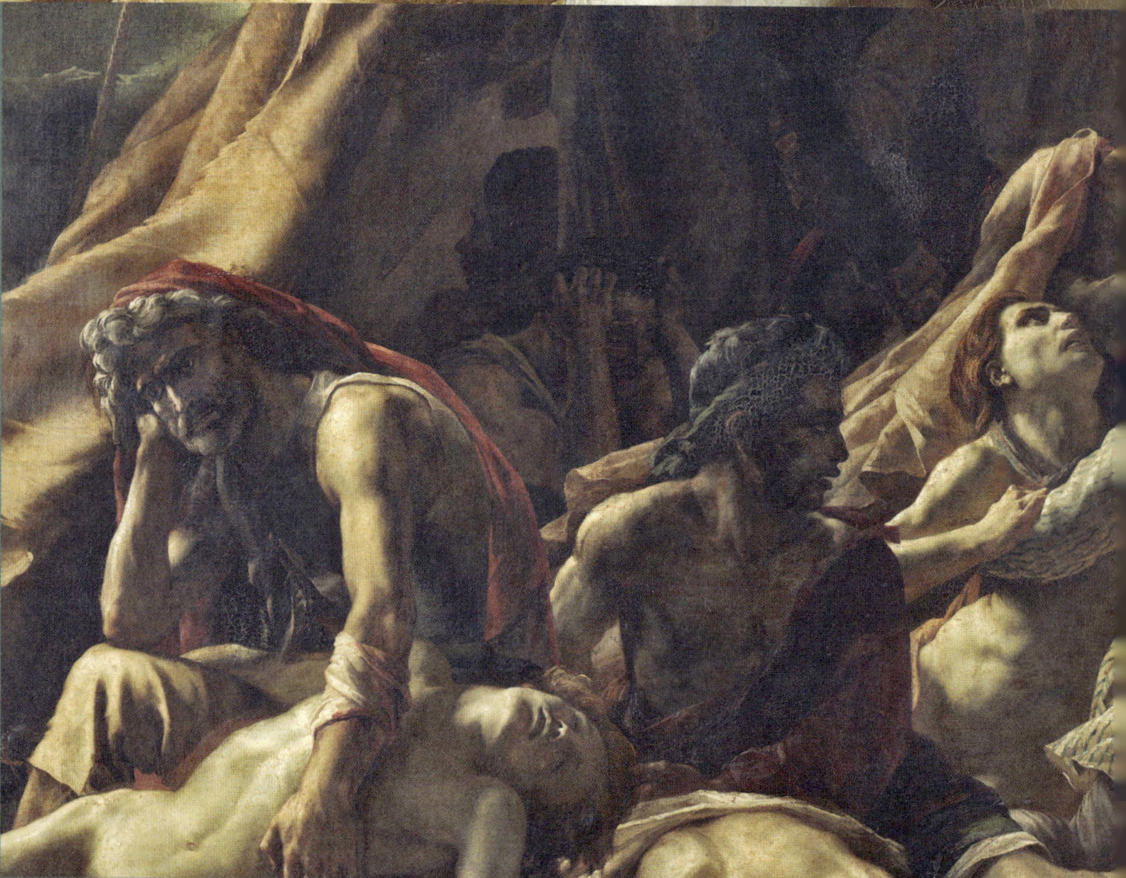

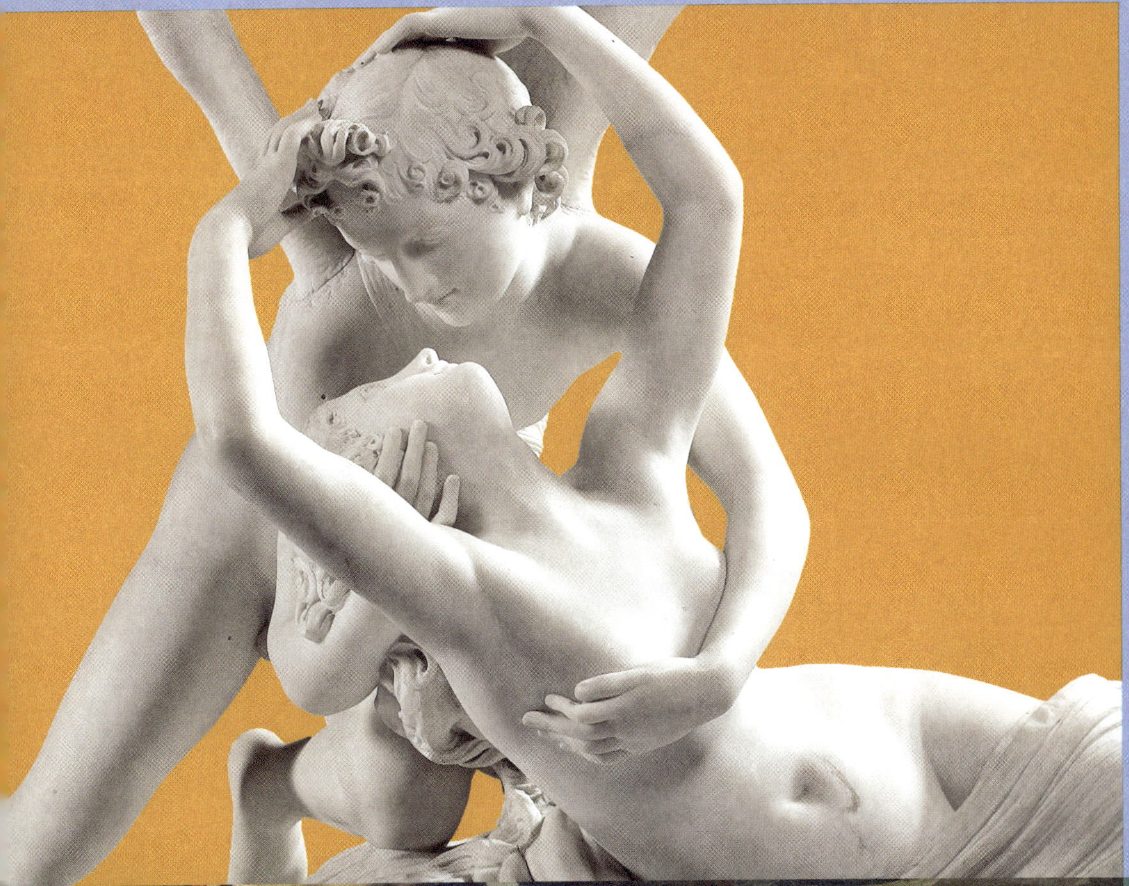
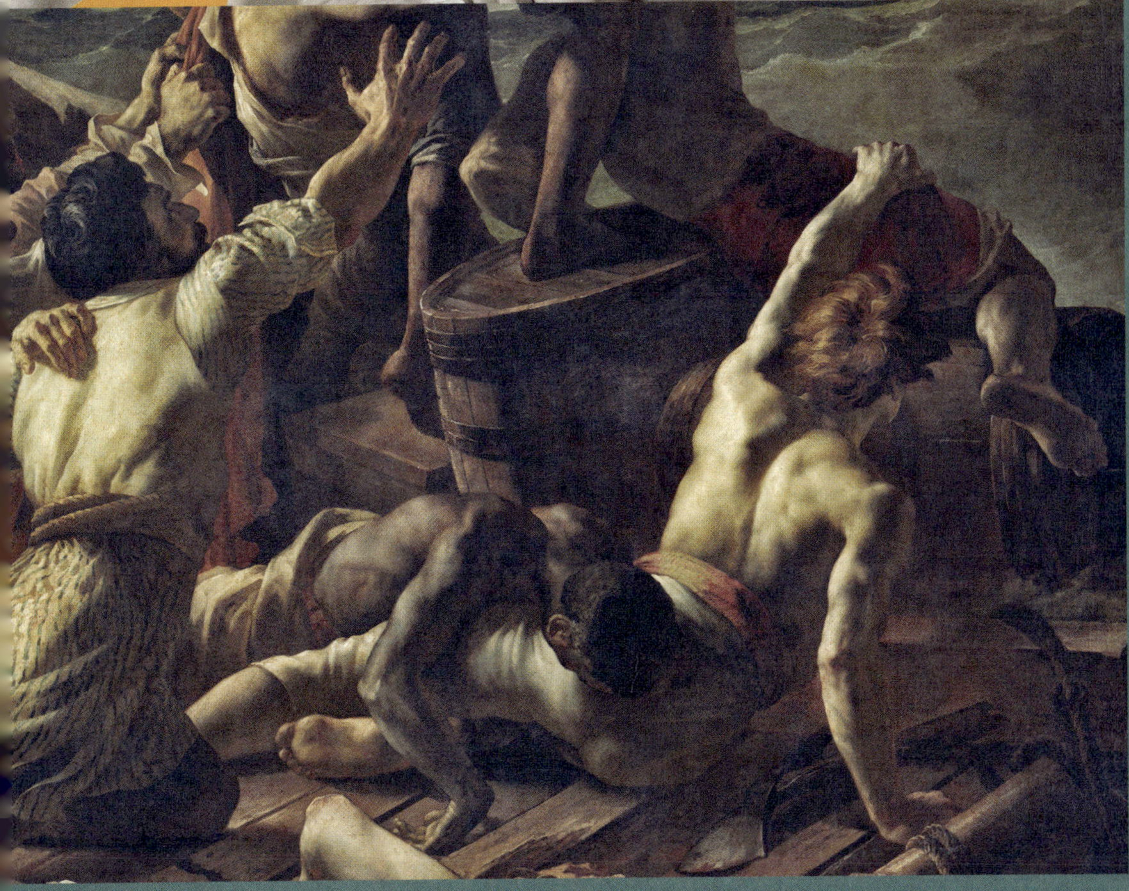

Why is it ...

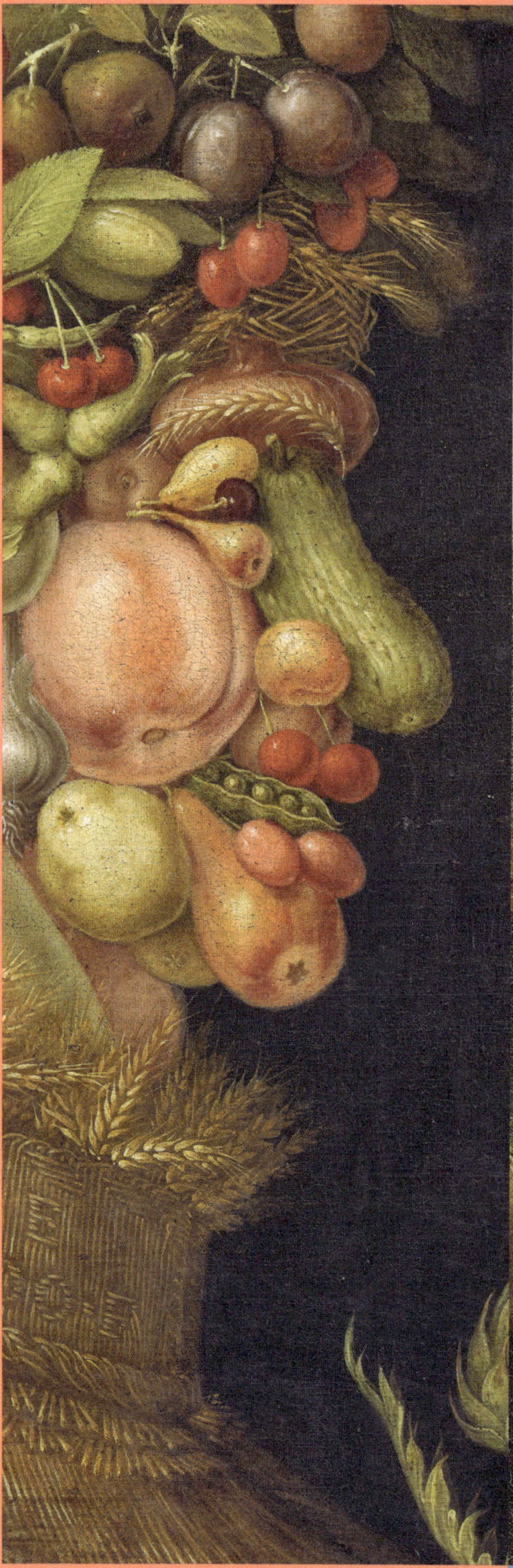

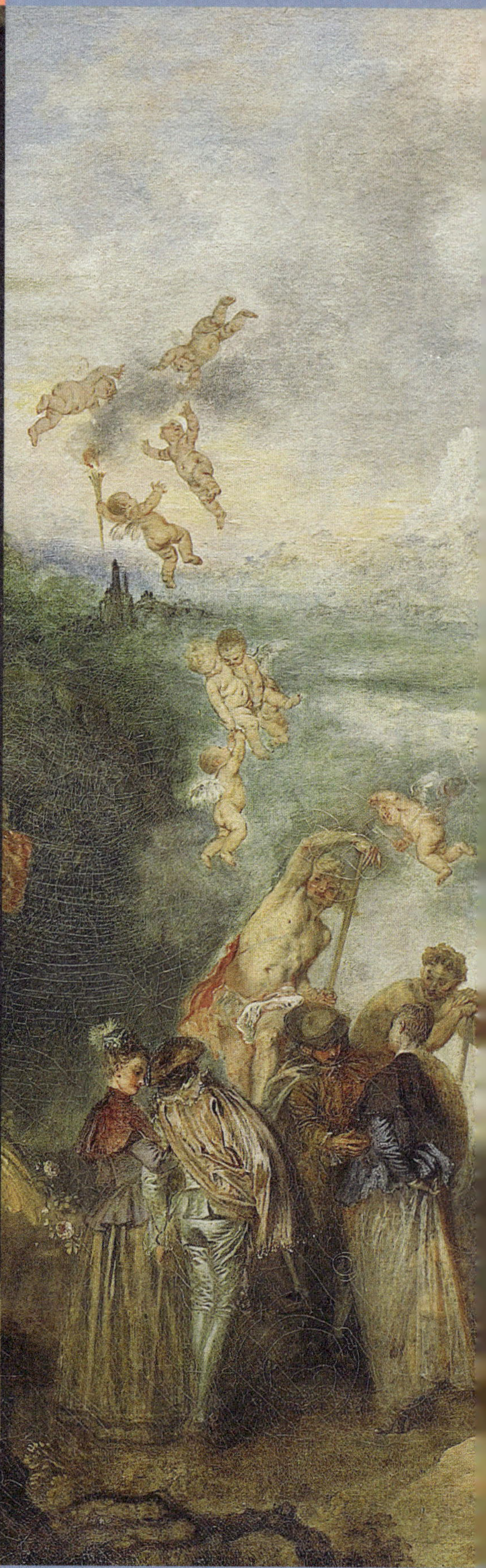

The Road to Fame

You have probably heard of the armless marble statue; the winged figure standing proud at the top of a staircase; the king of France striking a pose in his ermine coat; the granite lion with a pharaoh's head; the bare-chested woman holding a flag; and the one with the enigmatic smile. Sound familiar? Any one of these masterpieces is so popular that its mere mention is enough to evoke an image, a title, or even the creator's name. Why is it famous?

What lies behind the fame of a particular artist or work? The answers to that question are manifold, instructive, and sometimes quite startling. Who would have thought that the once famous, then long forgotten, painter Georges de la Tour would rise to glory again when a young tennis player bought a painting from an antique dealer on the Île Saint-Louis in Paris? Read on for the full story.

There is no recipe for fame. Of course, there are basic ingredients such as technical virtuosity, wonderful colors, a particular subject—but no such thing as a magic wand. Success may stem from the artistic gesture itself, from the lives of the artists, or from the way the latter were defended by their peers or vilified by critics. Anything can lead to fame, even scandal: the public found Ingres' *Grande Odalisque* appalling at first.

Some paintings and sculptures were acclaimed from the start, then copied and reproduced so often that they seem familiar even to those among us who have never seen them. This is the case, for instance, with Renaissance masterworks such as Michelangelo's slaves, Raphael's Madonnas, Titian's portraits, and of course, Leonardo da Vinci's paintings.

But masterpieces can hold surprises. The *Mona Lisa* is said to hide a mystery, and we often hear in the news that its secret is about to be unveiled. Not a year goes by without yet another development in the striking Renaissance portrait's fascinating—and relatively recent—saga: it became a universal icon a mere century ago.

Nothing is ever set in stone. Archaeological excavations could reveal treasures. A painting can fall into oblivion only to reemerge triumphant, as was the case with Louis Le Nain's *Peasant Family in an Interior* and Vermeer's *The Lacemaker*. Conversely, certain painters like Paul Delaroche rose to fame in their time but have been more or less forgotten since.

Some masterpieces have endured incredible trials and tribulations. A student of the painter Jacques Louis David wrote in his diary that his peers used to throw bread pellets at Watteau's *Pilgrimage to Cythera* because it represented the ancien régime and the frivolity of *fêtes galantes*. But no need to worry: the work is still in good condition. Similarly, *Liberty Leading the People* by Delacroix was kept hidden for twenty years because Louis-Philippe feared it would stir up popular revolt.

This book recounts the incredible journeys of the Louvre's icons by observing how our appreciation of art has evolved over the centuries, and how literature, movies, series, video clips, and social media have helped shine new light on some of the world's most famous masterpieces.

You already knew about the armless marble statue, the winged figure, and the woman with the enigmatic smile. You are about to find out why.

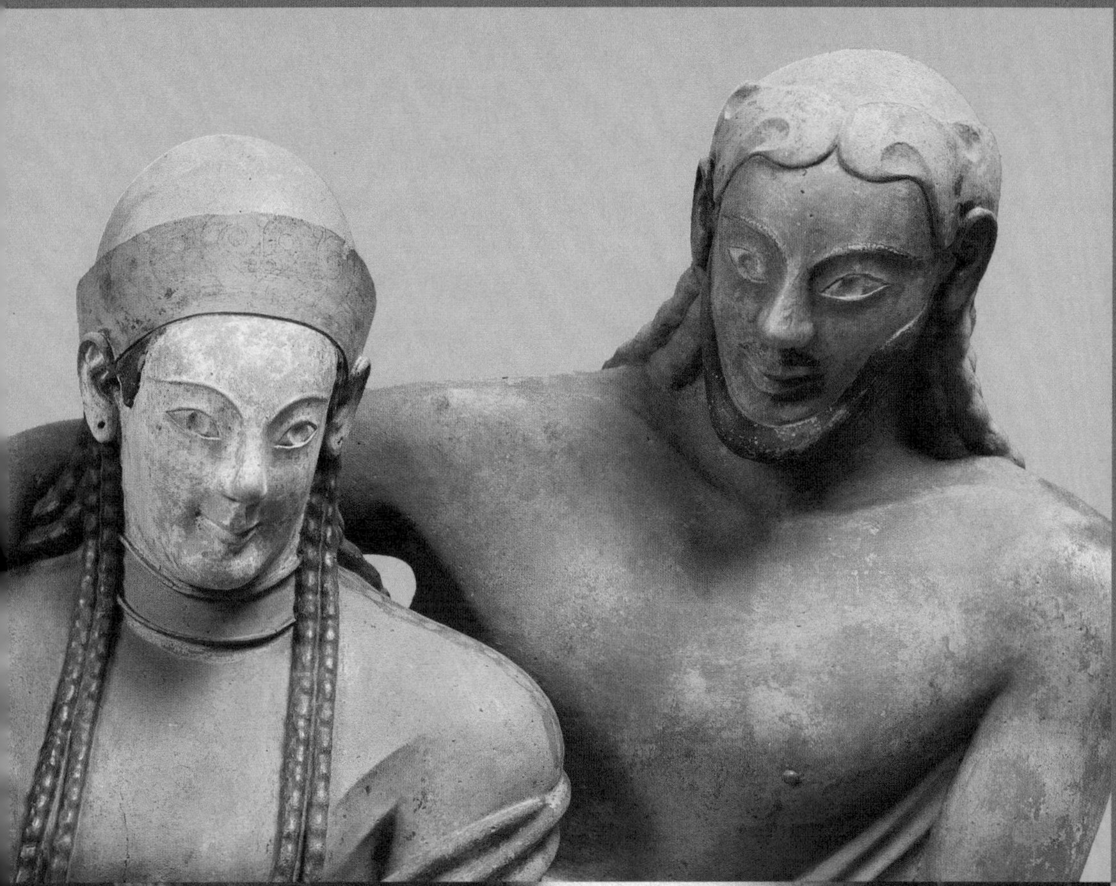
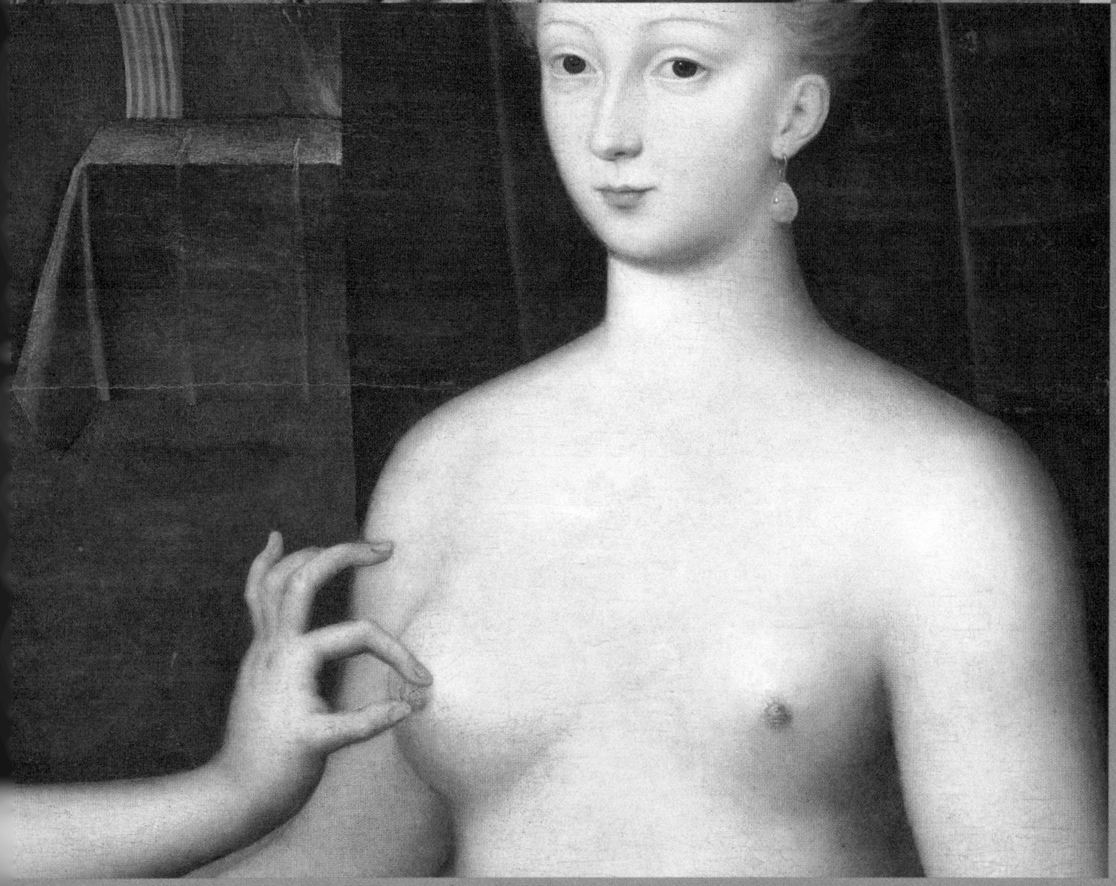

Head of a Cycladic Idol

Making Something New with Something Ancient

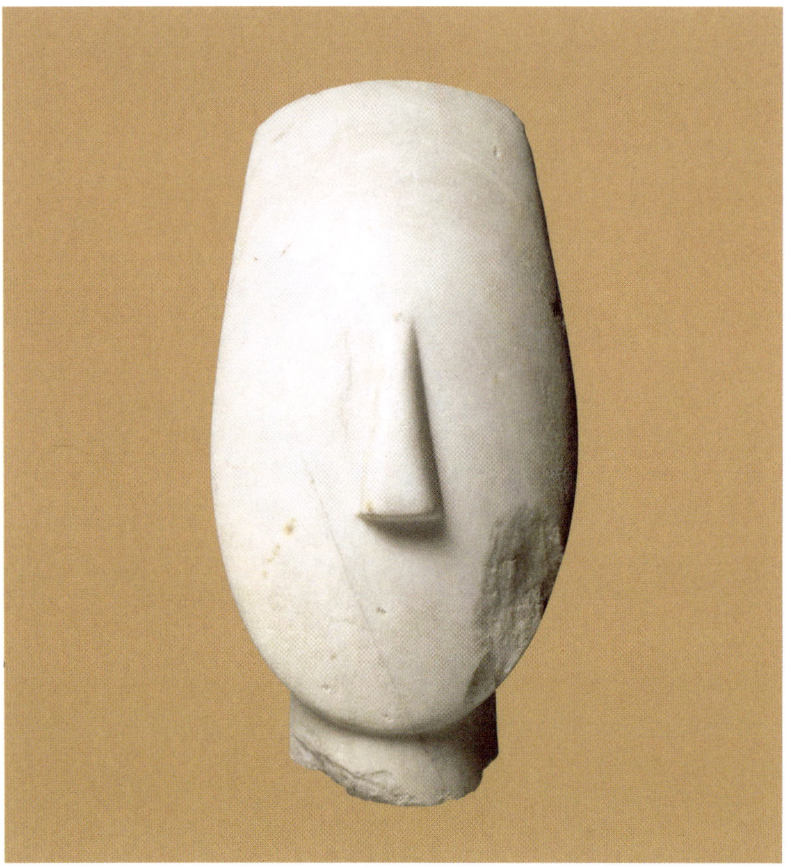

Head of a Female Figurine,
also known as Head of a Cycladic Idol,
c. 2700–2300 BC,
marble,
27 × 14 cm

On display in the most important archaeological museums of Athens, London, New York, and Paris, this stylized face is a fragment of a polished marble idol. It originates from the Cyclades archipelago and marks a major period in Greek sculpture. It also represents a mysterious form of creativity, a geometric simplification that has largely inspired modern art since the twentieth century.

Primitive

Artists such as Constantin Brancusi, Alberto Giacometti, Pablo Picasso, and Henry Moore preceded the archaeologists and historians in wanting to know how the idols were made. In particular, the avant-garde wondered how to achieve a simplified form while respecting the material, by carving rather than modeling. Following the Impressionist era inspired by Far Eastern—and especially Japanese—art, the Fauvists, expressionists, and cubists developed a passion for African and Oceanic art. Paul Gauguin, Henri Matisse, André Derain and Maurice de Vlaminck, among others, collected so-called "primitive" objects that served as models of inspiration for their own work. The artists were also inspired by the Cycladic figurines (Henry Moore acquired three of them). Avant-garde artists thus helped promote and protect an ancestral art.

Made-up woman

Prehistoric Cycladic artisans used to enhance the bright white of the marble by coloring the eyes and mouth and adding tattoos or scarification marks on the body.

A protective figure?

"I am sure that the famous Cycladic head on display in the Louvre influenced Brancusi and that it was the prototype for his sculpture."

Henry Moore

The Cycladic idol on display at the Louvre is a simple silhouette, a presence that mirrors our humanity. Originally 1.5 meters tall, the statue depicts a female figure standing naked on tiptoes with her arms crossed under her chest and her head slightly tilted back. Her face is flat, with a protruding nose and seemingly no mouth and eyes. It is thought that this type of figurine may have been used as a substitute for human sacrifices, or, like in ancient Egypt, to keep the dead company in the afterlife; it may also have represented a mythological deity, such as the goddess of fertility or a similar protective figure. Perhaps it was everything at once. The answer was lost over the centuries.

When the first discoveries were made in the late eighteenth century, the scientists and archaeologists of the time paid little attention to these figurines. They saw them as crude and associated them with the East to explain the lack of harmony and finesse compared to classical Greek statuary. And despite a change in appreciation in the late nineteenth century, the works of art still did not spark much interest. It was not until 1960, however, archaeological research intensified in the Cyclades. With the systematic study and periodization that ensued, the figurine was dated to around 2700–2300 BC.

The Seated Scribe

Pioneer

The Seated Scribe is a famously unknown figure. The man thus represented remains a mystery, and although no one knows his name, his position in the hierarchy, or the exact period when he was sculpted, he never fails to impress visitors as they enter the Department of Egyptian Antiquities.

The origins of Egyptology

Egyptology began when Jean-François Champollion deciphered hieroglyphic writing in 1822. In 1850 François Auguste Ferdinand Mariette was sent by the Louvre to purchase Coptic manuscripts. He ventured some 30 kilometers from Cairo to Saqqara, a place that would turn out to be one of the main necropolises in the country—a fact Mariette was unaware of at the time. In a way, he was a pioneer. One day, he discovered a stone on which he deciphered the names Apis, Osiris, and Serapis. With the help of about thirty workers, he cleared the sphinx alley leading to the sanctuary—surely the "Memphis Serapeum" he had read about in various writings. To get around the ban on excavating imposed on him, he worked at night. Our famous scribe was buried in the sand. Mariette then managed to gain access to a subterranean tomb that was 250 meters long. It contained thousands of objects.

"The Scribe doesn't look at you. He has glass eyes, which bothers me in spite of my adoration for The Scribe."

Alberto Giacometti

Amazing eyes

The technique used to make the scribe's eyes is quite impressive, for it draws on the human eye's anatomical characteristics. In 1995 the Centre de Recherche et de Restauration des Musées de France analyzed the eyes and found that they consisted of a piece of red-veined white magnesite (for the cornea) embedded with a piece of rock crystal (for the pupil) that was polished at the front and colored at the rear. A slightly off-center perforation representing the iris further accentuates the apparent mobility of the gaze.

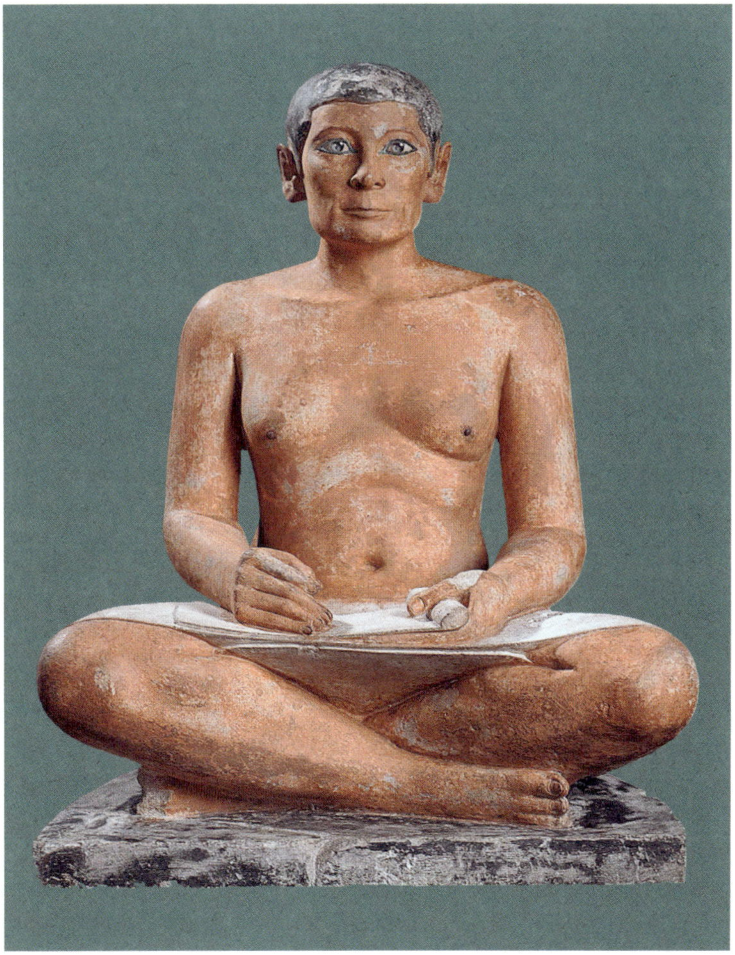

The Seated Scribe,
2620–2500 BC,
painted limestone,
alabaster, copper,
53 × 44 cm

Scriveners

Scribe figures in art and literature have become a rarity. To find famous scriveners one needs to go back to the nineteenth century, at the time of *Bartleby, the Scrivener* and *Bouvard and Pécuchet*. The figure of the scribe refers to a distant past: the monks who illuminated manuscripts in the Middle Ages, the mandarin's scroll in China, the imperial civil servant bust from Roman times. Scribes were senior officials in ancient Egypt and the figures most often represented after the pharaoh. They held great historical and symbolic importance in the centralized state.

What's so special about this guy?

The Great Sphinx

Colossal

The sphinx is a chimera, a mythological creature with the body of a lion and the head of a man. It guarded the ancient Egyptian necropolises. Its imposing size is said to have instilled fear and inspired many riddles.

The Eye of Ra

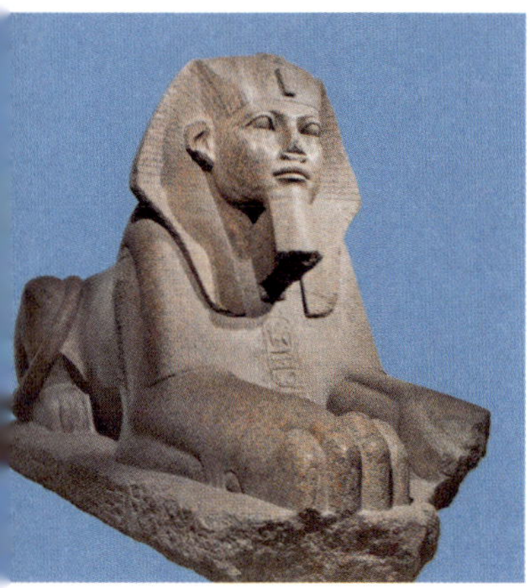

In the Egyptian pantheon brimming with hybrid creatures, the sphinx was an exception for the gods were most often depicted with a human body and an animal head. To the Egyptians of ancient times, the sphinx—a lion with a human head—embodied the union of the sun god Ra and the pharaoh. It is a "living image": the association with a god conveys strength to the king.

The pharaoh is characterized by the nemes, a pleated and striped headcloth crowned by the uraeus, the snake symbolizing the eye of Ra. The distinctive braided beard was also a ceremonial feature.

The Riddle

The sphinx stands guard at the entrance to the temples. It is meant to scare off the unwelcome intruders and protect the secrets within the sanctuary. According to legend, the sphinx posed a riddle to those who sought to penetrate the sacred place. The most famous one, solved by Oedipus, refers to our own condition (it is a clue): "What is the creature that walks on four legs in the morning, two legs at noon, and three in the evening?"

Is it really a statue?

Monolithic

According to certain Egyptologists, the great sphinx is thought to be the image of a king of the early Old Kingdom, perhaps Snefru, the father of Khufu who gave his name to the largest of the Giza pyramids. The dating of the work has often been questioned and the granite statue has long been attributed to Amenemhet II.

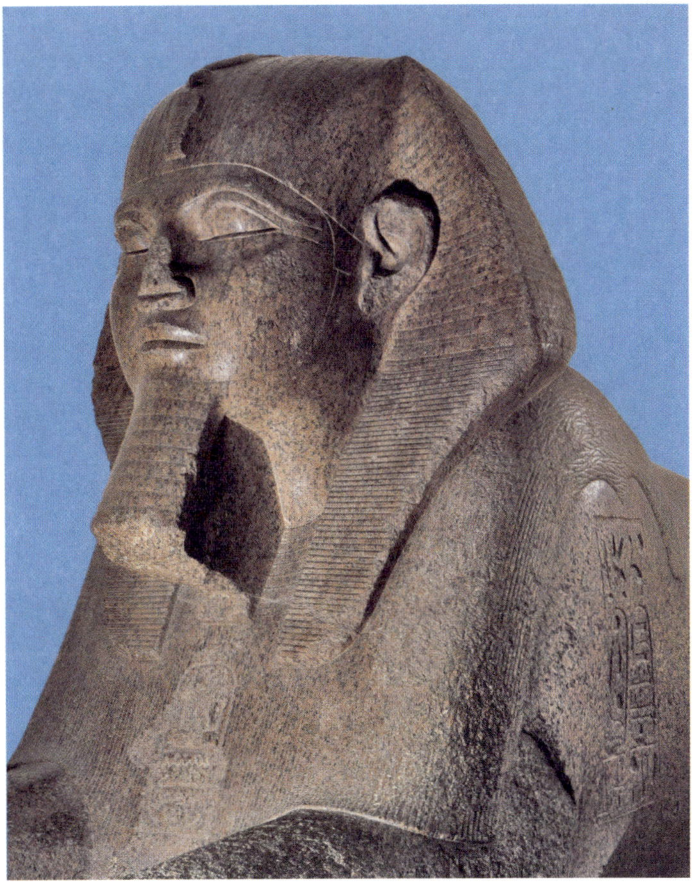

"The sphinx was an emblem of strength and wisdom, godly attributes granted to the living images of divinity on earth: the Pharaohs."

Jean François Champollion

The Great Sphinx of Tanis, Fourth Dynasty (2620–2500 BC) and Amenemhat II's reign (1901–1866 BC), granite, 183 × 154 cm

The sphinx in the Louvre was discovered in 1825 in the Nile Delta, in Tanis, the capital of Egypt during the 21st and 22nd dynasties, by the English Egyptologist Henry Salt. Cut from a single block of pink granite, it weighs about 12 tons. Thanks to the French Egyptologist Jean François Champollion, the Louvre acquired Henry Salt's collection of 4,000 pieces, including the Great Sphinx. In the first of the thirty or so rooms that make up the Department of Egyptian Antiquities, where 50,000 works cover 4,000 years of civilization, the stone creature standing guard by the eponymous crypt marks the beginning of the visit. Naturally, the most famous sphinx remains in Giza, to the southeast of the pyramids. Measuring 20 meters at its highest point with its head facing upward, it was probably carved around 2500 BC by Khafre, son of Khufu, from a natural promontory of rock. Its broken nose has given rise to many a wild guess as to what damaged it: some blame a cannonball fired by soldiers under the reign of Napoleon, others put it down to the clumsiness of a strongman like Obelix in *Asterix and Cleopatra*. But in all likelihood, it was an act of iconoclasm perpetrated in the fourteenth century.

The Statue of Ebih-Il

Glory to Ishtar

The 4,500-year-old Statue of Ebih-Il is one of the most remarkable pieces on display in the Department of Near Eastern Antiquities. The statuette owes its renown to its great state of preservation and craftsmanship, and above all its expressive style. It bears witness to the mores and customs of the ancient cradle of civilization.

The highest bidder

In August 1933, a French officer was doing a round about 10 kilometers from the village of Abu Kamal in northern Syria, not far from the Middle Euphrates River. He met a group of Bedouins who were digging up stones to make a new grave. A few days later, one of the nomads went to see the officer about a headless man they had discovered; they did not know what to do with it. Arms crossed on its chest and weighing about 200 kilograms, the mutilated statue suggested that the Bedouins had probably discovered the vestiges of a Mesopotamian site. The officer called on the antiquities inspector who immediately launched a major excavation. This is how the ancient Mesopotamian city of Mari was uncovered. Fortifications, tombs, and sanctuaries were found, including the Ishtar temple, which took two months to dig up. The archaeologists unearthed ex-votos, offerings, and statuettes of various sizes, including the famous Statue of Ebih-Il. Ebih-Il served as a *nu-banda* in the royal palace; in other words, he held high administrative and military offices and duties. He had his effigy sculpted with his name engraved on his shoulder as an offering to the goddess Ishtar.

Here is the report written by archaeologist André Parrot after he found the statuette in two parts on the pavement of the temple's outer court, not far from a statue of King Lamgi-Mari: "Small white alabaster statue of a seated man wearing a fluffy petticoat. The figure differs from the previous one in type and costume. Unlike the king's, his head is fully shaved, but his beard reaching up to his eyes on the sides and cut short around the cheekbones, cheeks and lips is rather short and curly. The embedded eyebrows meet in the middle and bring out the fine aquiline nose. The eyes are particularly expressive. The artist artfully combined schist, shell, and lapis lazuli to represent respectively the eyelashes and eyelids, the cornea, and the iris. The very thin lips stretch into a faint smile. The rest of the body was also carefully crafted."

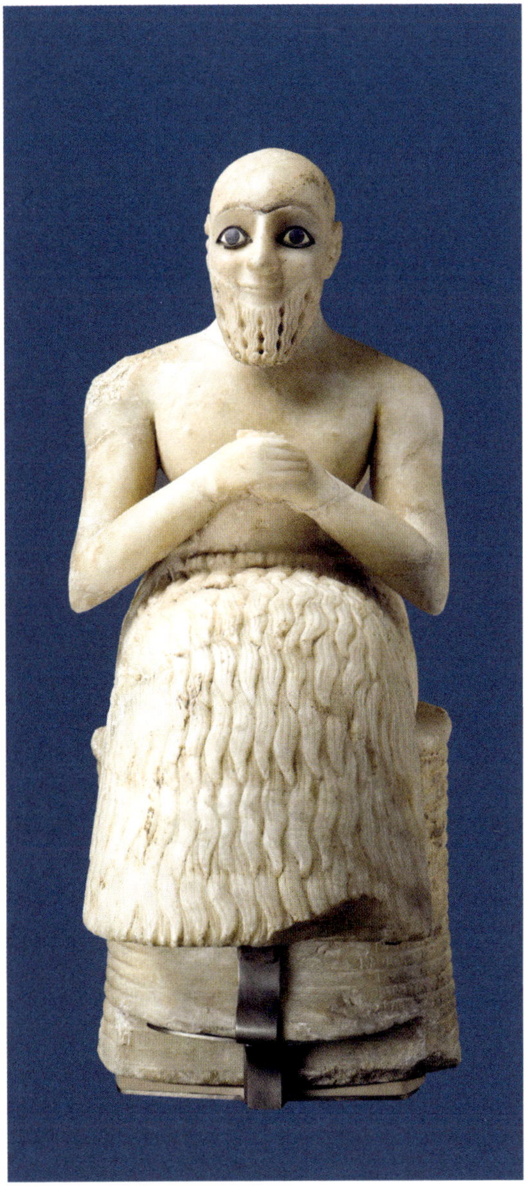

The Statue of Ebih-Il,
c. 2400 BC,
alabaster,
shell, lapis lazuli,
bitumen,
52 × 20 cm

Mari

The site of Mari is the archetype of Mesopotamian city-states and one of the most beautiful archaeological discoveries of the twentieth century. It is a legendary capital, along with Ur and Babylon. Founded in the early third millennium BC, the city oversaw the trade route linking the Euphrates, the mountainous plateaus, and the wealthy urban centers of central and southern Mesopotamia. It had great political and cultural influence. Today, unfortunately, the site of Mari is bearing the consequences of the Syrian conflict. The damage is made worse by rampant looting and the use of mechanical shovels for illegal large-scale excavations.

The second sex

The ecstatic face of Ebih-Il refers to a time when Ishtar the mother goddess of love and war was worshipped. Ishtar was sometimes depicted as virile and warlike with a lion as her animal attribute. In her famous essay, *The Second Sex,* Simone de Beauvoir recounts how the queen of heaven, Ishtar in Babylon or Astarte to Semitic peoples, was ousted in favor of male gods in a world "reconquered by males."

Code of Hammurabi, King of Babylon

The Jurists' Bible

This basalt stela bears eloquent testimony to the political and social history of Mesopotamia. It alone represents the influence of Babylon, the importance of writing, the creation of cities, their complex administrations, and the formation of the first empires.

An eye for an eye

Erected by King Hammurabi in the eighteenth century BC, the high stela is engraved with a code of law on its entire surface. It once stood more than 2 meters tall in a Babylonian public square for all to see. The "citizens" of the time could read or have someone read what was relevant to them. The 282 articles of law carved in Akkadian could also be copied by the scribes onto tablets.
The laws state the gradation of punishments according to the crimes committed, such as the application of the law of retaliation—meaning the sentence must match the offence—and the principle of presumption of innocence whereby both the accused and the accuser have the opportunity to provide evidence as to whether or not the alleged facts are true. Generation after generation, Mesopotamian scribes studied the Code of Hammurabi whose legal principles were passed on for more than a millennium.

Code of Hammurabi,
King of Babylon, 1792–1750 BC,
basalt,
225 × 79 cm

Particular attention was paid to the code itself, in the formal beauty of the 3,500 lines of cuneiform characters, in the literary power of the language used, and in the iconography chosen to depict the king receiving the law from God's hands. The Code of Hammurabi was so renowned that, in the twelfth century BC, it was stolen and brought to Iran to be exhibited with other masterpieces on the Susa acropolis. It was there, in this museum ahead of its time, that an archaeological mission discovered the code at the turn of the twentieth century. Eminent Assyriologists managed to decipher the inscription unfolding in three stages: a prologue celebrating Hammurabi's great actions at the end of his reign; the "laws," or rather the decisions rendered by the king; and an epilogue stating the king's wish for his word to be transmitted throughout the ages and the curses that shall befall whoever damages the code.

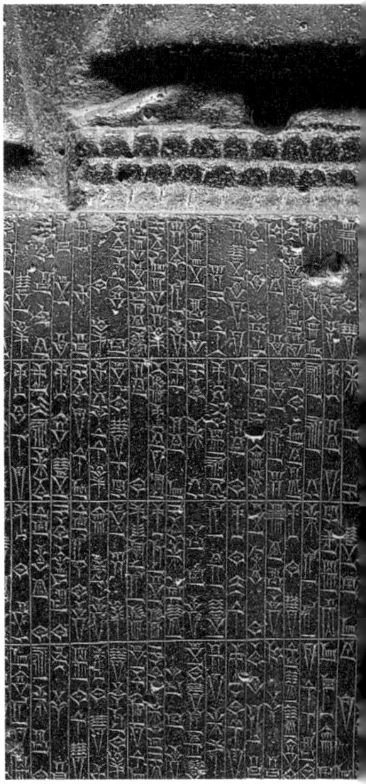

The law of retaliation

"If a man has caused a man of rank to lose an eye, one of his own eyes must be struck out. If someone breaks the tooth of a free man, who is his equal, his tooth will be broken." In Exodus, the law of retaliation is formulated as follows: "Thou shalt give life for life, eye for eye, tooth for tooth."

The Tables of the Law

How does one do justice to such a treasure?

The Hammurabi code is the most complete collection of laws from antiquity. A synthesis of more ancient texts, it predates biblical laws and has inspired some of them. Among other similarities, Hammurabi represented at the top of the stela can be compared with Moses receiving the Tables of the Law.

The code is of paramount importance to epigraphy (the study of ancient inscriptions) experts and legal historians. Many copies of the stela can be found around the world, including a life-size cast first exhibited in Baghdad and then in Tehran. A copy is also on display next to the Rosetta Stone at the British Museum in London.

Although better known as a great empire builder and conqueror, with the stela Hammurabi became a notable figure among the legislators of antiquity. He is represented in bas-relief at the Capitol and the Supreme Court of the United States.

The Goddess Hathor Welcomes Seti I

A Match Made in Heaven

This large bas-relief is one of the rarest and most admirable works exhibited in the Department of Egyptian Antiquities. It represents King Seti I receiving a necklace from the goddess Hathor while she holds his hand. The fragment's exceptional character lies in the beauty of the bodies, the soft yet serious faces, and the vividness of the colors.

In the torchlight

Was Egyptomania a bad habit?

The bas-relief was first observed by Giovanni Battista Belzoni, an Italian engineer who worked for the English Egyptologist Henry Salt (who discovered the Great Sphinx, page 24). Belzoni was active on all fronts: he cleared the entrance to the Abu Simbel temple; he was the first to enter the pyramid of Khafre in Giza; he found the tomb of Rameses I in the Valley of the Kings; and in October 1817, he discovered *The Goddess Hathor Welcomes Seti I*. In the torchlight, Belzoni first came across two pillar rooms and corridors decorated with painted scenes. "The paintings became more perfect as we advanced," said the mesmerized engineer. In the tomb that sank 137 meters beneath the mountain, seven corridors and ten rooms sheltered the highest degree of perfection in Egyptian art. Coming out of a four-pillar room, Belzoni walked between two symmetrical bas-reliefs at the foot of a staircase leading to a corridor. The masterpieces represent the goddess Hathor welcoming King Seti I as he enters the tomb. The naturalness of their poses, the sensuality of their gestures, and the preciousness of the jewels all echo the Amarna style, which had developed during the reign of Akhenaton and which may be recognized here in the fluidity of the garments and the refinement of the colors (evoking gold, silver, lapis lazuli, turquoise, etc.).

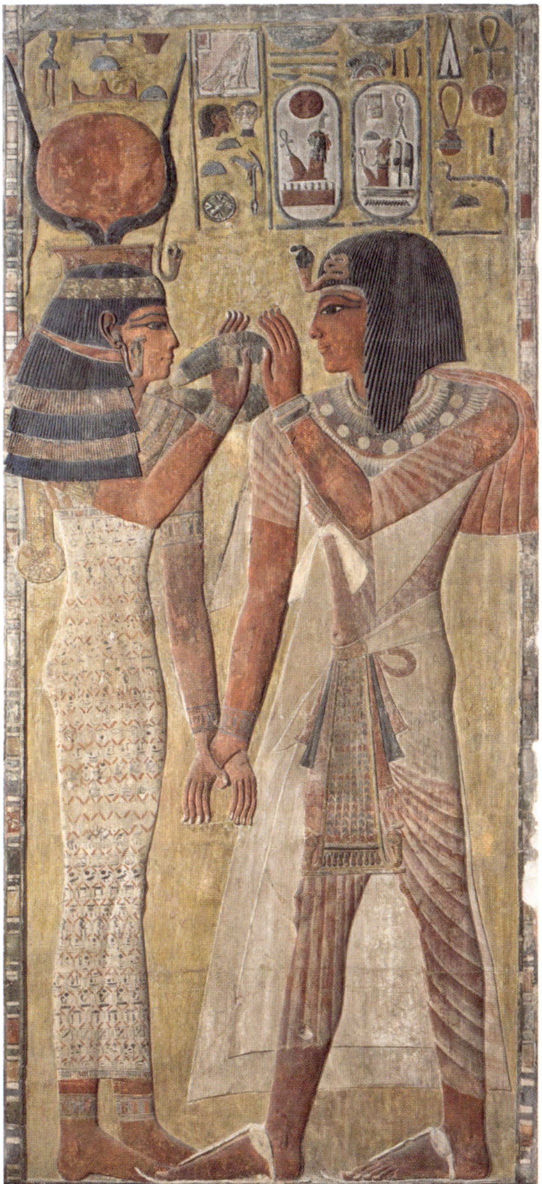

The Goddess Hathor Welcomes Seti I, New Kingdom (c. 1550–1069 BC), painted limestone, 226 × 105 cm

The heyday of Egyptomania

Europe's renewed interest in ancient Egypt dates to the early nineteenth century. Napoleon Bonaparte's Egyptian campaigns made a lasting impression. Upon his return from an expedition, Dominique Vivant-Denon (the future director of the Louvre) wrote *Voyage dans la Basse et la Haute Égypte*, a chronicle that was regularly republished and acclaimed by scholars. Similarly, the series *Description de l'Égypte* (1809–26) influenced the worlds of literature, art, and architecture. It was in this context that Belzoni decided to organize an exhibition in Europe, to present a life-size replica of the tomb of Seti I.

It was during the same period that Jean François Champollion deciphered the hieroglyphs on the Rosetta Stone. Upon visiting the tomb of Seti I a few years later, the French Egyptologist noted the damage caused by floods and the constant flow of visitors. The two bas-reliefs were removed from the tomb in September 1829. One was sent to Florence and the other to the Louvre in Paris, where they continue to fascinate visitors two centuries later.

The Sarcophagus of the Spouses

An Eternal Feast

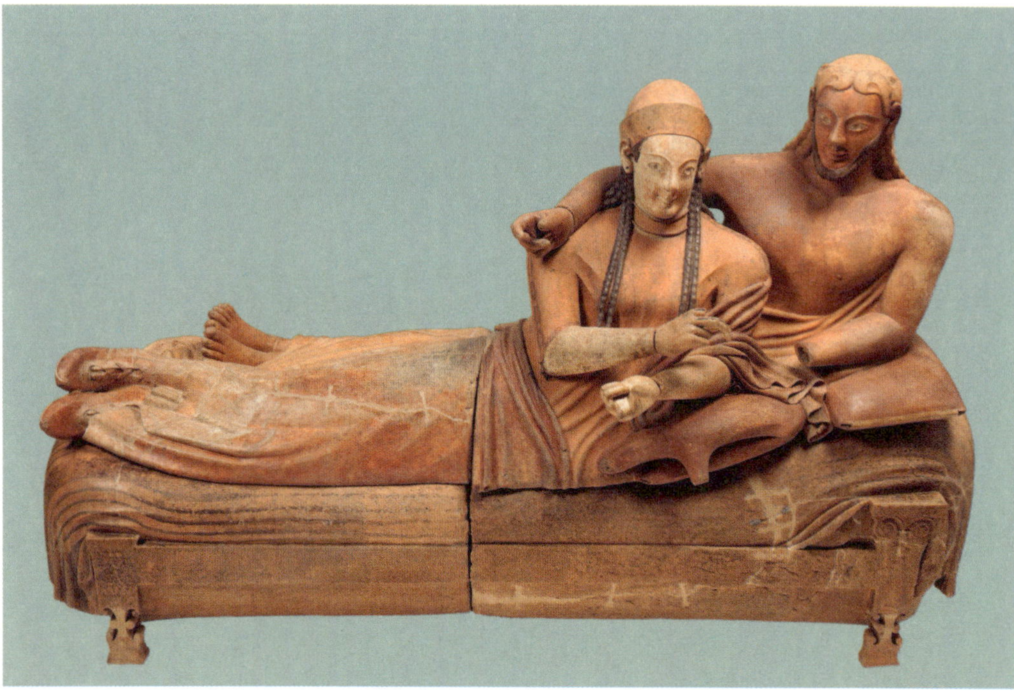

The sarcophagus sparked great interest when it was shown in Paris for the first time in 1862. What were the origins of this couple of banqueters reclining on cushions in the form of wineskins? Did the two figures really come from Italy? They looked Tatar or Chinese. The age-old question of the Etruscan people's origin and disappearance has still not been resolved.

The Sarcophagus of the Spouses,
c. 520–510 BC,
polychrome terra-cotta,
114 × 194 cm

Etruscan revival

In the nineteenth century, the antiquities market thrived on the many excavations carried out throughout the Mediterranean basin, notably by Italian landowners who sought to take advantage of their property. As many of the archaeological finds thus collected were sold in private collections, their origin could not always be traced or certified.

In 1826 some 800 terra-cotta pieces were found near the city of Cerveteri by the archpriest Alessandro Regolini. In 1834 about fifty tombs were discovered in the same area. A renewed surge of interest in Etruscan art and culture ensued: a new institute was founded in Rome by German and French archaeologists; the Etruscan museum exhibiting the Vatican collections was inaugurated in 1837; the Altes Museum in Berlin acquired a thousand or so pieces, while London held the first major exhibition on the theme; Cerveteri and its necropolis were soon featured among the sites of the Grand Tour. The Etruscan civilization was in fashion, it inspired the decorative arts of the time in terms of furniture and jewelry, tomb robbers and counterfeiters thrived. When the banker Giovanni Pietro Campana visited the region in 1844, he was granted permission to search the estates of Prince Giovanni Ruspoli. The following year, in a tomb in the necropolis of Banditaccia, the art and antiques aficionado discovered the Sarcophagus of the Spouses in several broken pieces.

A nightcap?

An Italian dream

Campana wanted to put together an exemplary collection. Not only did he lead excavations and amass objects, he also sought to show the continuity of Italian genius from the antiquity through to the modern day. His passion coincided with the Risorgimento political movement. Back then, Italy was divided into several city-states; hence, promoting the indigenous origin of the Etruscans contributed to the greatness and unity of the country. Already during the Renaissance, Lorenzo and Cosimo I de' Medici studied the history of the Etruscans to find glorious roots for the Tuscan people. In the eighteenth century, an academy was founded in Cortona for scholars to further study the Etruscans and their origins, language, and alphabet, mostly to understand why they spoke a different language from their neighbors. Some believed the roots were indigenous while others stood by an oriental contribution.

Campanagate

In 1857 the Marquis of Campana was accused of financial malpractice after he embezzled funds from the pawnshop of which he was in charge. The pontifical authorities seized his collection and put it up for sale. The works were subsequently dispersed in Russia, Britain, and France, which acquired more than 11,000 artworks including a panel of Paolo Uccello's *The Battle of San Romano* (see page 64) and *The Sarcophagus of the Spouses*.

The Frieze of Archers

The Other Terra-Cotta Army

The Frieze of Archers is a stunning element of architectural decoration that once adorned the palace built in the Persian city of Susa by Darius I in the sixth century BC. It has since been dispersed in the departments of Near Eastern antiquities of the main museums.

The puzzle

The countless bricks that make up The Frieze of Archers were found in the rubble of the Apadana, the royal court in the Palace of Susa, in what is now western Iran. First, the British archaeologist William Kennett Loftus identified the frieze motifs, then in the late nineteenth century, the Frenchman Marcel Dieulafoy began to assemble the puzzle. The latter's wife, who actively participated in the excavation campaign, kept a journal: "Every evening we would ship thirty to forty white slabs, compact and solid, adorned on the edges with wonderful enamels. first, the superimposition of three bricks revealed a long sleeve; later, black feet in yellow ankle boots, and black legs and hands appeared. From the subject and the cutting of the joints, Marcel could piece fragments of figures together; then, bringing these fragments together, he reconstituted two life-size archers" (Jane Dieulafoy, December 31, 1885). Typical of Persian art, the frieze, a simple arrangement of polychrome glazed bricks, draws on techniques used in Mesopotamia for centuries. The martial motif evokes the court of Darius I and the Greco-Persian Wars, at a time when the empire was at its apogee. The fact that the figures are all the same size conveys a sense of power and immutability to the ensemble: perhaps the archers represent Herodotus' Ten Thousand Immortals, popularized once again in the series *Game of Thrones* as the Unsullied, or the Persian people in arms, or subjects of the king, or else members of a multiethnic empire—and all without any form of individual variation.

Darius the Great

Darius I, king of Persia (522–486 B.C.), was a conqueror, as was Alexander the Great of Macedon. He extended the Achaemenid empire from the Nile Valley to the Indus Valley and built Persepolis. His expedition against the Greeks (the Greco-Persian Wars) failed at Marathon in 490 BC.

Darius had a palace built in Susa; it was completed by his son Xerxes and later restored after a fire by Artaxerxes. Some vestiges of the monument remain. The characteristic frieze fragments were dispersed at the Pergamonmuseum in Berlin, not far from the walls of Babylon; in London, not far from the lions of Persepolis; in Tehran; and in Paris, at the Louvre where most of the few hundred fragments have been sorted according to the motifs (feet, boots, spears). Several series of archers have thus been recreated. A team of restorers at the Louvre-Lens selected twenty-one bricks to reconstitute a new archer. The fragment of the Department of Near Eastern Antiquities masterpiece was subsequently exhibited at the opening of the Galerie du Temps.

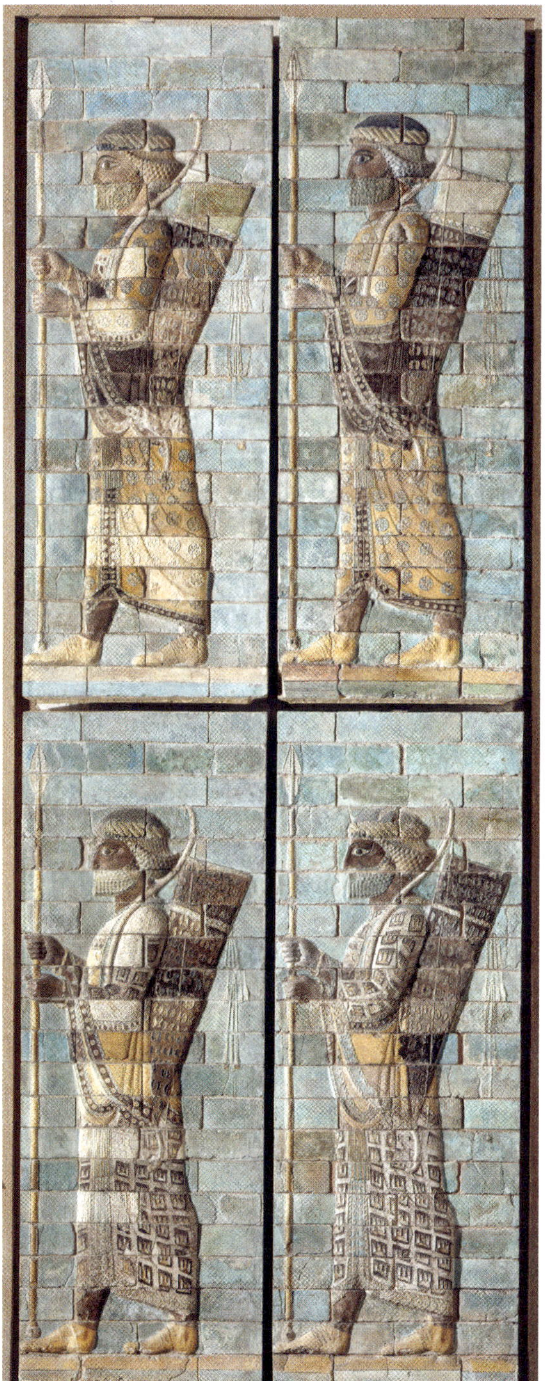

The Frieze of Archers,
c. 510 BC,
glazed siliceous bricks,
475 × 375 cm

Parthenon Frieze

The Glory That Was Greece

A classical Greek masterpiece, the frieze representing the great Panathenaic procession initially adorned the Parthenon colonnade. It is now dismantled.

"Mighty indeed are the marks and monuments we have left. Men of the future will wonder at us, as all men do today."

Pericles, 430 BC

In the shade of the colonnade

The Parthenon is the most famous and most characteristic building of Ancient Greece. It was a monument dedicated to Athena, the patron goddess of the city. At almost 70 meters long and 30 meters wide, it took a mere fifteen years to build in replacement of another "temple" destroyed by the Persians.
The statesman Pericles wanted the architectural masterpiece to establish the supremacy of Greek thought and technology in the world. The extensive and impressive construction was supervised with great skill by the sculptor Phidias. It had to stand the test of time.

The Elgin Marbles

At the turn of the nineteenth century, the map of the Mediterranean was very different from that of today. Greece was under Ottoman rule. The British-Turkish alliance reclaimed the city of Cairo from the French. Lord Elgin, the ambassador to Constantinople, was granted a permit to access the Acropolis ahead of French archaeologists. He removed sculptures and marbles under the pretext of "refining English taste." In five years, about half of the Parthenon's ornaments were shipped to England in hundreds of containers. A dozen statues were dismantled, as well as fifteen metopes (rectangular panels decorated with bas-reliefs) and more than one

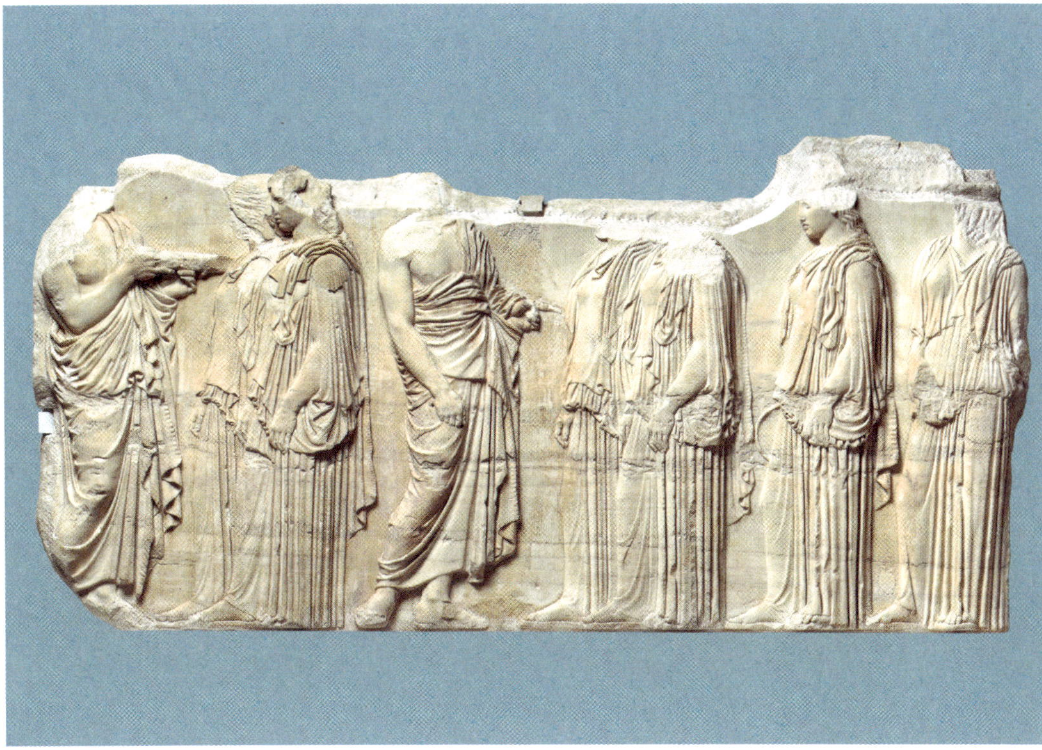

hundred and fifty frieze slabs—some were sawn in half to facilitate transportation. Lord Elgin sold the pieces to the British Museum, where they have been exhibited since 1816. This sparked an ongoing controversy: ever since the wars of independence (1821–32) restored Greek sovereignty, the Greeks have asked for the frieze to be returned to Athens, notably in the 1980s and 1990s by Melina Mercouri, at the opening of the Acropolis Museum in 2008, and more recently when Brexit was announced. Although Greece's attempts to recover the ancient frieze over the past two centuries have failed, they have contributed to its worldwide fame.

Parthenon Frieze,
445–438 BC,
marble,
101 × 207 cm

Greek Revival

Architects and artists were greatly influenced by the marbles as they were moved from the Parthenon to London, Paris, Rome, and Vienna. Two major frieze molding campaigns were carried out in London, in 1816 and 1838, to meet the demand of art schools and museums worldwide. Many artists copied the frieze as part of their training.

Sleeping Hermaphroditos

A Telling Detail

The *Sleeping Hermaphroditos* represents a myth that evokes the very foundations of our humanity. The ambivalent and contradictory piece is still as fascinating and troubling as ever.

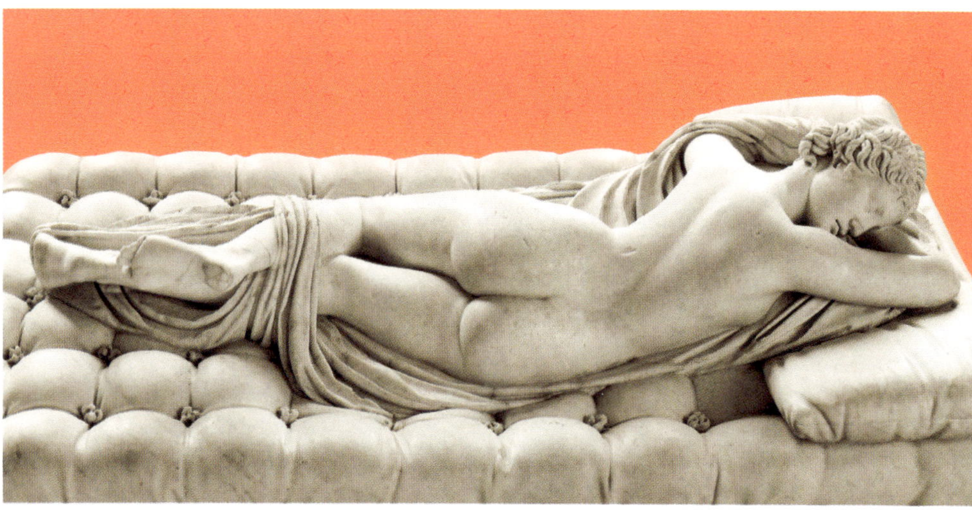

Cherchez le garçon

Have visitors' caresses really worn down the marble?

At the Louvre, visitors usually approach the marble from behind, observing the curvaceous body reclining on the padded mattress. The buttocks accentuate the arch of the back and the shapely hips. The perfect profile is further softened by the hair curls. Walking around the marble, viewers discover a breast, a soft stomach, and male genitalia. Visitor usually smile at this point—or even blush. Although the staging of the piece greatly contributes to the surprise effect, nineteenth- and twentieth-century literature suggests that cultivated audiences were familiar with the sculpture. Théophile Gautier was inspired by the statue's "disturbing beauty" when he wrote the poem "Contralto." In *The Picture of Dorian Gray*, Oscar Wilde built on it to portray the torment caused by contradictory desires. Anatole France reported an urban legend according to which marble is being harassed:

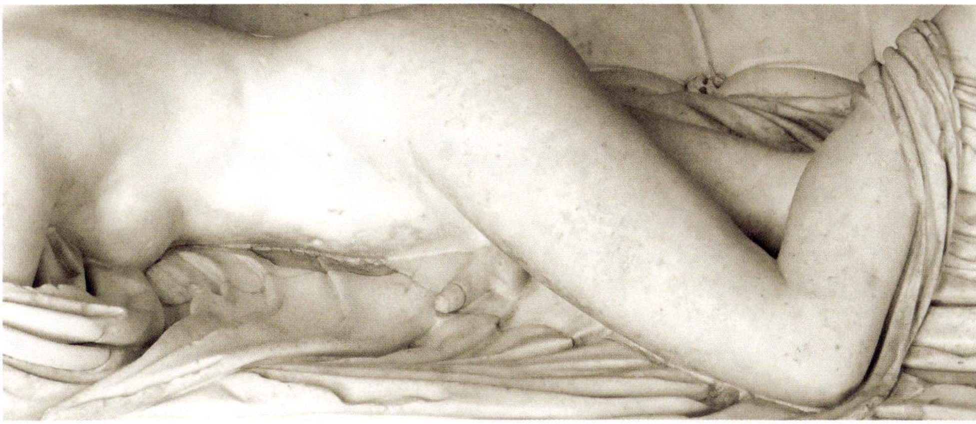

"Did you not know that the Louvre Hermaphrodite's marble was worn down by visitors' caresses, and that the administration of museums had to protect this monstrous and charming figure with a barrier?"

Sleeping Hermaphroditos,
c. 100–150 BC,
marble,
46 × 173 cm

A disturbing beauty

"In the ancient museum
On a carved marble bed
Lays an enigmatic statue
Of disturbing beauty."

Théophile Gautier, "Contralto"

Viewers may not see it at first glance, but the marble is a composite piece resulting from the stratification of different styles and periods: sculpted after a Greek bronze original from the second century BC, it dates from the Roman Imperial Period and was discovered in the early seventeenth century near the Baths of Diocletian. After the work was restored and a mattress was carved by the Baroque sculptor Bernini, it entered the Borghese collection (see *Gladiator*, page 48). Two centuries later, the collection was bought by Napoleon I and entered the Louvre.

As the son of the god Hermes and the goddess Aphrodite, Hermaphroditos embodies one of the founding myths of antiquity. His mesmerizing beauty wooed the nymphs, one of whom, Salmacis, convinced Zeus to unite them for all eternity. Playful, Zeus merged their two bodies into a single androgynous form. According to the myth, hermaphrodites combine two genders into one body; they form ambivalent beings that question the boundaries between male and female, and between what is normal and monstrous. Thus, like the androgyne in Plato's *Symposium*, the myth finds an echo in fields as diverse as alchemy, psychoanalysis (C.G. Jung), gender studies, medicine, and literature (Balzac wrote three short stories on the subject).

The Winged Victory of Samothrace

Breathtaking

As in ancient times when it stood on mountainside on the island of Samothrace, one must climb a few steps in order to admire the Winged Victory of Samothrace. The Hellenistic masterpiece was put together from more than a hundred fragments to form the now familiar stunningly poised figure.

« When the head is gone, so what, the marble has bled . . . »

Paul Cézanne

With the angels

The Winged Victory is the mother of angels. Indeed, the messenger (*angelos* in Greek) of the Gods is the oldest incarnation of the heavenly beings who play the trumpet to be heard and who bring a palm branch, a laurel wreath, or a trophy to victors (or the chosen one) as a sign of their triumph. It is omnipresent in Greek art. The Romans adapted it to mark their domination over the world, and it inspired the messenger angels in Christian iconography: pleated dress, colored wings, smiles, and so on.

The sculpture's *élan vital*

As the name suggests, the Winged Victory of Samothrace represents a winged victory (or the goddess Nike) alighting on the prow of a ship. The colossal statue was probably made in honor of the great gods to celebrate the naval victory of the Rhodians over the Macedonians, but this cannot be confirmed for the sculptor's name is missing. The finely sculpted white marble represents a strong and triumphant body as the seemingly windswept stone garment reveals a perfectly shaped stomach and bosom.

The stunning messenger of Zeus was discovered in 1863 by the vice-consul of France, Charles Champoiseau, an amateur archaeologist, on an island located in the northeast Aegean Sea.

The ancient sanctuary in honor of the Great Gods is located near the coast, in a ravine crossed by a stream at the foot of a mountain. The workers uncovered parts of a large female statue, numerous fragments of drapery and feathers, but no head nor arms. Champoiseau had the white marble pieces packed and shipped to France. After one year of transportation and two of restoration, the statue's main block was first exhibited in 1866 in the Room of the Caryatids. Archaeologists concluded that the

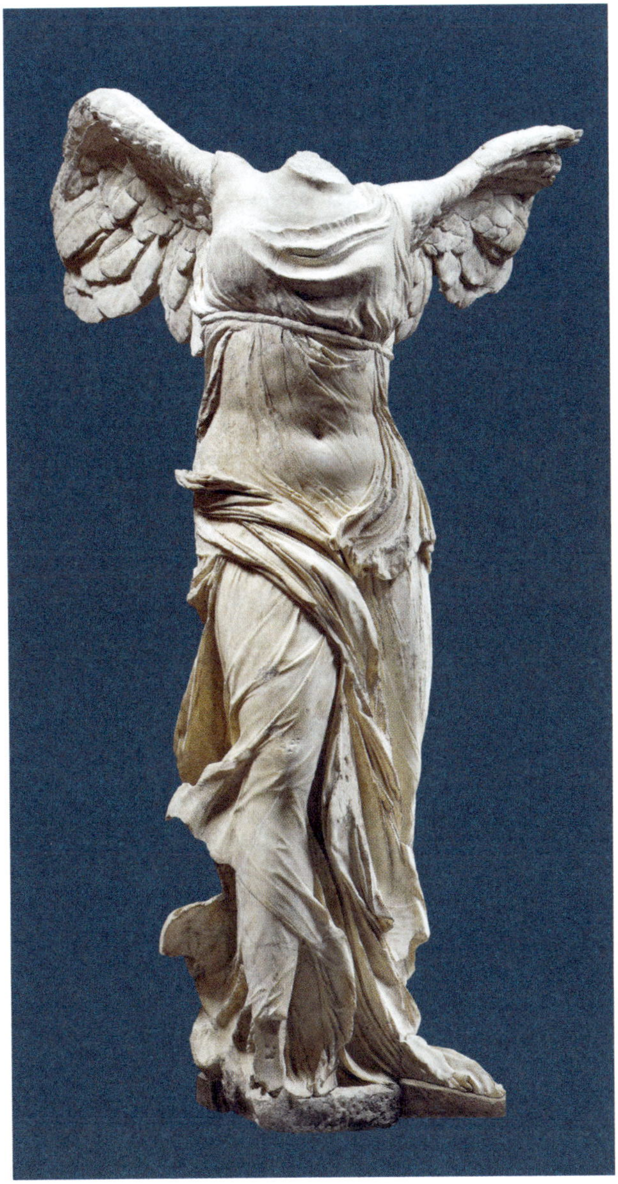

Swoosh !

Many commercial companies were won over by the beauty and sculptural dynamism of the Winged Victory of Samothrace. Famous examples are the *Spirit of Ecstasy* bonnet ornaments on Rolls-Royce cars and the Honda logo; but American sports equipment manufacturer Nike, named after the Greek goddess, whose name means Victory, has the most famous logo of all: it is a highly stylized representation of the statue's wings. Known as the "swoosh," it went on to become one of the most easily recognizable commercial logos in the world.

The Winged Victory of Samothrace, c. 190 BC, marble, 275 cm

gray marble blocks surrounding the Winged Victory at the site were part of a tomb. In 1875 the archaeologists of an Austrian mission drew the pieces of gray marble that remained at the site, compared them with ancient medals, and concluded that they had initially formed the prow of a ship that was the statue's base. The monument appeared to have three elements: a rectangular base, the prow of a ship, and the winged figure. The left wing was reconstructed from the original fragments while the right wing was made with plaster.

After the restoration was completed in 1884, the statue was placed on the upper level of a newly built staircase for maximum visual effect. This marked the Hellenistic masterpiece's public consecration.

Where does this spectacular statue come from?

Posing for posterity

A major restoration campaign was launched between 2013 and 2014, after thousands of Internet users helped raise the hefty sum of 4 million euros. More than ten people were assigned full-time to this project for ten months. Extensive scientific research has unveiled new secrets about the origin of the marbles and the colored decoration on the statue. An intermediate block was removed; a long feather was replaced on the left wing. A thorough cleaning highlighted the finesse of the garment and the original hue. The Winged Victory has been given a new lease of life in the spotlight.

Samothraces

The Louvre's casting workshop has sold reproductions of the statue since the late nineteenth century. The architect Frank Lloyd Wright acquired life-size copies which he subsequently placed in a number of his buildings. In 1962, the artist Yves Klein produced a series of replicas coated in blue pigments. The casts greatly contributed to the Winged Victory's fame.

"My eyes landed on a very beautiful fragment of white marble, barely emerging from the ground, that I identified as an admirably carved woman's breast."

Charles Champoiseau

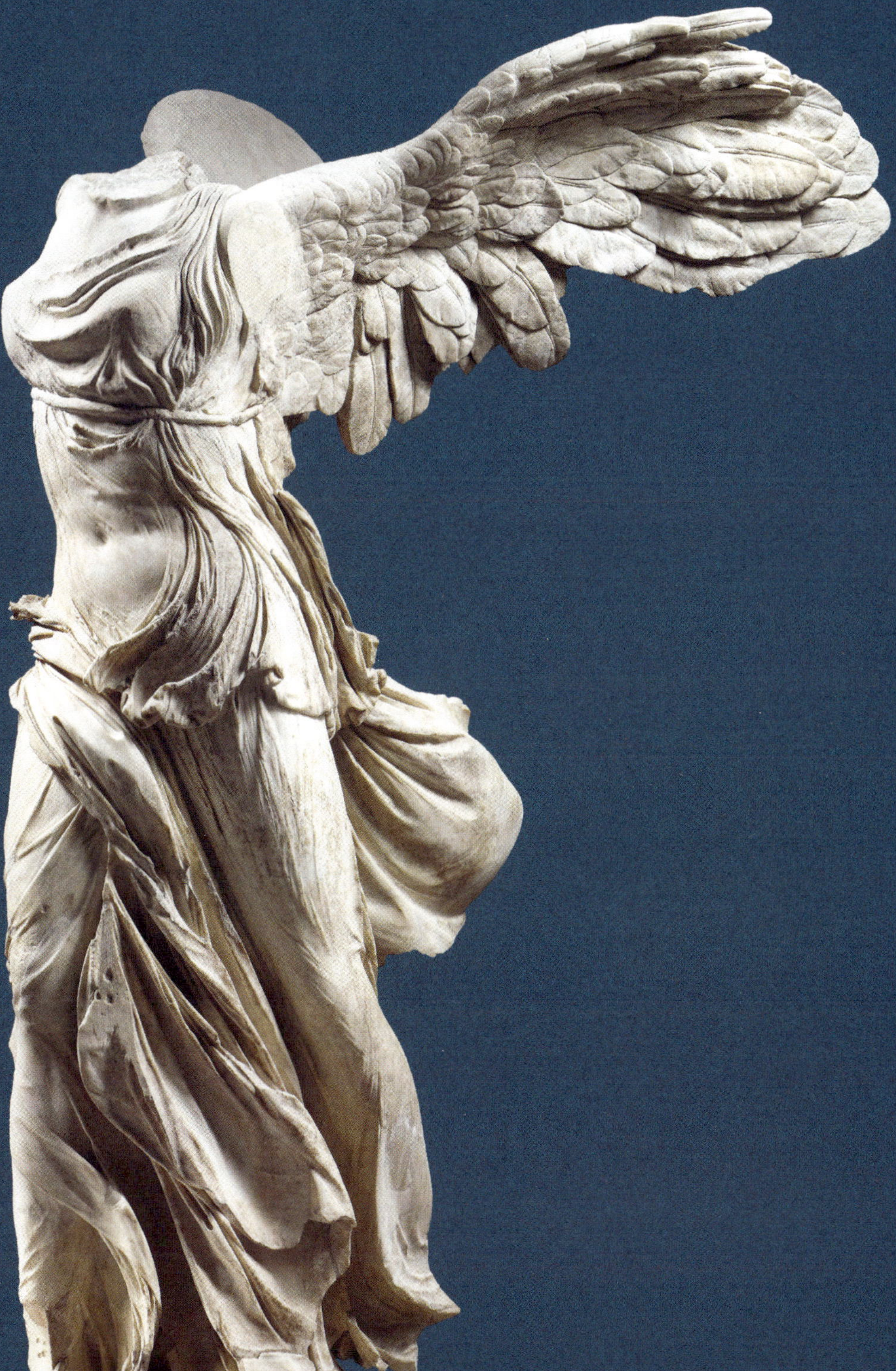

Venus de Milo

Total Beauty

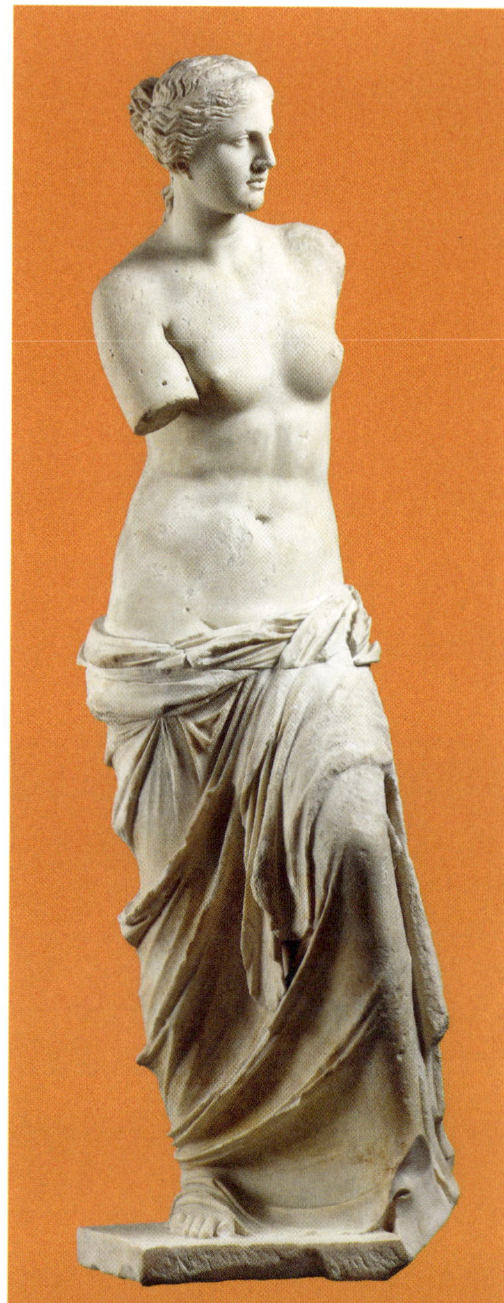

In turn a Hellenistic masterpiece, a copy freely inspired by an original marble, a "history of taste" monument in the nineteenth century, and a muse to the surrealists, the Venus de Milo has lived several lives. The draped garment gradually slipping down her hips, her small bust, and her perfect face are universally attractive.

The Venus de Milo was discovered in April 1820 by a Greek peasant on the Cyclades island of Melos (Milo in modern Greek). He found cut marble blocks and dug further to look for more. The man, whose name was Yorgos, located a chapel where several sculptures were buried. In addition to the Venus de Milo, broken into two main parts and a few fragments, he discovered carved pillars and a dedication to the god Hermes. Yorgos told several people about his find, including Jules Dumont d'Urville, a young French naval officer who took notes on site and paid the peasant to set aside the treasure. When the French ambassador, Marquis Charles François Riffardeau de Rivière, was informed, he sent a purchase order, at the same time as an Ottoman dignitary who was also seeking to buy the statue's fragments. The diplomatic imbroglio was resolved in extremis: France secured ownership of the work before it could be sent to Constantinople. After a few stopovers, the Venus de Milo reached Toulon; then, it was taken by river to Paris where it was presented to Louis XVIII by the Marquis de Rivière. A special medal was struck on the occasion, with the king on one side and the beautiful Venus on the other. Its entry into the Louvre marked the beginning of its fame.

The choice morsel

How to produce a masterpiece

When the statue was restored the following year, several fragments—including the hip and chignon—were brought back to the marble statue. Plaster was used to seal the joints, and the sculpture's dazzling white was restored with vigorous cleaning. The question of whether arms should be added, and in which position, was raised. The permanent secretary to the Académie des Beaux-Arts Quatremère de Quincy chose to keep the work as it was: "I believe that, as it is, it will never cease to unveil the style and taste of one of the most famous schools of ancient sculpture; it will be no less instructive for artists, nor less precious to true amateurs who may see it as the rarest and most precious piece of our Museum." The stakes were high. The curators thought they had in their possession a Greek original from the classical period that filled an obvious gap in the collections. Indeed, the Louvre had been the world's main museum under the First Empire. Following the defeat at Waterloo and the signing of the Treaty of Vienna, masterpieces such as the *Laocoon*, the *Apollo Belvedere*, and the *Medici Venus* had to be returned to Italy. The antique statuary rooms were partly emptied while the great European museums engaged in a new form of national competition: the fame of the works, the capitals, and their institutions ought to be combined. Of course, the Louvre presented the Borghese collection, which had been purchased by Napoleon from his brother-in-law Prince Camille Borghese in 1807 and could thus remain in France. The opportunity to showcase the work of a great sculptor—a Greek original and not a Roman copy—could not be missed. The event was a resounding success. The image of the Venus was disseminated through the intermediary of casts of her body; she served as a model to fine arts students and became the canon of female beauty.

Venus de Milo,
150–125 BC,
marble,
204 cm

The Venus de Milo embodied a new ideal of Greek beauty. She crystallized both fantasies and praise during the Romantic period. Balzac spoke about her, Lecomte de Lisle dedicated a poem to her. She was even mocked, as if she were shown at the Salon, notably by Jules Vallès who saw her as an overrated old thing with an undersized head, an oversized neck, and overly perky breasts. In any case, whether she was mocked or fantasized, she entered the creative world of artists. She dazzled the poet Mallarmé as one of the great "scintillations of beauty on this earth," the sculptor Rodin, who saw her as "the wonder of wonders," cast two versions of her, in plaster and bronze, titled *Cybele* and *The Inner Voice*. In the twentieth century, the Venus de Milo was chosen as a muse by the surrealists. She even inspired Giorgio de Chirico's *Premonitory Portrait of Guillaume Apollinaire*. Dalí turned her into an "anthropomorphic cabinet," complete with drawers in her forehead, bust, and legs—the goddess of love was suddenly nothing more than a piece of furniture.

About the arms

The left arm is outstretched, the right arm is folded under the bust. What gesture is the Venus de Milo making? Is she Aphrodite with the apple (in reference to the Judgment of Paris), or a Victory holding a shield in which she admires her own reflection? The question remains unanswered to this day.

Just the right dose of classicism

Researchers are still debating representations of the Venus de Milo. To most, her half-nakedness and sensual face evoke Aphrodite, the goddess of love (Venus in Latin). But she could just as easily be the sea goddess Amphitrite, revered on the island of Milo. The theory put forth by the sculptors Phidias and Praxiteles has been discarded. Although it has not been verified, the sculpting technique seems typical of the Cyclades studios where marble blocks were carved separately before they were assembled. The sculpture does not date from the classical period (450–323 BC) but from the Hellenistic period (323–31 BC). It was probably produced in the classical style, e.g., in the manner of the Capuan Venus, or perhaps it was a free copy, a late Hellenistic masterpiece.

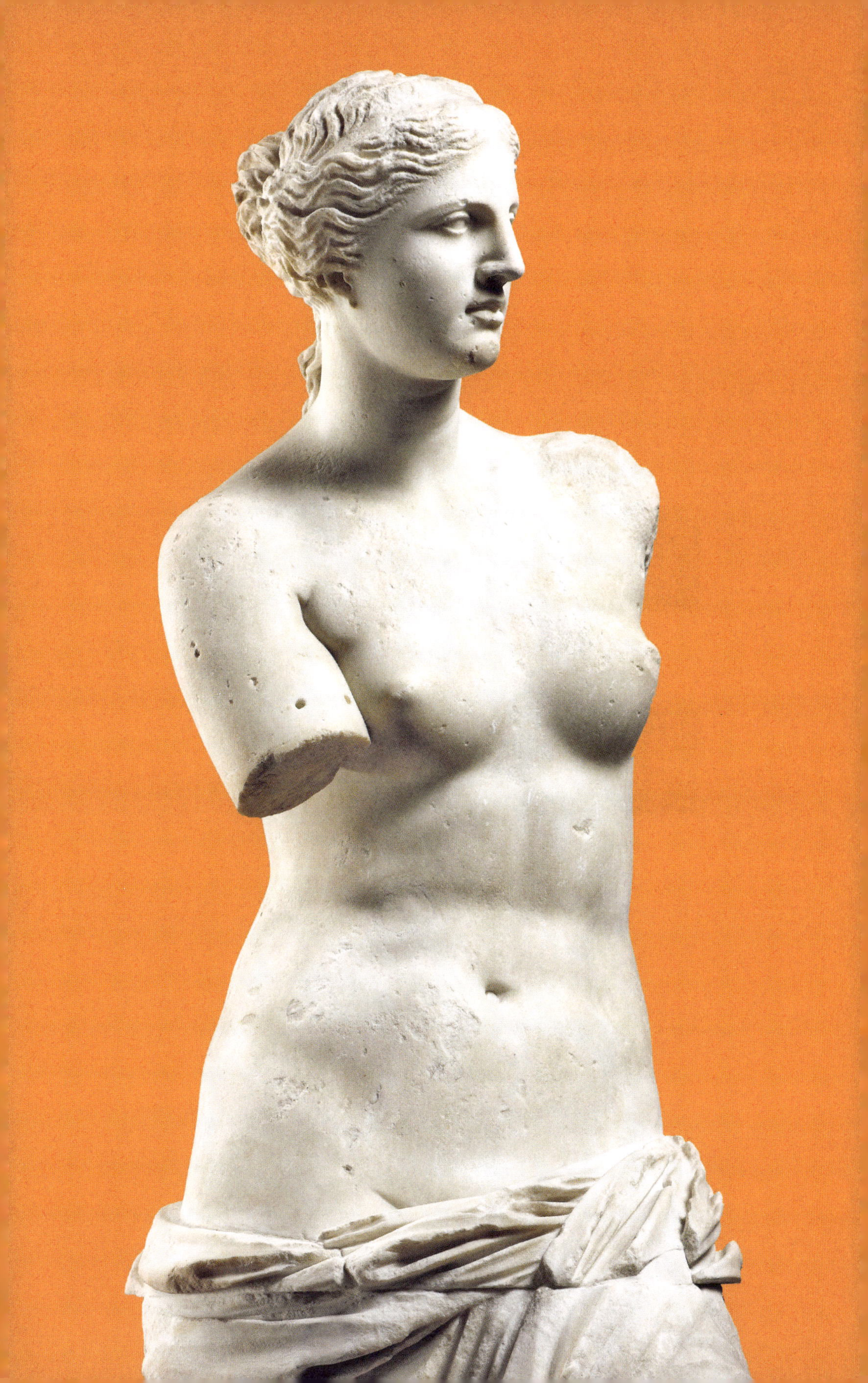

The Borghese Gladiator

Bravura

The Borghese Gladiator is aesthetically impressive with his muscular body, dynamic pose, and expressive face. Now among the most famous works in the Louvre, the sculpture is a powerful legacy from ancient times.The work was commissioned by a Roman client from Agasias of Ephesus, a Greek sculptor, in around 100 BC (his signature appears on the tree trunk). Inspired by classical Greek athletic aesthetics, perhaps from an original bronze, the sculpture's anatomy and proportions are perfect from all angles. In addition, the work was carved from a single block of marble—quite a technical feat. The gladiator's torso is leaning forward. The figure is thrust in an oblique angle coined by art historians as the "heroic diagonal," a dynamic posture that became widespread in Greek sculpture, painting, and mosaics.

"It epitomizes what was most beautiful about the ancient world."

Joseph Jérôme de Lalande, 1765

Epic epoch

What makes him stand out?

The seventeen parts of the Borghese Gladiator were found in around 1610 in the Roman port of Antium, where the ruins of Nero's villa remain. Cardinal Scipio Borghese, the nephew of Pope Paul V, was an art lover and collector who used his rank to acquire everything that came from Rome and Italy. He gathered hundreds of sculptures, including this marble to which a right arm, a hand holding the hilt of a sword, an ear, and genitals were added. It was exhibited in the Casino Borghese to wide acclaim. Bernini's *David* was inspired by the Borghese Gladiator. The model's renown thus grew throughout the seventeenth and eighteenth centuries.
In 1807, as for *Sleeping Hermaphroditos*, Prince Camille Borghese sold the sculpture to Napoleon. The gladiator was considered the most important piece in the lot (it represented a quarter of the total sum of the transaction). After being transported in an oxcart specially designed for the occasion, the sculpture arrived in Paris and found its place in a room dedicated to it until 1922, when it was transferred to the Room of the Caryatids.

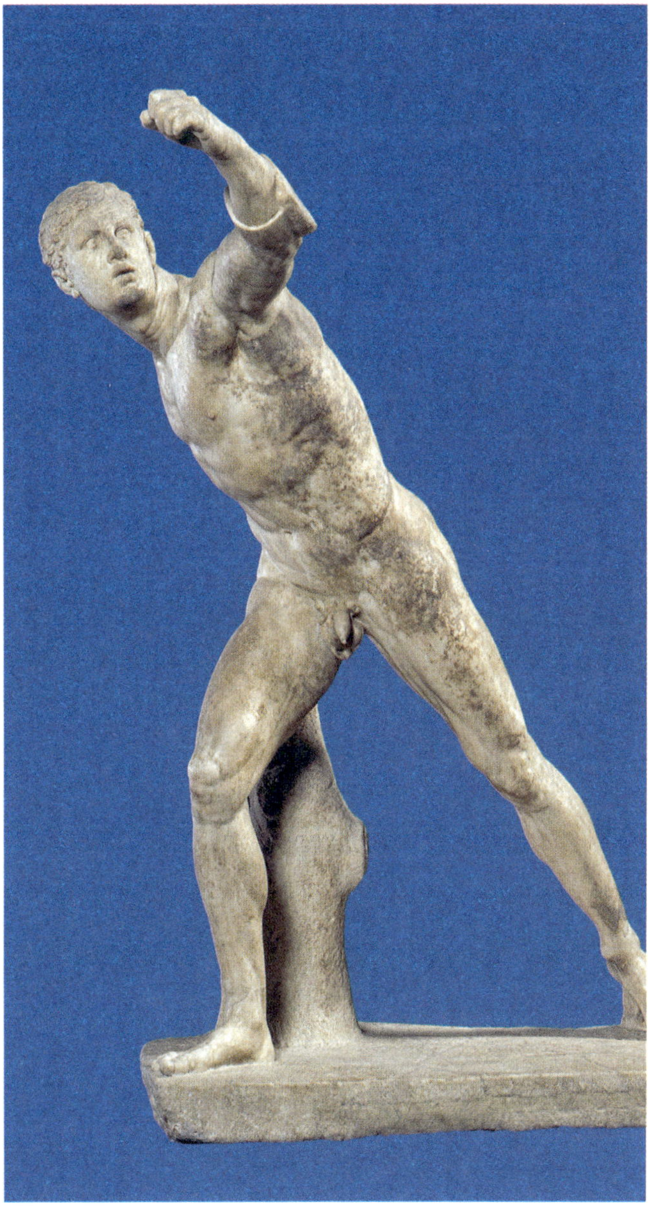

A gladiator?

As the art historian Winckelmann remarked in the nineteenth century, "The Greeks did not play gladiator games!" This sparked a series of theories about the sculpture's real subject. Could the fighter be a boxer, a discobolus, or an armed dancer? He most certainly had a shield strapped to his arm. Perhaps was he a king (Leonidas) or a Trojan War hero (Ajax). The name Borghese Gladiator was given to the statue in reference to its initial collection.

Agasias of Ephesus, son of Dositheus
The Borghese Gladiator, c. 100 BC, 173 × 172 cm

The marble was restored from 1995 to 1997. The Borghese Gladiator was brought to the Saclay laboratory, where gamma rays revealed that the new arm had been attached to the original torso with dowel pins, cramps, and an iron bar. The restoration was complicated mainly due to the various Italian and French casts that had altered the marble's surface, not to mention the marks left by knives, chemicals, and waxes. Fortunately, the work could eventually be restored. The Borghese Gladiator is now proudly displayed in the Galerie Daru.

Pyxis of al-Mughira

A Scent of the East

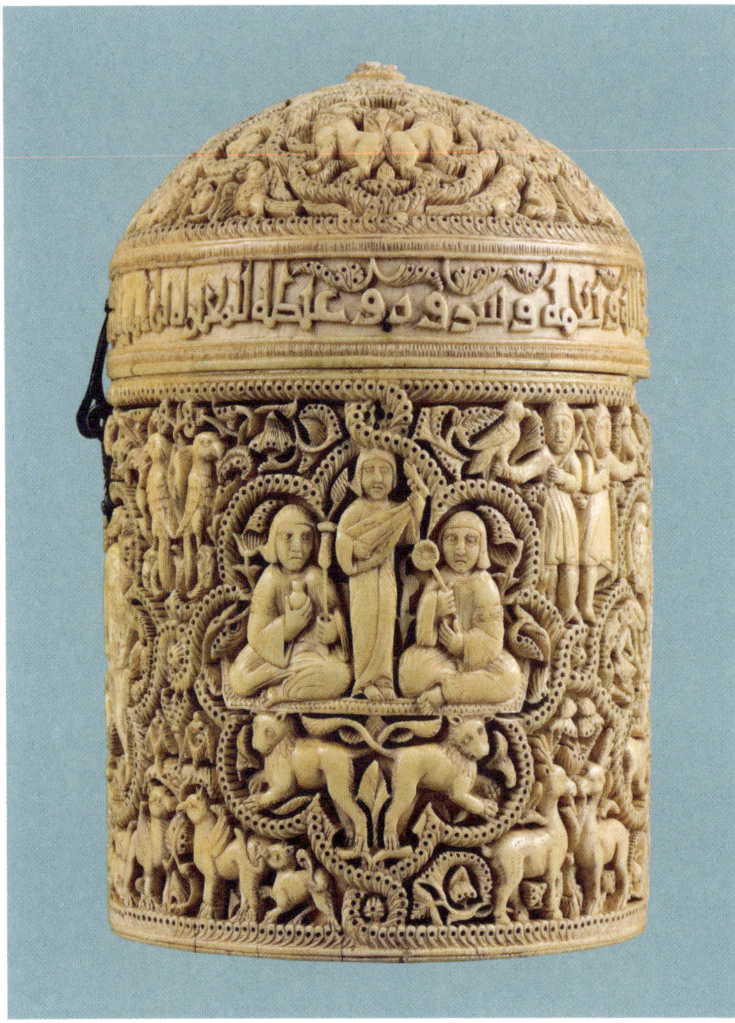

Pyxis of al-Mughira,
968 (AH 357),
carved ivory with traces of jet,
18 cm

Produced in Andalusia during the caliphate of Córdoba, the Pyxis of al-Mughira exhales an air of splendor and political intrigue. Fashioned out of ivory, a material as precious as gold, the pyxis represents both an accomplished civilization and its imminent decline.

The symbols of power

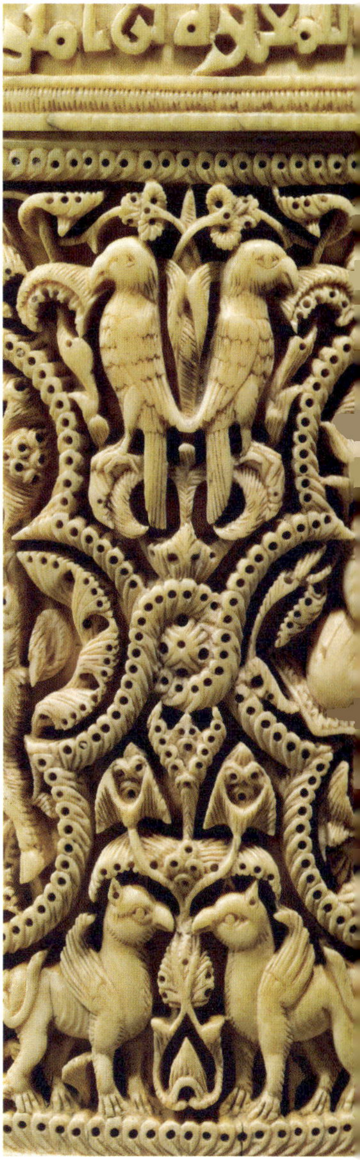

The pyxis is a small box carved in a single block of ivory that holds a mysterious and enchanting world. It takes a magnifying glass to see every detail. When the Louvre acquired the piece in the late nineteenth century, viewers admired a garden of wonders where figures play, pick dates, and listen to music. The masterpiece of Islamic art bears witness to the grandeur of the Umayyad civilization. The falcon of al-Andalus is depicted more than ten times. The engraved palm tree symbolizes the East and caliphal power. The object is so refined that it softens the violence of some of the scenes: a donkey being bitten by dogs; lions fighting with bulls; cheetahs trying to catch the tails of falcons; figures stealing eggs in a nest. Around the base, the inscription dedicated to Prince al-Mughira reads: "Blessing from God, goodwill, happiness, and prosperity to al-Mughira, son of the Commander of the Faithful, may God's mercy [be upon him], made in the year 357 [AH 357 or AD 968]."

Today, medieval art historians are considering the object in the context of a dispute over Caliph Abd al-Rahman III's succession. More than a perfume box, it held a message sent to the caliph's younger brother al-Mughira, who had just come of age. The choice of iconography (date picking, endangered falcon nests, etc.) evokes a political parable: he who fends off the dangerous rival claimants to the prophet's succession will reap the fruits of power. The rest of the story is tragic: despite the ivory talisman and the prayer to Allah, Prince al-Mughira was murdered the day after his own brother died. The killing was ordered by a concubine of the caliph whose son soon rose to power as Hisham II.

AD 2012

The new Department of Islamic Art at the Louvre was created in 2003 and moved to an impressive architectural showcase in 2012. Designed by Rudy Ricciotti and Mario Bellini, it contains spaces conceived as a movement through time and features a panorama of art works from the Hegira to the nineteenth century, from Spain to India. The space forms a mesh of golden glass and undulating metal in the Cour Visconti.

Saint Francis of Assisi Receiving the Stigmata

Giotto

A Real Miracle

This magisterial work opened a door onto a new space. Before Giotto, the figures were most often expressionless and portrayed full-face against a gold backdrop. The Florentine painter's representation of Saint Francis introduced new elements that contributed to a revolutionary conception of painting.

The ungilded legend

This large altarpiece, over 3 meters high, is most likely from a chapel in the church of San Francesco in Pisa. It depicts four scenes from the life of Saint Francis of Assisi. In the main one, the saint is praying on La Verna, facing Christ with three pairs of wings like a seraph. The missionary who founded the Order of Friars Minor (the Franciscans) receives the stigmata, that is, the marks of the wounds on Jesus' body after he was crucified. The five wounds are transmitted to Saint Francis through five beams of light.

The recipe for a successful revolution?

Why is Giotto famous?

To make a long story short, the pre-Giotto era was about Byzantine virgins, gilded backgrounds, mosaics, and Cimabue and Duccio's great hieratic figures, while the post-Giotto era saw the emergence of a form of freedom and sensitivity: the painter emphasized the major events in the saints' lives rather than represent them standing with their arms along their bodies, motionless, like statues. With him, the compositions vary, they are rich and lively, the space gains depth and legibility, the faces become expressive, the eyes shine with humanity.

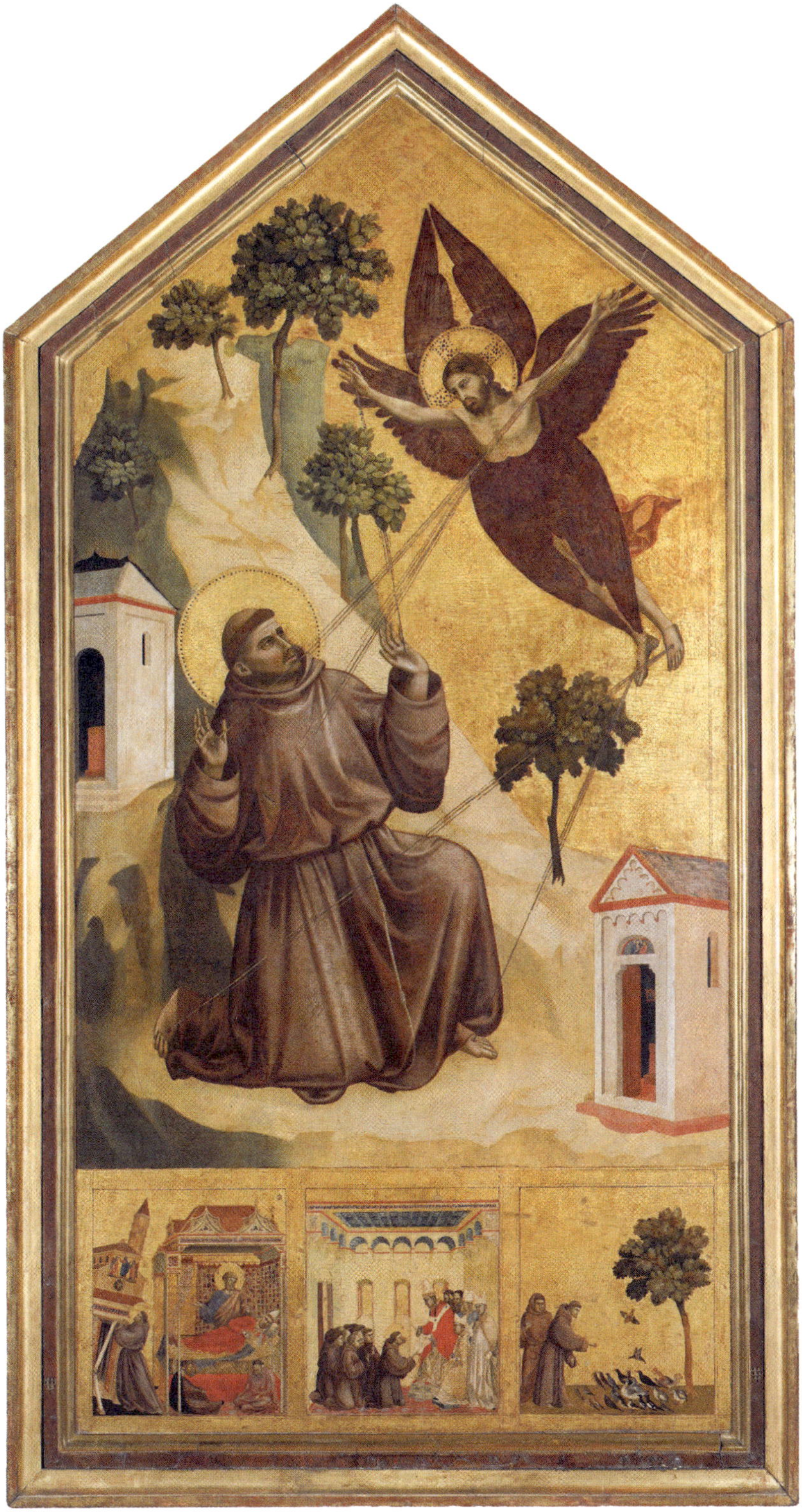

Giotto di Bondone
Saint Francis of Assisi Receiving the Stigmata,
c. 1300–25, tempera on panel, 313 × 163 cm

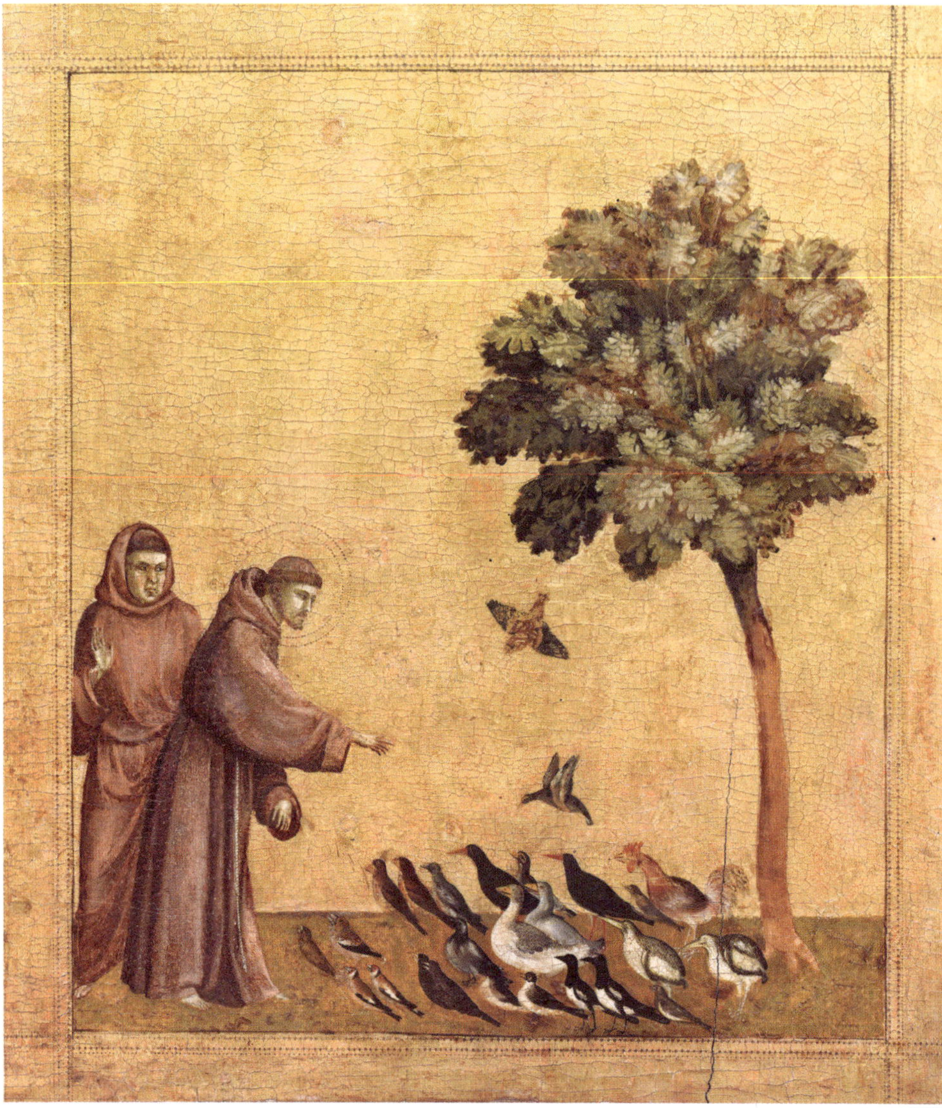

The three scenes painted at the foot of the altarpiece (the predella) represent Innocent III dreaming of Saint Francis supporting a Roman church on the verge of collapse; the Pope approving the statutes of the Order of the Franciscans; and lastly, Saint Francis preaching to birds. This parable, along with that of the stigmata, forms the most famous and edifying scene: the good word can be passed on to all living beings, regardless of their species. Giotto portrays the religious man as a person who shares and communes with all beings.

Even though it was studio work and other painters such as Cimabue or Cavallini contributed to the aesthetic renewal at the turn of the Trecento, Giotto's talent was widely recognized during his lifetime. He was honored by Pope Boniface VIII, knighted by the king of Naples, and appointed "master and governor" in charge of architecture in Florence. The artist was capable of producing several frescoes at the same time, the most famous of which are still visible in the basilicas of Santa Croce in Florence and of San Francesco in Assisi, as well as in the Cappella degli Scrovegni in Padua.

The cycles of Saint Francis painted by Giotto retrace the monk's life: his calling, the scene where he renounces his worldly goods, the trial by fire, and the stigmata. Francis of Assisi (1182–1226) was extremely popular; he was canonized as a saint a mere two years after his death. The stigmatization in particular made a lasting impression in Italy and even north of the Alps. Similar iconography can be found in works by Fra Angelico and Jan van Eyck.

"Giotto artfully suffuses the evangelical scenes—the wonderful episodes that unfold in the life of a kind and charitable saint—with a meditative state that enfolds the viewer in absolute purity and simplicity."

André Chastel

The birth of the artist

Giotto owes part of his posthumous fame to Dante, who told how Cimabue's fame was eclipsed by the other artist's in the Purgatorio of his Divine Comedy: "Cimabue believed that he held the field/ In painting, and now Giotto has the cry/ So the fame of the former is obscured." Similarly, in *The Decameron*, Boccaccio wrote that Giotto's painting delights the eyes of the ignorant as well as the mind of the scientist. Thus hailed by the two founding authors of Italian literature, Giotto's name was soon equated with the model of the "artist"—a concept slowly replacing that of the artisan. The artist emancipates himself from the icon; he finds his own voice to represent the world from a new angle. Like Giotto, an artist is an individual with his own name, style, and legend.

Baptistery of Saint Louis

A Crucible of Civilization

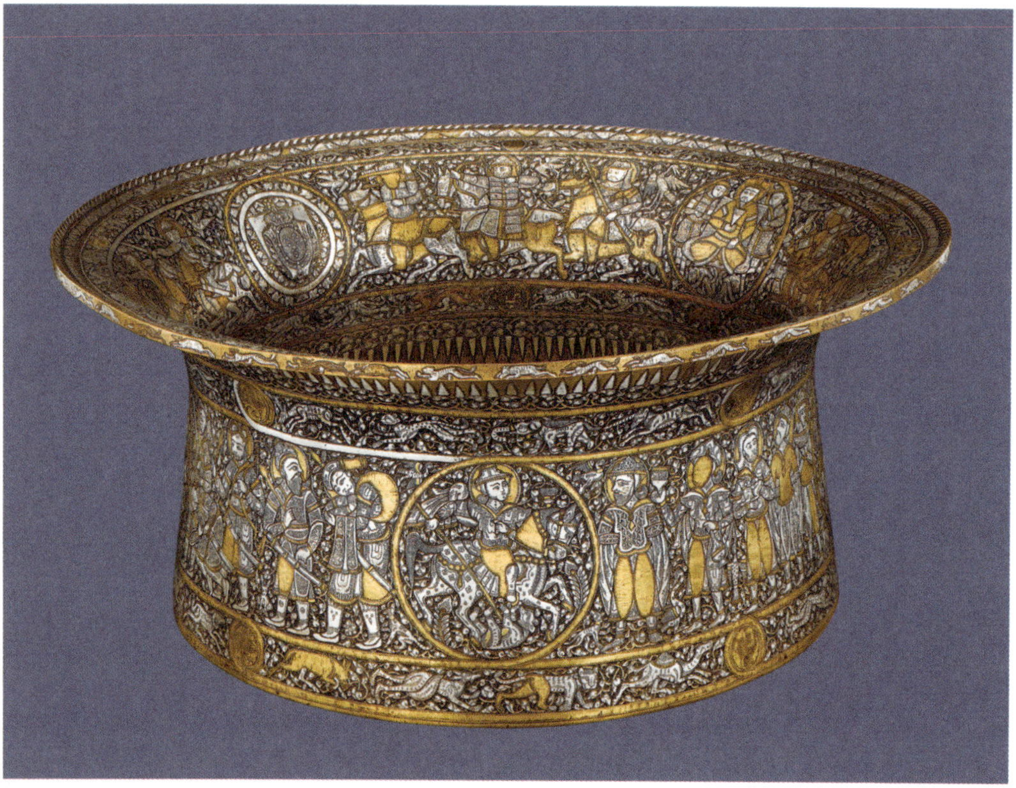

Basin known as the Baptistery of Saint Louis,
c. 1325–40,
hammered brass,
gold, silver,
black paste inlay,
23 cm

Why is this basin made by Muhammad ibn al-Zayn known as the Baptistery of Saint Louis? Is it the result of a Crusades legend, or an attribute of royal power passed on from generation to generation? Long held in the treasury of the Sainte-Chapelle in Vincennes, the princely object was moved to the Louvre after the Revolution.

A thousand and one legends

The origin of the basin and its use have given rise to a number of theories that have contributed to the legend. Eighteenth-century scholars such as Millin and Hurtaut surmised that Louis IX (Saint Louis) had returned from a crusade with the basin that depicted the persecution of Christians by the Mohammedans, or that it was a gift from Harun al-Rashid to Charlemagne. It is still known as the Baptistery of Saint Louis today, even though a baptistery is not a basin but an architectural construction similar to a presbytery, and Saint Louis died in the thirteenth century—that is, before Muhammad ibn al-Zayn's time. The fleurs-de-lis concealing the Seal of Solomon (the star of David) have also sparked much debate.

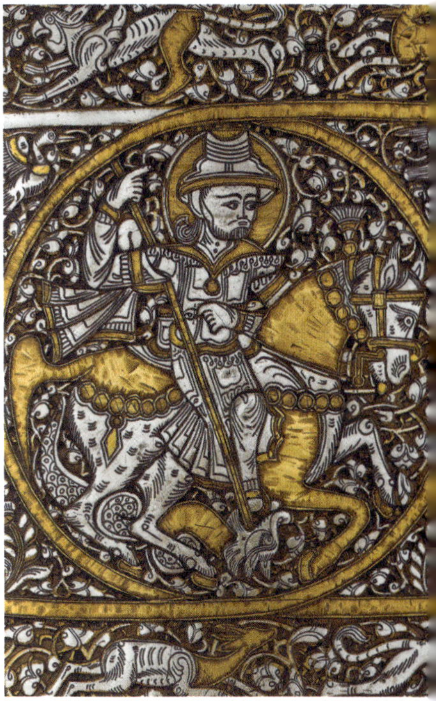

Spectacular

"The basin was probably brought back from a crusade. It was used to baptize French princes."

Pierre Thomas Nicolas Hurtaut

The birth of a prince is a major event for it seals the alliance between two dynasties and anchors the reigning line. Spectacular celebrations culminate with the baptism ceremony, the perfect opportunity to impress one's subjects and forge new alliances by way of the child's godparents. In 1856 the baptism of Napoleon III's only son proved a great opportunity to shine through Europe, legitimize the regime, and rally the traditional elites, the bourgeoisie, and the intellectuals. Between two universal expositions, Pope Pius IX and Queen Josephine of Sweden became the prince's godparents; 400,000 francs were spent to decorate Notre-Dame Cathedral; and Muhammad ibn al-Zayn's basin was taken out of the Louvre for the occasion. Nearly 500 guests gathered in the large Galerie de l'Hôtel de Ville to eat crayfish bisque, ortolans, and truffles, washed down with champagne and Château d'Yquem.

Charlemagne's Scepter

Good-Old Charlemagne

Half-magic wand, half-episcopal crosier, the scepter is a fascinating symbol of power. With the crown, it represents the monarchy and is part of the regalia—clothing, accessories, and insignia—used during a king's coronation ceremony.

Treasure hunt

What does regalia mean?

We have grown accustomed to seeing regalia represented in official portraits or coat of arms. The king is portrayed with the crown, of course, but also with the scepter and other royal insignia. Hence, the coronation sword known as Joyeuse reminds one that the king can take up arms to protect the Church if necessary. Another attribute of power is the Hand of Justice, a wooden staff topped with an ivory hand whose first three fingers are open. The holy ampulla used to anoint kings, the Scepter of Dagobert, and the Chalice of Saint Rémi can also be considered regalia. They were used during the coronation of the kings of France and were kept at the abbey of Saint-Denis the rest of the time. In the early eighteenth century, the monk Dom Michel Félibien made an inventory of the regalia and listed 445 different items, thus making it possible to identify which ones had been melted during the Revolution (mainly crowns) and which masterpieces had been preserved or reconstituted.

Charlemagne's scepter was named after the statuette that surmounts it. It was commissioned by Charles V (1338–1380), probably in anticipation of the coronation of his son, the future Charles VI. The monarch—from the Valois dynasty, the cadet branch of the Capetians—wanted his dynasty to be in the direct line of the illustrious king of the Franks, then venerated as a saint by the court of France. This manner of placing the royal insignia under the patronage of Charlemagne dated from the previous century and was to continue until the reign of Napoleon I.

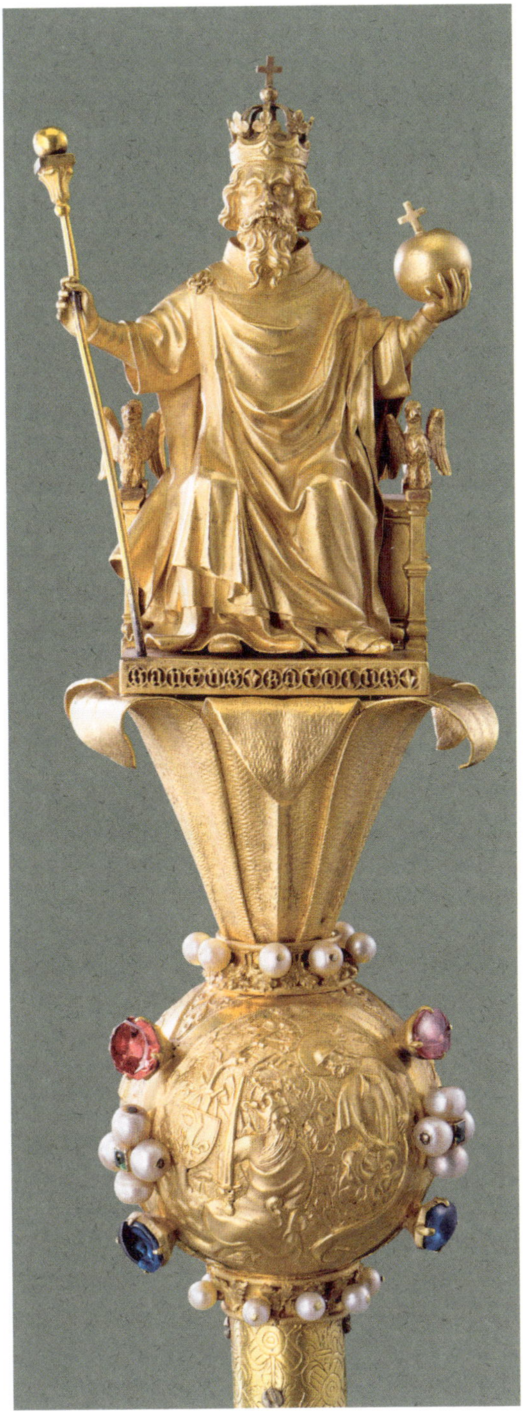

The Scepter of Charles V, known as Charlemagne's Scepter, c. 1364, gold, gilt silver (handle), rubies, colored glass, beads, 60 cm

Centerpiece

The "knob" at the end of the shaft also features on bishops' croziers. It is adorned with pearls, set stones, and a historical depiction of three major events in Charlemagne's life. The finely crafted scepter bears witness to the flourishing precious arts during the reign of Charles V, who was also a great collector and a patron.

How the relics came to be

When Napoleon became emperor in the nineteenth century, he had to bear the symbols of his immense power—even if it meant making up illustrious predecessors. Dominique Vivant Denon, who had been appointed director of the Musée Napoléon and director of arts, looked into the matter. With the help of an architect and a goldsmith, he redesigned some insignia and restored some regalia, and devised a synthesis of the coats of arms that had to appear on the imperial seal. The aim was not only to make a connection with the Merovingians and Carolingians, but also to bypass the Capetians since Louis XVIII, exiled in Poland, had refused to abdicate. Hence the Merovingian king Childeric's bees on the purple mantle, the reconstitution of an ivory hand of justice, and the restoration of Charlemagne's scepter for the coronation whose splendor was immortalized by David (page 138).

The Most Detailed of Prayers

This small wooden panel is fascinating both in its manifold details and complexity of meaning. A true milestone in both Van Eyck's career and Flemish painting, *The Madonna of Chancellor Rolin* has sparked countless debates.

Treasures

The *Madonna of Chancellor Rolin* owes its fame mostly to Van Eyck's use of technique, inventiveness, perhaps even trickery.
The humility of Rolin's gesture is counterbalanced by his luxurious fur-lined garment, on a par with the Virgin's embroidered mantle. The viewer is drawn to the profusion of details, from the elaborate tiles to the carved friezes on the arches, from the peacocks to the magpies, rabbits, and fruit. A vast landscape stretches beyond the loggia. The moss on the paving stones, the circles in the water—these "lesser details" as Dürer used to call them—reveal the painter's technical prowess. The meticulously composed background includes a variety of buildings, fields, a river, a bridge, and various figures. The perspective seems endless as the hues gradually blend into the horizon.

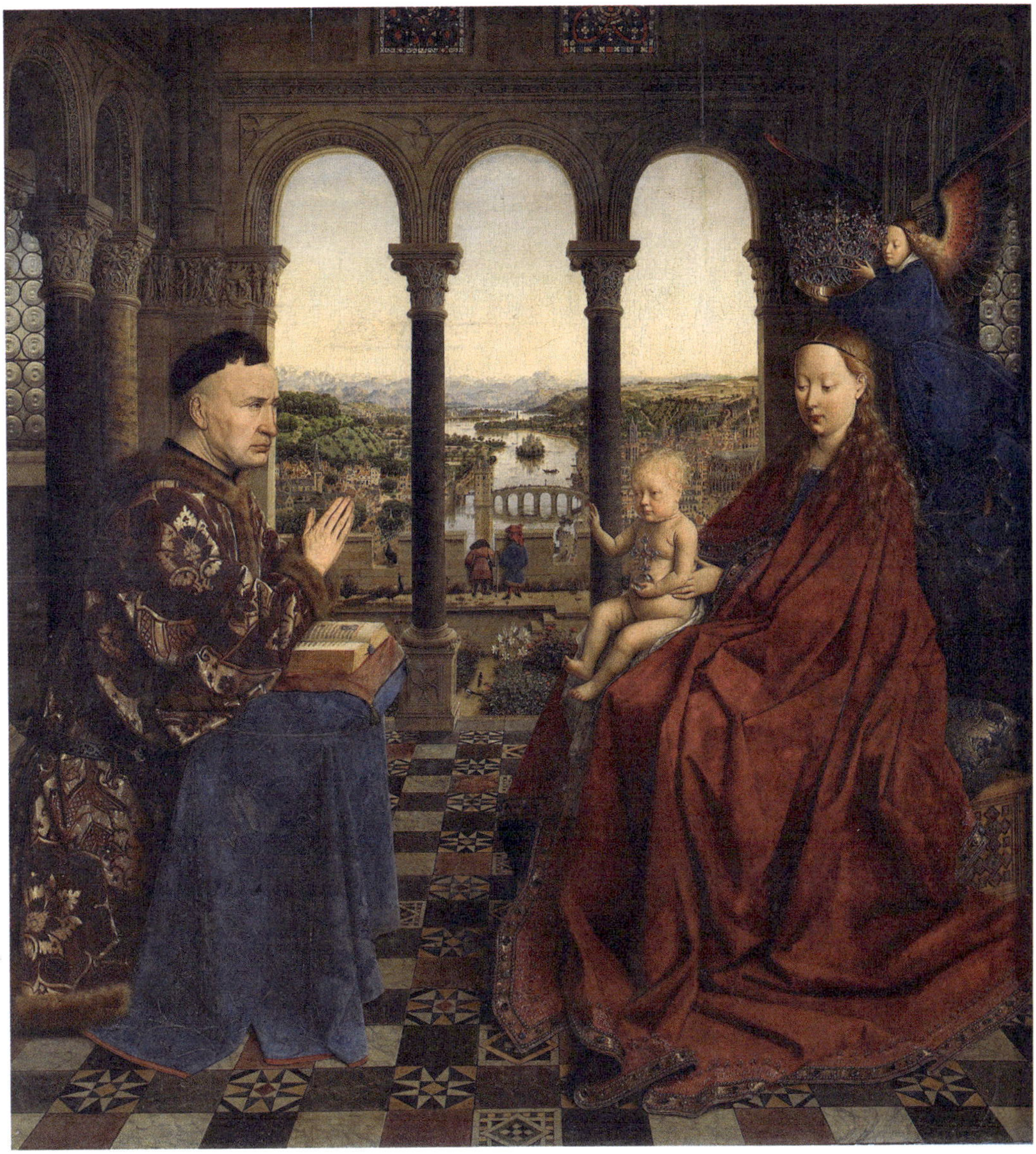

Jan van Eyck
The Madonna of Chancellor Rolin, c. 1430,
oil on panel,
6 × 62 cm

Did Chancellor Rolin buy his seat in Heaven?

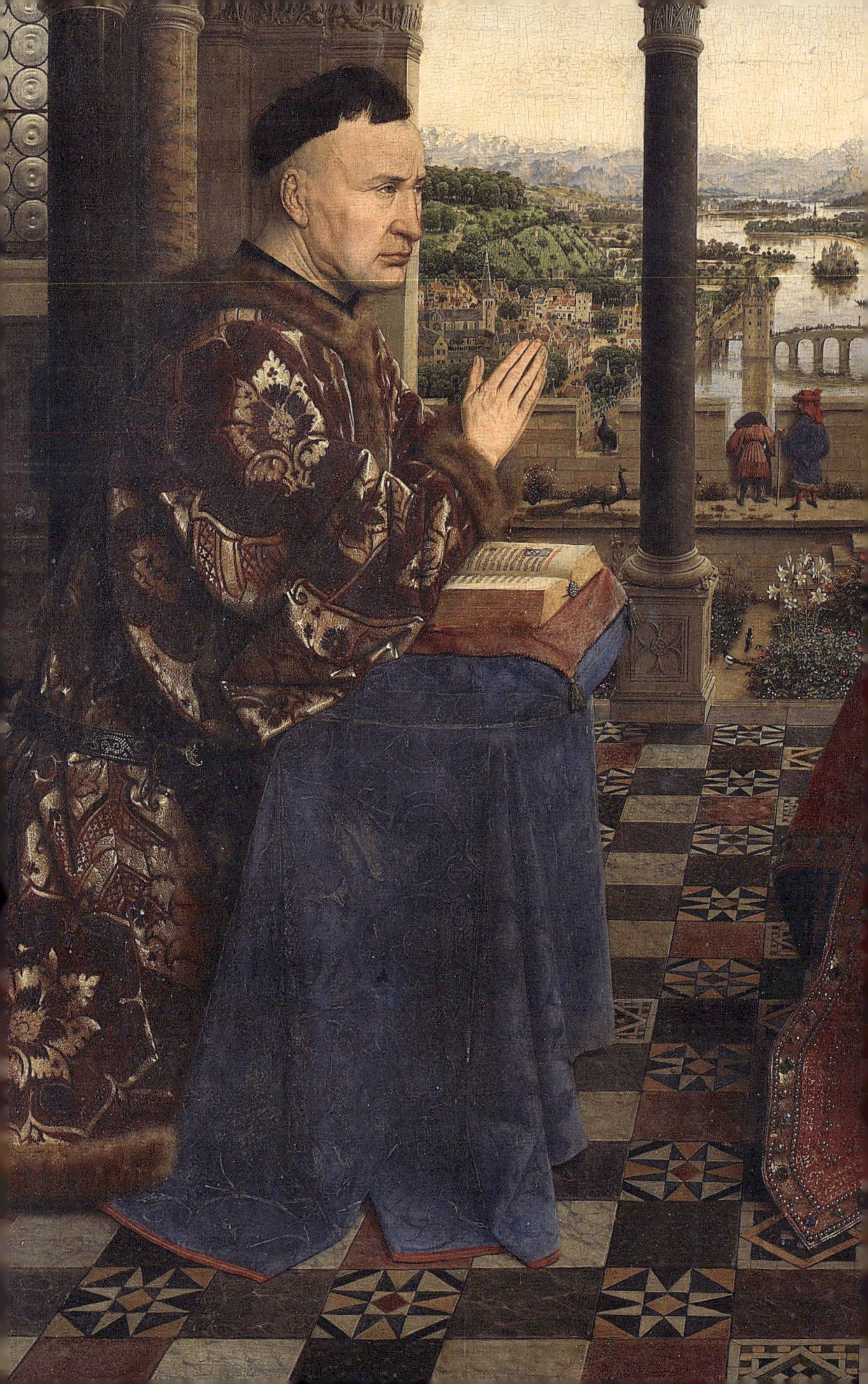

A conversation

Beyond the countless details, the painting depicts a mental image: it portrays the commissioner before the object of his devotion, namely the Virgin and the Child. Chancellor Rolin commissioned this work from Jan van Eyck to adorn a family chapel in the church of Notre-Dame du Châtel in Autun. Rolin is depicted as the believer engaged in holy conversation. He addresses his prayers to the Virgin and receives the blessing of the Child. The book of hours placed atop the prie-dieu is the object of intercession, and the two figures on each side are absorbed in contemplation.
That said, what one remembers about the painting is not the intimate and silent prayer characteristic of *devotio moderna*, the spiritual movement that developed in northern Europe in the fifteenth century. The details galore were more impactful and intrigued commentators as did those of *The Arnolfini Portrait* by the same artist.

The advent of oil painting

Contrary to claims by some of his peers (Vasari), Jan van Eyck did not invent oil painting. Still, along with Robert Campin and Rogier van der Weyden, he was one of the Flemish Primitives who perfected the technique with meticulous rendering of detail and transparent glazes obtained with successive liquid layers.

VIP

The position Nicolas Rolin (1376–1462) held as chancellor to the duke of Burgundy, Philip the Good, was equivalent to that of a head of state or an attorney general. Then a large state including Burgundy and Flanders, the duchy played a central role in the European political arena. The chancellor would accumulate considerable assets through annuities and pensions. Furthermore, Rolin was an enlightened patron who built castles, mansions, and the renowned Hôtel-Dieu in Beaune, whose *Last Judgment* polyptych he commissioned from Rogier van der Weyden.

The Battle of San Romano

Uccello

A Huge Miniature

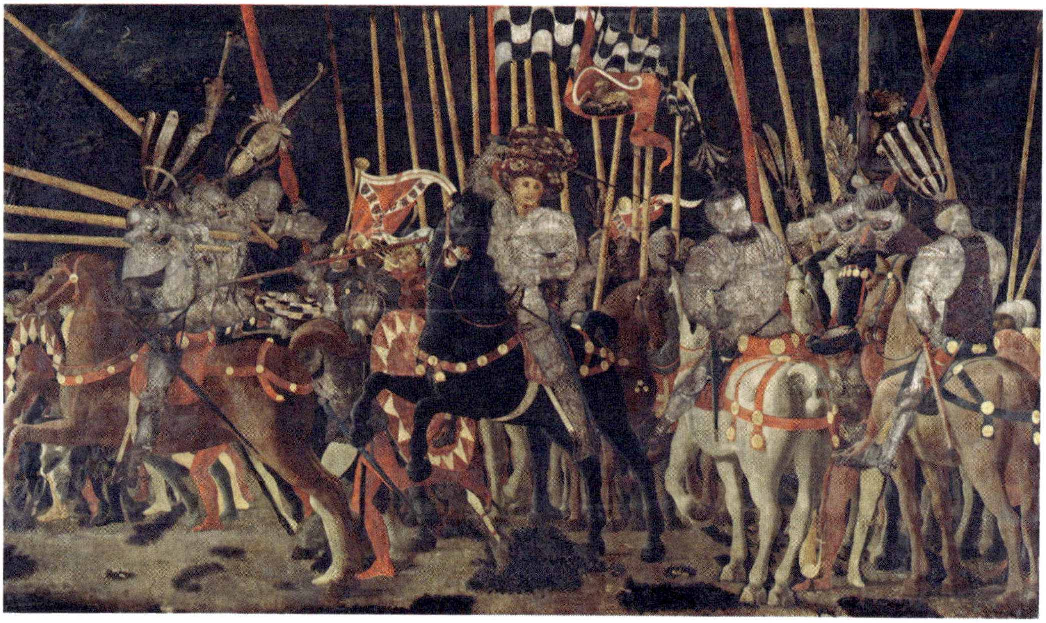

Paolo Uccello's *Battle of San Romano* is strangely appealing: stylized like a bas-relief, it commemorates the victory of the Florentines over the Sienese in 1432. The historical feat is now of less interest to viewers than the painter's take on perspective, despite the fading colors.

The origin of the battle

It was long believed that the work had been commissioned by Cosimo de' Medici for his palace, but it was more likely Leonardo Bartolini Salimbeni who asked Paolo Uccello to produce a series of paintings about the Battle of San Romano. The works initially consisted of curved panels that were probably cut and/or completed to form rectangles by the time they were hung on the walls of Lorenzo de' Medici's bedchamber, as was recorded in the inventory of 1492. Eager to appear noble through their collection and patronage, the Medicis could relate to a tradition of chivalry with this type of war paintings.

Can you see this hanging on your bedroom wall?

Paolo Uccello
The Battle of San Romano: The Counterattack by Micheletto da Cotignola,
tempera on panel,
c. 1435–75,
182 × 317 cm

Dispersal

The first panel, *Niccolò da Tolentino Leads the Florentine Troops*, is currently on display at the National Gallery in London. The second panel, *The Counterattack by Micheletto da Cotignola*, was part of the Marquis Campana's collection before entering the Louvre's Department of Paintings. The third panel entitled *Niccolò Mauruzi da Tolentino Unseats Bernardino della Ciarda at the Battle of San Romano* is still in Florence, at the Galleria degli Uffizi. The spectacular side of battle is striking. These large panels must have responded to each other when they were together. When the silver leaf patterns on the armor were still new and shiny, viewers must have felt as if they were standing amid the roar of battle.

A fantastic ride

Paolo Uccello's painting is so striking because of the artist's research on perspective and because of the fantastical nature of his oeuvre. He excelled at interweaving objects and figures while balancing color and space. His painting was quite unusual as a result—it is both turbulent and still.

On the silver screen

In Roger Vadim's contribution to the film *Spirits of the Dead*, Uccello's painting illustrates the strange relationship between Countess Frederique, played by Jane Fonda, and a superb black stallion escaped from a wall tapestry. More recently, in the series *The Borgias*, life-size copies of the Louvre and National Gallery panels are displayed side by side in the filmset of the reception hall of the Palazzo Medici in Florence.

The hats

Some of the figures in *The Battle of San Romano* wear surprising ring-shaped hats decorated with checkerboard or plant patterns (opposite), which contributed to Uccello's fame as they impressed his contemporaries. Art historians, who call them *mazzocchios*, read the headgear's geometric pattern as a study of shape and color, and of concavity and convexity. It shows an artisan or artist's ability to create perspective.

Another startling hat can be seen in a work entitled *The Thebaid*. Indeed, in the painting, a cardinal's red headdress seems to be floating in space. It was mistaken for an alien and gave rise to an unexpected renewal of interest in the artist during the twentieth century.

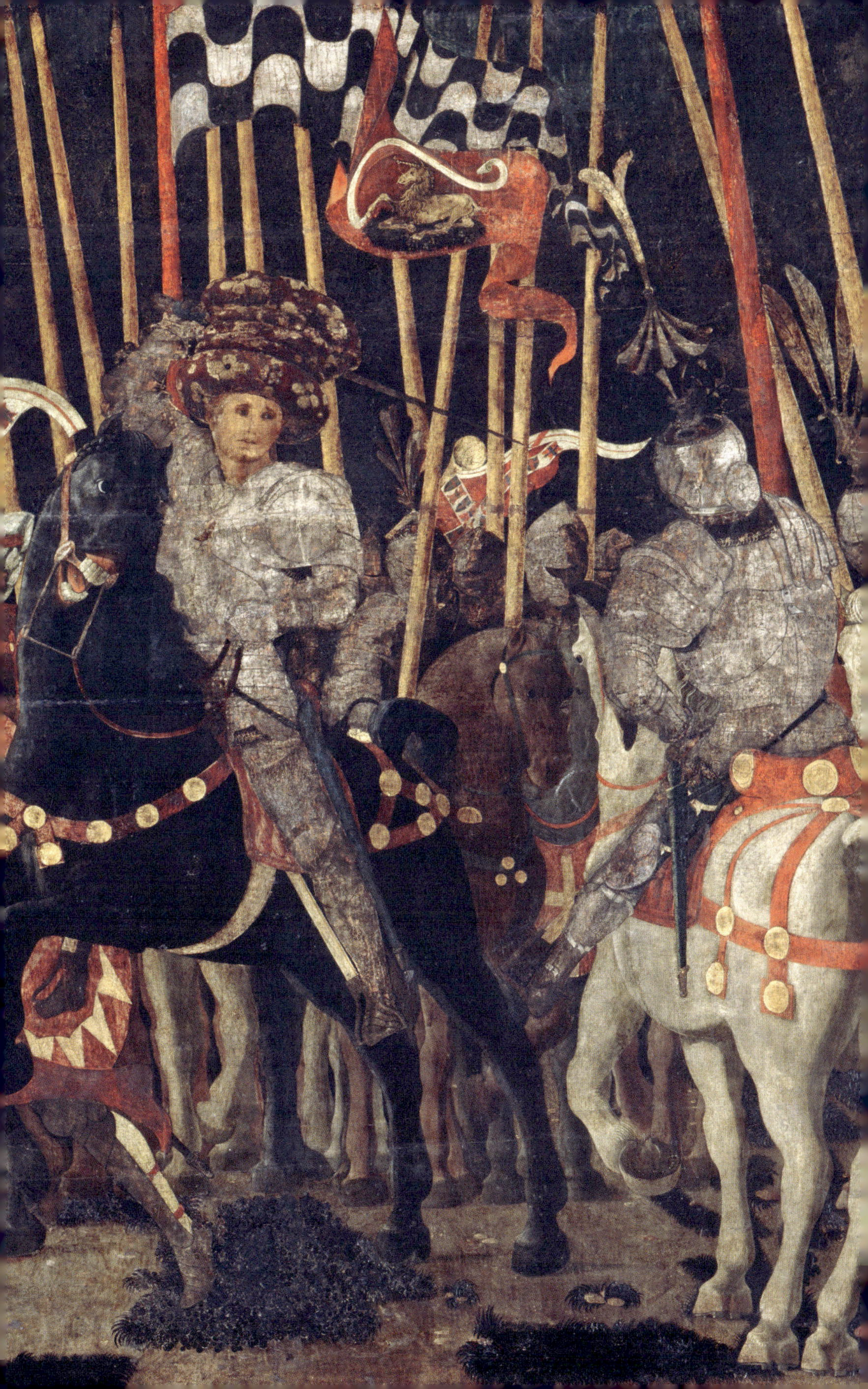

The Pietà of Villeneuve-lès-Avignon Quarton

Devotio Moderna

The pietà, where Mary cradles her son's body following his descent from the cross, was widely represented in fifteenth-century European art. The tragic scene is portrayed with restraint in *The Pietà of Villeneuve-lès-Avignon*. It is a touching testimony to the medieval sensitivity and pictorial genius of Enguerrand Quarton, a painter rediscovered in the nineteenth century and acclaimed in the twentieth century.

The new idol

The Pietà of Villeneuve-lès-Avignon marked an entire generation when it was first exhibited at the Louvre in the early twentieth century. Indeed, according to curator Sébastien Allard, head of the Department of Paintings, "back then, the large painting must have had a strange resonance with other new objects from Africa or Oceania." Audiences of the day were interested in the geometry of some "primitive" works (see the Cycladic figurine, page 20). In this altarpiece, they probably admired the abstract textures, the frontality of the faces, the gestures, the angles of the bodies, the contrasting earth and gold—all the things that could echo modern art, cubism, constructivism, abstract art, and so on. As it turned out, Mondrian made a copy of it in 1913. The viewers were paradoxically drawn to the modernity of the Middle Ages and—more so than Michelangelo's—it was *The Pietà of Villeneuve-lès-Avignon* that appeared on record sleeves and concert posters to advertise the new versions of *Stabat Mater* by Vivaldi, Pergolese, and Rossini.

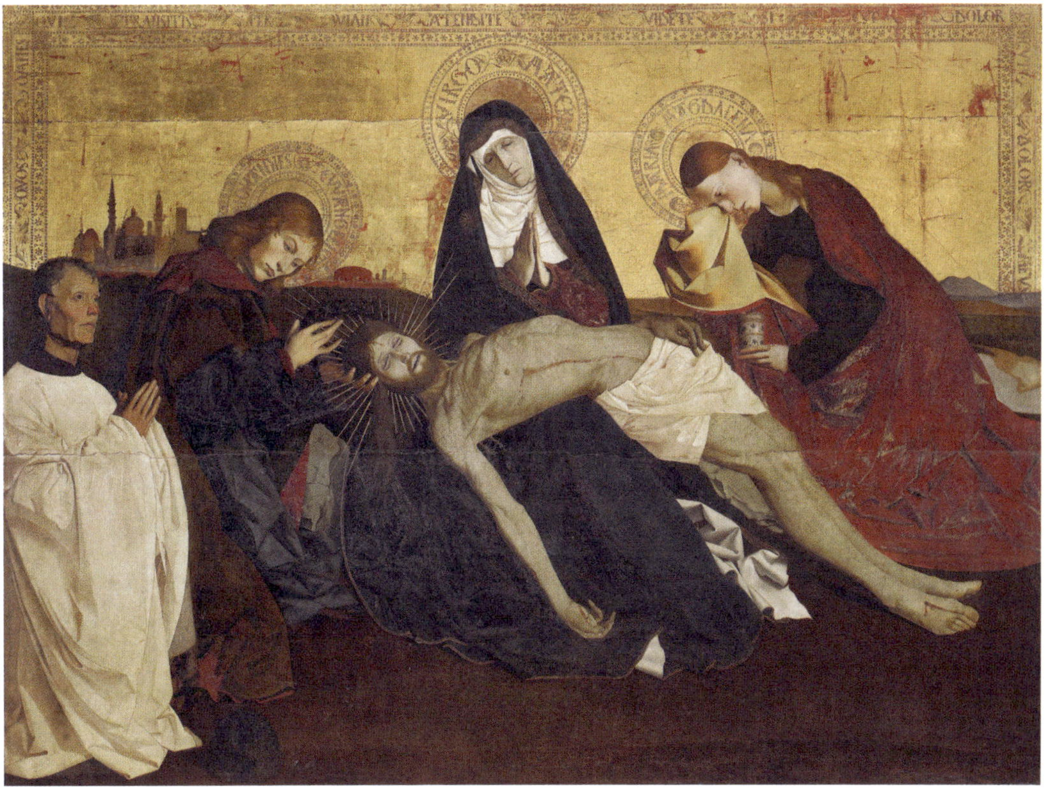

Enguerrand Quarton
The Pietà of Villeneuve-lès-Avignon,
c. 1450–75,
tempera on panel,
163 × 218 cm

Why is it modern?

Now famous

The Pietà of Villeneuve-lès-Avignon was the central—and only remaining—panel of the altarpiece in the Villeneuve-lès-Avignon charterhouse. It stayed there until 1834 when it was discovered by Prosper Mérimée, the young inspector-general of historic monuments in charge of inventorying the works found in French churches and châteaus. The author of *Carmen* brought *The Pietà of Villeneuve-lès-Avignon* out of the shadows and into the limelight.

Seventy years later, it was acclaimed by visitors of the French Primitives exhibition at the Louvre. Hung next to the famous portrait of Jean Le Bon under the title *Pietà with Donor*, neither its commissioner nor its creator were known. Mérimée thought it was perhaps the work of Bellini. But wasn't the Avignon masterpiece of Spanish or Portuguese descent rather than Italian? To avoid confusion until the issue was resolved, the art history expert Charles Sterling spoke of the "Master of the Avignon Pietà." In 1959 his research led to the conclusion that the panel was by Enguerrand Quarton, a painter from northern France who worked in Provence in the middle of the fifteenth century. The artist must have been familiar with Parisian miniatures, Sienese art, and that of the Flemish primitives. Art historians now agree that he painted four works from four altarpieces: *The Virgin of Mercy of the Cadard Family* (1452, Musée Condé, Chantilly); *The Coronation of the Virgin* (1453, Musée de l'Hôpital, Villeneuve-les-Avignon); *The Requin Altarpiece* (c. 1450–55, Musée du Petit Palais, Avignon), and the now famous *Pietà of Villeneuve-lès-Avignon* (1455).

"The great 'Pieta' of Avignon is one of the summits of the harmony. It is now like the sound of a violoncello arising alone above the tombs."

Élie Faure, *History of Art*

A festival of piety

In Italian, *pietà* means compassion. Like the Crucifixion and the Virgin and Child, from the late Middle Ages the pietà became a popular iconographic theme. Viewers were touched by its clear and simple message. The words engraved in Latin on the gold background are from the Book of Lamentations: "Oh, all ye that pass by the way, attend, and see if there be any sorrow like to my sorrow."

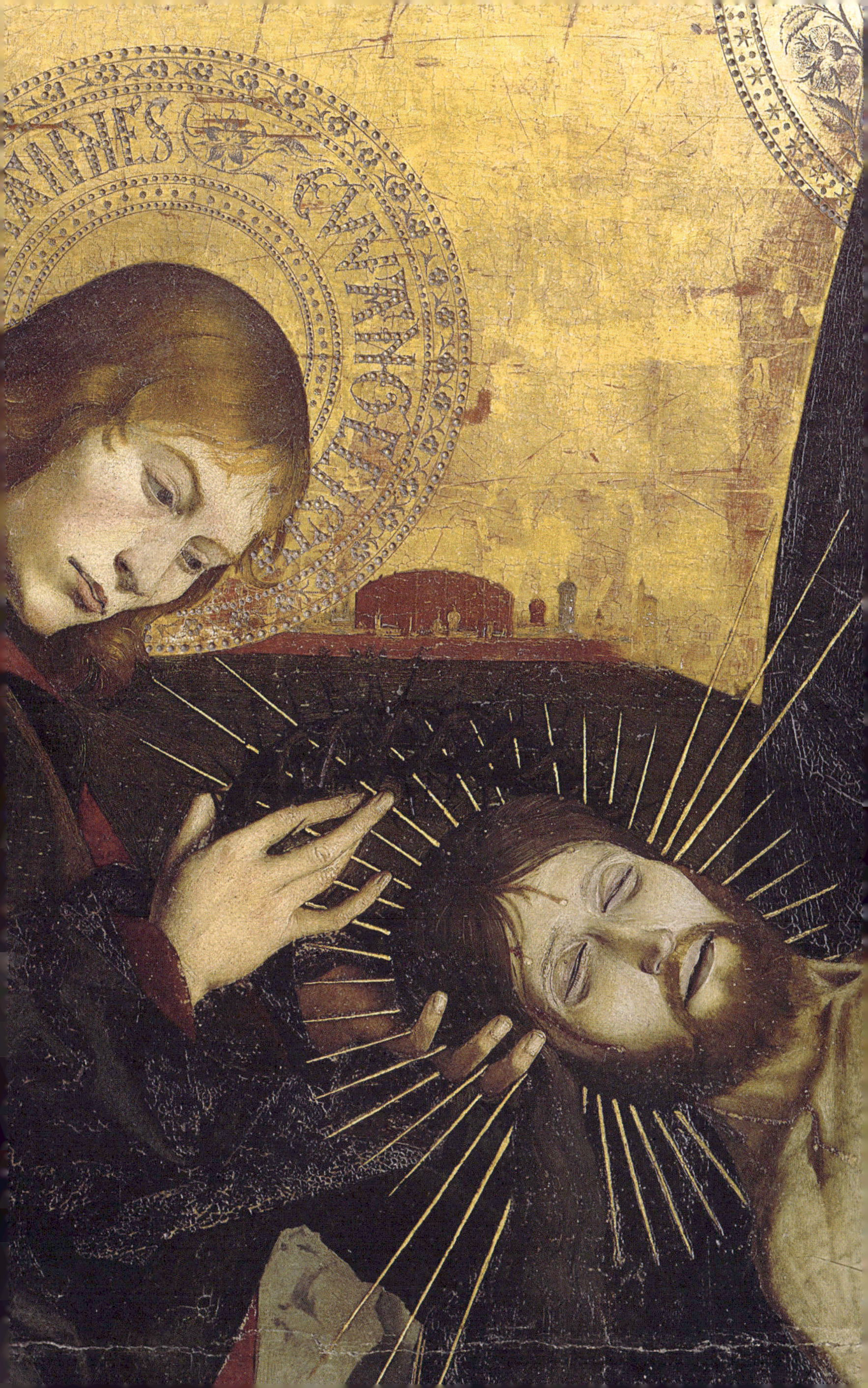

Saint Sebastian Mantegna

Exemplary

Mantegna's *Saint Sebastian* is on display in the Grande Galerie of the Louvre. Guides and art lovers can address major Italian Renaissance issues based on it alone. Furthermore, it arouses a sensual curiosity and represents a male counterpart to Venus and a model in the fight against homophobia.

How to sum up the Renaissance in a single painting

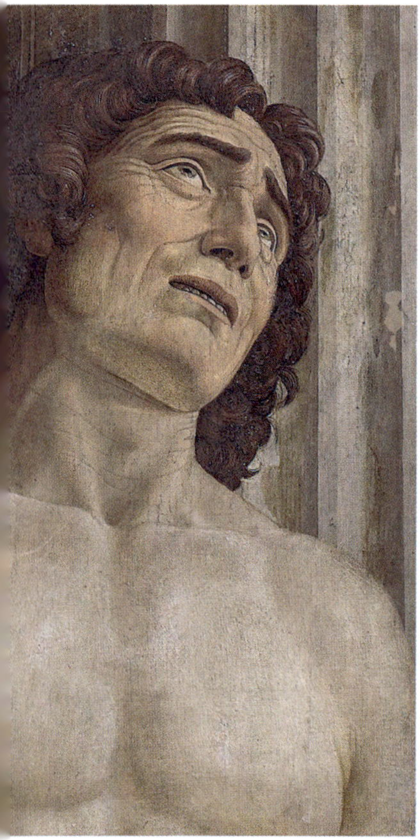

The epitome of the Renaissance

The work exemplifies the Renaissance period: the painting was structured like a window open onto the real world and composed in keeping with the laws of perspective and anatomy. The viewer is firmly steered into the work through a trompe-l'oeil porphyry frame that creates a fake opening. Then the half-naked body, arrows, and executioners give away the theme: it is a martyrdom. At that stage, the viewer delves deeper into the layers of meaning: Sebastian replacing a broken statue of which a foot remains, the Corinthian capital matching the ancient style of the Palace of Diocletian, the gaze drawn to the right in a serpentine movement. In the background, a forum and inverted columns overlook a steep path leading to more modern city, the clouds above, etc. Gone are the medieval golds.

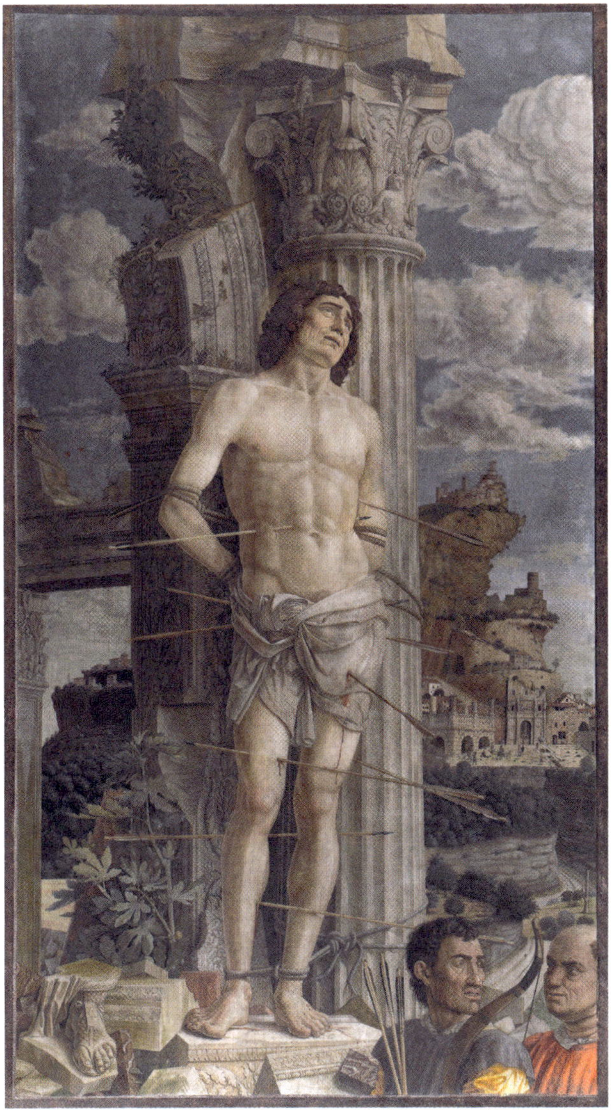

Andrea Mantegna
Saint Sebastian,
c. 1480,
tempera on panel,
255 × 140 cm

Riddled with arrows

After joining his army as a simple soldier, Sebastian was appointed commander by the Emperor Diocletian. But, as a Christian, he was condemned to death after he defended the prisoners who were persecuted for their faith. "And the archers hit him until he was riddled with arrows like a hedgehog is covered with thorns," Jacobus de Voragine wrote in *The Golden Legend* in 1266.

Remaining fabulous

In the fifteenth century, Saint Sebastian evolved into a charming figure with a more alluring body, a languorous pose, and translucent skin. The piece of cloth wrapped around his waist hugs the appendage it is meant to conceal. He becomes an erotic figure when painted by Mantegna, Perugino, and Guido Reni. Twentieth-century literature, photography, and cinema associated the martyrdom of Saint Sebastian with homosexuality. In *Confessions of a Mask* (1949), the great Japanese writer Yukio Mishima reveals how he became aware of his own homosexuality upon discovering Guido Reni's version of the martyrdom.
Of the saint whose face never betrays the agony of having a body riddled with arrows, the essayist Susan Sontag—who combated AIDS and died of cancer—says he is "the exemplary sufferer." To her, beauty and suffering were two separate things. The attitude that enabled him to resist the plague must continue to serve as an example.

Venus and the Three Graces Botticelli

Eternal Spring

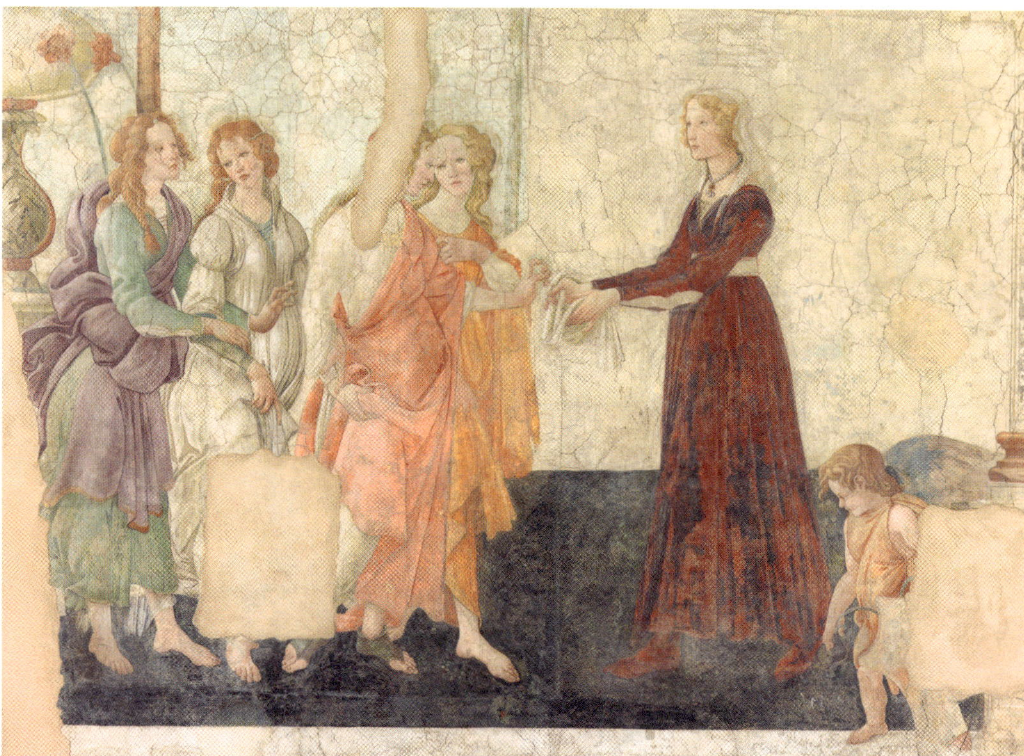

Alessandro Filipepi,
known as **Botticelli**
Venus and the Three Graces Presenting Gifts to a Young Woman,
c. 1483–485, fresco,
211 × 283 cm

Upon leaving the Winged Victory of Samothrace on their way to see the Italian masterpieces, visitors to the Louvre discover this fresco that once adorned the loggia in a villa near Florence. Passing through the Salle Percier et Fontaine is both an immersion in Botticelli's world and a reunion with his ideal beauties.

Full of grace

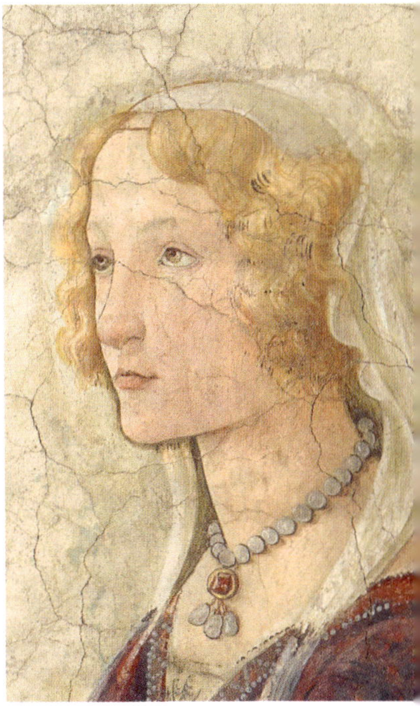

Botticelli's works are now iconic, in the same way as his vision of women most certainly influenced our own. But Botticelli's painting was out of fashion at the time of his death, whereas all eyes were focused on the great Leonardo da Vinci, Raphael, and Michelangelo. Botticelli sank into a relative oblivion until the nineteenth century and John Ruskin's writings hailed him once again as a master of the first Florentine Renaissance, that of Medici refinement and elegance. Pre-Raphaelite painters favored Botticelli's allegorical aesthetics magnified by sumptuous drapery and translucent faces. Late nineteenth-century dandies fell in love with the inaccessible figures. Botticelli's fame has not ceased to grow since his twentieth-century revival. Andy Warhol turned Venus into a silkscreened Pop art icon, and fashion designers Dolce & Gabbana printed her effigy on their clothes.

The Florentine ideal

Beauty is at the heart of Botticelli's art. In Florence, the painter was regarded highly among the learned circles of the Medici family. He shared the humanist views of Marsilio Fisino, Poliziano, and Giovanni Pico della Mirandola. His painting was an interpretation of Neoplatonist thoughts whereby Venus was a goddess of "the love of knowledge," who granted immortality of the soul to men. The Graces represent the generosity of giving and receiving. The fresco depicts a young woman accessing Ideal Beauty and the world of ideas with the help of Greco-Roman deities. The gracefully painted figures familiarize the viewer with this ideal.

At the same time, Botticelli produced his two most famous works: *Primavera* and *The Birth of Venus*. Both represent the same figures that went on to leave their mark on the Western psyche; indeed, there has since been countless representations of curvaceous young blondes stepping out of water or scantily dressed and laughing with friends in an eternal spring.

An Old Man and his Grandson Ghirlandaio

The Beauty of the Ugly

The double portrait fascinates and raises questions about its allegorical meaning. *An Old Man and his Grandson* touches everyone, and its clever staging deepens our perception of ugliness and aging.

As plain as the nose on his face

"What is commonly called ugliness in nature can in art become full of great beauty."

Auguste Rodin, sculptor of *Man with the Broken Nose*

At the exact point where the medians and diagonals meet in the middle of the painting, as in the middle of the face, there is a bulbous nose. It cannot be missed. The old man is suffering from "rhinophyma," an acute form of rosacea where reddish lumps appear on the nose. The old man in the painting also has a bald head and a wart on his forehead. Although the contrast with the child's delicate features is obvious, the painting's composition gives a more nuanced interpretation of the difference between ugliness and beauty, old age and youth: the elder looks benevolently down at the boy, who places his hand on the old man's shoulder as if looking for support. They exchange a look of mutual trust, affection, and acceptance of the other's difference. The open window behind them reveals a stylized landscape in the outside world. According to art historians, the *cappuccio* on the old man's shoulder indicates that he was a patrician. The double portrait could be a tribute to him, and by extension to the continuing generations of Florentine nobility.

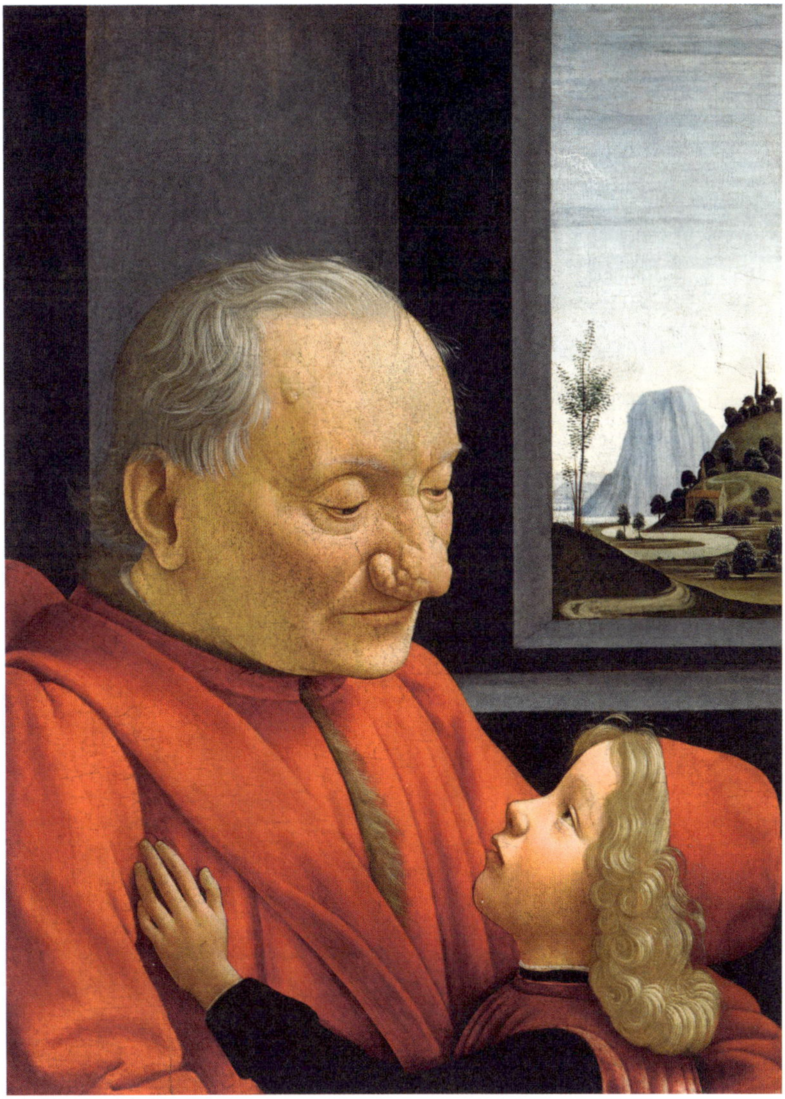

Domenico Ghirlandaio
An Old Man and his Grandson,
1490, tempera on panel,
62 × 46 cm

Can we find ugliness attractive?

The entrepreneur

At the end of the Quattrocento, Domenico Ghirlandaio was the most famous and sought-after painter in Florence. He worked with his brother in the family business—where Michelangelo did his apprenticeship—which could employ ten people or so to help produce large frescoes for chapels. The studio was known for its easily readable religious images. The wide distribution of prototypes of the then highly popular veiled Virgin, with her haloed head tilted down and her gaze lowered, was attributed to Domenico Ghirlandaio instead of Raphael.

The Drunken Boat

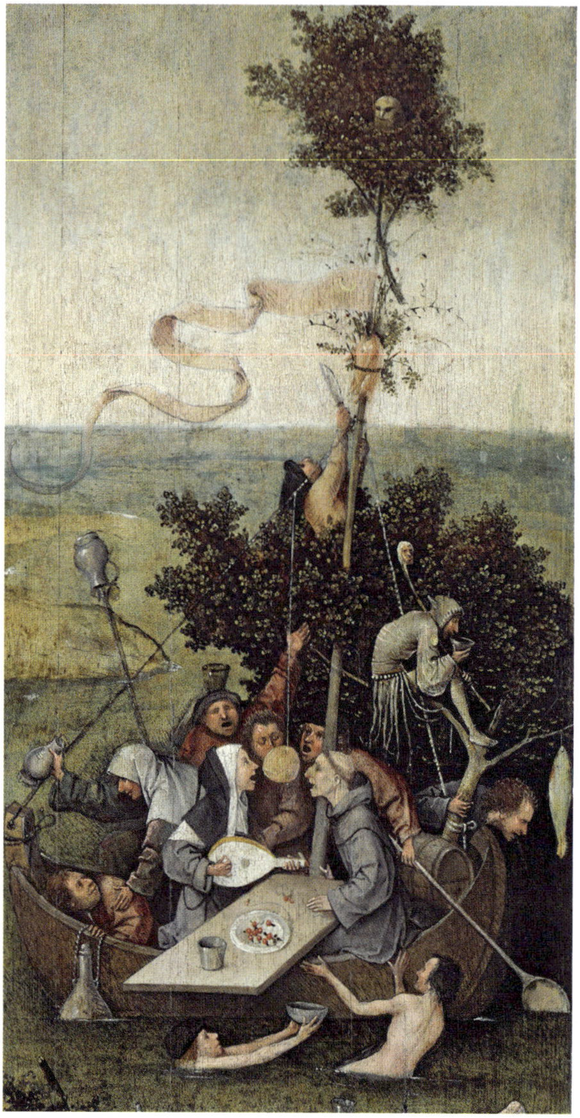

The world is changing. Humanity appears on the verge of downfall. The figures flail about, the details abound. In *Ship of Fools*, Hieronymus Bosch gives a striking depiction of the upheaval about to befall society and the clergy. The small wooden panel is a fragment of a fascinating triptych on the seven deadly sins.

Hieronymus van Aken, known as **Hieronymus Bosch**
Ship of Fools,
c. 1500,
oil on panel,
58 × 33 cm

The impulses of the imagination

The painting represents a group of ten gluttons gathered in a boat. A Franciscan monk faces a nun playing the lute. Both have their mouths open, about to swallow a suspended pancake. Rowers wield a broken jug and a ladle. There is a general sense of unrest. A roasted goose and a banner with a crescent moon are hung from the mast, itself topped with a bouquet of leaves sheltering an owl or a skull. Where did the artist get his inspiration from? The painting is reminiscent of *Das Narrenschiff* (Ship of Fools), an illustrated book of folk tales in the context of the Reformation published in 1494 by Sebastian Brant. It was probably by analogy with the famed eponymous book that the small painting was named *Ship of Fools* in the late nineteenth century.

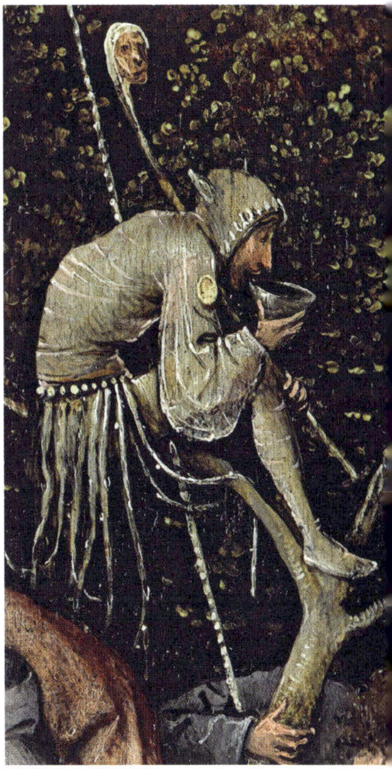

A European bestseller

At the very end of the fifteenth century, Brant's *Ship of Fools* was a huge success. The book was reprinted in Nuremberg and Augsburg in the year of its very first publication in Basel. An enriched edition was published in Strasbourg, and a Latin version was published in Freiburg. Two English versions ensued, one in verse and the other in prose. Albrecht Dürer (page 80) was one of the artists who worked with the author and his woodcuts contributed to the book's fame.

In *Madness and Civilization: A History of Insanity in the Age of Reason*, the philosopher Michel Foucault observes the tales of folly in the context of the late Middle Ages. Before Erasmus praised it, folly was seen as a form of comic punishment. The insane were cast out of the cities in convoys filled with gesticulating and sniggering fools. According to Foucault, Bosch's painting shows the dark side of man, fueled by his weaknesses, dreams, and illusions. More generally, *Ship of Fools*, *The Garden of Earthly Delights*, and *The Temptation of Saint Anthony* are peopled with whimsical figures whose actions escape us. We are both troubled and intrigued by the irreducible force that drives them.

What the heck is going on here?

Revelations

Between 2014 and 2015, the restoration of *Ship of Fools* revealed elements of the landscape (blue horizon, architectural remains, etc.) and gave a new lease of life to the figures in the foreground. Once restored, the painting was sent to the Netherlands to commemorate the 500th anniversary of the death of the artist born in 's-Hertogenbosch.

Portrait of the Artist Holding a Thistle

Dürer

Renaissance Man

Albrecht Dürer's *Portrait of the Artist Holding a Thistle* is considered one of the first autonomous self-portraits in the history of art. Perhaps intended for his fiancée, the painting showcases the artist's technical skills as a token of his dedication and as a forerunner of his illustrious contribution to Germanic Renaissance art.

A universal artist

Dürer was a precocious painter and talented engraver who apprenticed with his father, a goldsmith in Nuremberg, before travelling throughout the Rhine region and copying the Italian masters (Mantegna, Carpaccio). At the age of twenty, the young artist began studying the German-Flemish style and the new Italian systems of representation. Dürer, who had inherited his father's sense of precision, had completed his southern Germany apprenticeship and was being introduced to the intellectual circles in Basel when he produced this self-portrait in 1493. The work is in line with the pictorial tradition of the time (bust turned to a three-quarter angle, sophisticated clothes against a dark background), but the apparently classical composition reveals the artist's singular ambition: whereas his predecessors and fellow painters mostly appeared as secondary figures in large religious compositions, he is represented as an artist. At once proud and humble. Autonomous.

The following winter, he went to Venice to study the proportions of the human body according to Leonardo da Vinci, as well as spatial geometry and perspective. He returned to Nuremberg where he devoted himself to the humanist movement through theory, drawing, and the production and distribution of engravings. He was granted the emperor's protection and was widely acclaimed throughout Europe. His renown was established.

Manifestoes

Perhaps Dürer painted his own portrait for his forthcoming engagement, as the thistle was a symbol of fidelity—or perhaps it was a symbol of Passion in reference to the thorns on Christ's crown. This last theory is backed by the lines written above the head: *Myj Sach die gat / Als es oben schtat*, meaning "my affairs follow the course allotted to them on high." In other words, the painter's career progressed according to the supreme order.

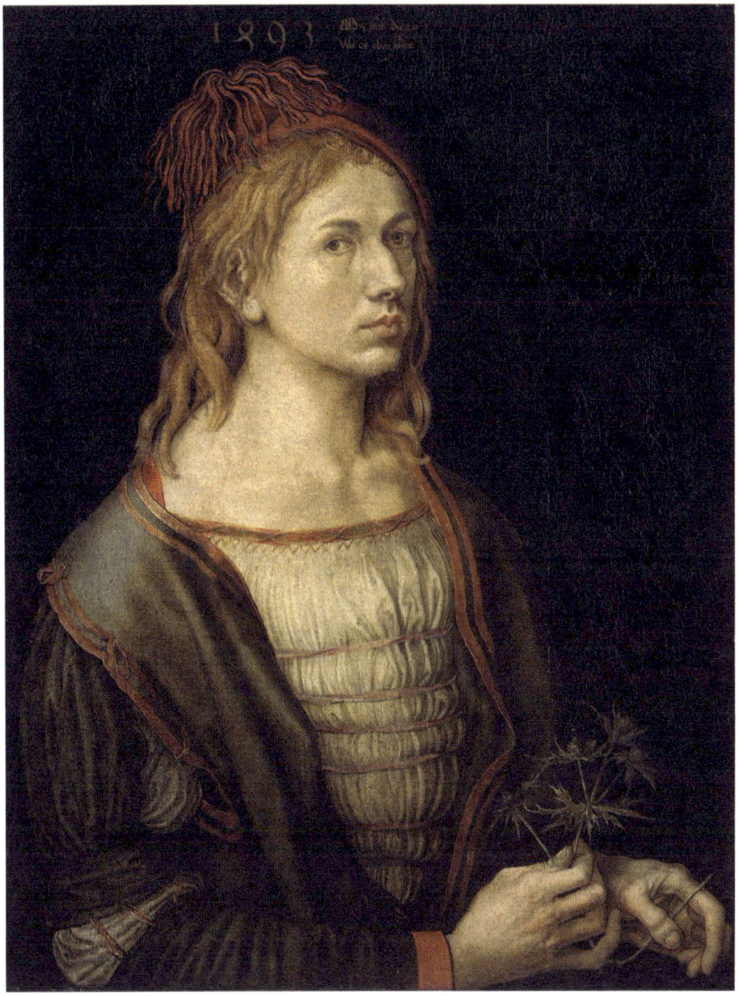

Dürer was only thirteen years old when he drew the first of a series of four self-portraits. Later, two paintings revealing the social status he sought to gain portrayed him in turn as a Venetian nobleman wearing grey lambskin gloves and as a Christ facing front, making a gesture like a blessing.

Albrecht Dürer
Portrait of the Artist Holding a Thistle, 1493, oil on parchment pasted on canvas, 56 × 44 cm

Effigies

Is this the ancestor of the selfie?

Dürer is considered a national treasure in Germany. Countless busts were cast in his honor and many schools bear his name. The Evangelical and Lutheran Churches dedicate the sixth and seventh of April of every year to the great artist. The German brand Playmobil even produced his effigy in plastic, complete with an easel and a miniature self-portrait.

Mona Lisa Superstar

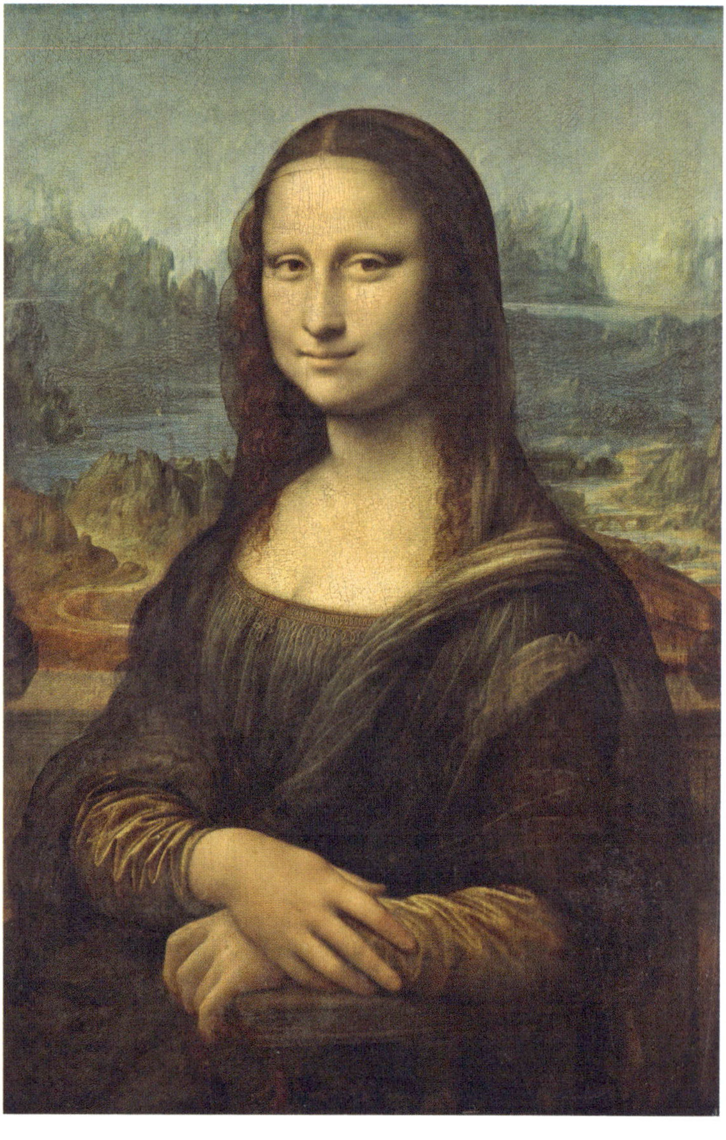

Leonardo da Vinci
Portrait of Lisa Gherardini,
known as *The Gioconda*
or *Mona Lisa*,
c. 1503–19,
oil on panel,
77 × 53 cm

No need to be an Italian Renaissance expert to know that the *Mona Lisa* was painted by Leonardo da Vinci and is located in the Louvre. Tourists from the world over come to the Louvre to see the *La Joconde* (in French) or *La Gioconda* (in Italian and Spanish). Every single day, 30,000 visitors converge on the Denon wing, most of whom leave almost immediately after having seen or photographed the universal icon. How did the *Mona Lisa* get to be so famous? It's a long story.

Why is it so loved?

The beginnings of the buzz

Painted around 1503 on a poplar panel, the picture most probably depicts Lisa Gherardini, the wife of Francesco del Giocondo. It appears Leonardo da Vinci delayed the delivery of the work commissioned by the Florentine fabric merchant because he finetuned the portrait until it embodied the quintessence of his art. In an enlarged frame, Da Vinci depicted a half-length figure whose hands are apparent. Although this composition, with its three-quarter model and its landscape in the background, was inspired by the Flemish manner (Memling, van der Weyden), the work has one particularity: the model is smiling. Those who visited the studio did not know if her smile was benevolent or mocking, but were marked by the astounding figure. All hailed its finesse, sense of detail, and the surprisingly lively aspect of the painting ("She was considered a marvelous thing for being no different than life," Giorgio Vasari).

Da Vinci brought the *Mona Lisa* to France, where it was acquired by François I in 1518. The portrait was considered one of the most precious items in the royal collection on account of the painter's extraordinary pictorial technique. During the reign of Louis XIV, the *Mona Lisa* was hung in the king's apartments in Versailles, and painters came to make copies of its (there are over 150 period copies). When it entered the Louvre in the late eighteenth century, the visitors admired the small panel as the Italian master's most accomplished work. But the *Mona Lisa* became truly famous in the following century when writers and art critics such as George Sand and Walter Pater took an interest in Leonardo da Vinci's universal genius as well as in one of his painting's main features: the mysterious smile. Because her smile is now associated with a mystery.

Femme fatale

Her mysterious past makes her all the more fascinating. Her smile contrasts with the chaotic landscape in the background, and her melancholic expression evokes a wide variety of feelings. While Jules Michelet wrote: "I go to her in spite of myself, as the bird to the snake," Théophile Gautier wondered: "From which planet fell, in the middle of a landscape of azure, this strange being with her look that promises unknown voluptuousness and her divinely ironic expression?" The *Mona Lisa* thus became the archetypical femme fatale. The mystery thickens.

Cheeeese!

In the words of the art historian Daniel Arasse: "Leonardo da Vinci invented the smiling portrait. None had been produced before the *Mona Lisa*, with the exception of Antonello da Messina's *Portrait of a Man*." The artist managed to capture his model's fleeting expression and render it in a particular way on a wood panel. The smile seems "uncatchable," as if the mouth changed the moment viewers look at it. To achieve this, the painter first sketched shadows of color; then, he superimposed layers of barely pigmented oil to create a sfumato effect (as if the shapes were seen through a light smoke). This conveys a sense of movement and hints at a smile depending on whether one focuses on the Mona Lisa's lips or face. Likewise, the finesse of the features makes the model particularly lively and makes us believe that Mona Lisa is following us with her gaze if we move right or left in front of the painting.

Thief! Thief!

The painting vanished in August 1911, leaving nothing but an empty space and four nails next to works by Veronese, Titian, and Correggio. When the museum opened its doors that morning, the copyists first thought that the portrait has been moved for technical reasons, probably to be photographed. But the frame and glass found in the staircase leading to the Cour du Sphinx left no doubt: the *Mona Lisa* had been stolen. The case was entrusted to Prefect Lépine. The first articles were published in the press. Everyone wanted to know where the painting was—a national subscription was even launched to reward whoever helped locate it. The Société des Amis du Louvre promised a reward of 25,000 francs. An anonymous person doubled that amount. The magazine *L'Illustration* offered to pay 45,000 francs to whoever brought the work to their headquarters before September 1. *Paris-Journal* outbid that amount, offering 50,000 francs. The burglary attracted massive press coverage: "The Mona Lisa is missing! This concerns all of humanity" (*Frankfurt Gazette*); "Whoever it was who stole Leonardo da Vinci's 'Mona Lisa' from the Louvre is sure of a place in history when his name comes out. He is sure of an extraordinary place, too" (*The New York Times*). But the thief remained discreet.

Jocondologie

What is the difference between readymade and made in Taiwan? Marcel Duchamp was a pioneer when he drew a mustache and beard on a simple reproduction of the *Mona Lisa* and captioned it "L.H.O.O.Q." The year was 1919. Since then, the famous face has been featured on all kinds of cards, posters, and gadgets (a beaded curtain, a pill box, a snow globe, and so on). The term "*jocondologie*" was coined to describe the study of the various ways in which the *Mona Lisa* has been caricatured, parodied, borrowed, and used for advertising. In 2014 more than 11,000 documents and objects were added to the museum's *jocondologie* collections.

The investigation was at a standstill. The poet Guillaume Apollinaire was arrested on September 7 and imprisoned on suspicion of illicit art trafficking. Pablo Picasso was also suspected. The scandal was reaching global proportions. As Jérôme Coignard explained in his remarkable work of investigation entitled *A Woman Disappears*: "A traffic of images, photographs, souvenirs, and illustrated ornaments thrives on the public calamity that is theft."

The *Mona Lisa* finally reappeared two years later when Vincenzo Peruggia, a glazier who had worked at the Louvre, putting its finest pieces under glass, contacted an Italian art dealer and offered to return the work to its hometown Florence for a fee. The merchant called the police and, after a farewell exhibition in Rome and Milan, the painting was reinstated in the Louvre. The *Mona Lisa* had become a popular heroine.

The triumphant tour

The now world-famous portrait had become a museum work for all to admire. She had acquired not only international fame but also the status (which seems obvious to us now) of a work in a museum meant to be contemplated by the greatest number. Like all heroines, she received tributes, went on triumphant tours, and became the object of parodies. In 1963 the Minister of Culture André Malraux accompanied the *Mona Lisa* to the United States in an effort to improve France's diplomatic relations with Washington. The painting was first received with great pomp by President John F. Kennedy and his wife. Then, it was presented at the National Gallery and exhibited at the Metropolitan Museum of Art in New York. In total, 1.7 million visitors admired the *Mona Lisa*. Ten years later, once again for political reasons, President Georges Pompidou decided to lend the painting to

Japan, including a brief stopover in Moscow. Since then, *Mona Lisa* spinoffs have kept proliferating worldwide: not a day goes by without the museum being asked for permission to use the iconic image and distribute it all over the world.

On your screens

Many curious people are drawn to the museum by a mysterious force. Dan Brown's novel *The Da Vinci Code* and its film adaptation have had a phenomenal impact. In 2006 the cryptologist Sophie Neveu (Audrey Tautou) and the "symbologist" Robert Langdon (Tom Hanks) are a box office smash, launching an esoteric fashion for ancient cults and sacred geometry as applied to painting. The Louvre designed a special Da Vinci Code visit of an hour and a half in a dozen stages that allow visitors to discover the museum Louvre from this novelistic angle and, in passing, correct some of the more extravagant misconceptions. Just as exciting, the visit dedicated to Beyoncé and Jay-Z allows visitors to find the key works in the video "Apest" and face the Mona Lisa with as much aplomb as the couple of singers.**

All the enigmas finally resolved

"The Mona Lisa enigma finally resolved" is a regular headline in newspapers that promise us to reveal the model's identity. You may not know that the Mona Lisa is a saint, is Monna's sister, is a Sforza, is a man, is Da Vinci himself—anything goes. The other mystery to solve urgently is that of the smile: the figure is either a stereotype ("gioconda" meaning "happy") or a woman delighted to be pregnant. But that's not all, you have probably noticed the shape of her face, which is a nearly perfect oval. There is surely an explanation for all that. Da Vinci must have arranged the geometric shapes to conceal a message. Moreover, a closer look at the picture reveals numbers and letters, such as an "s" engraved on the pupil. Even if these signs result from a yellowed or cracked varnish, they are intriguing, don't you think?

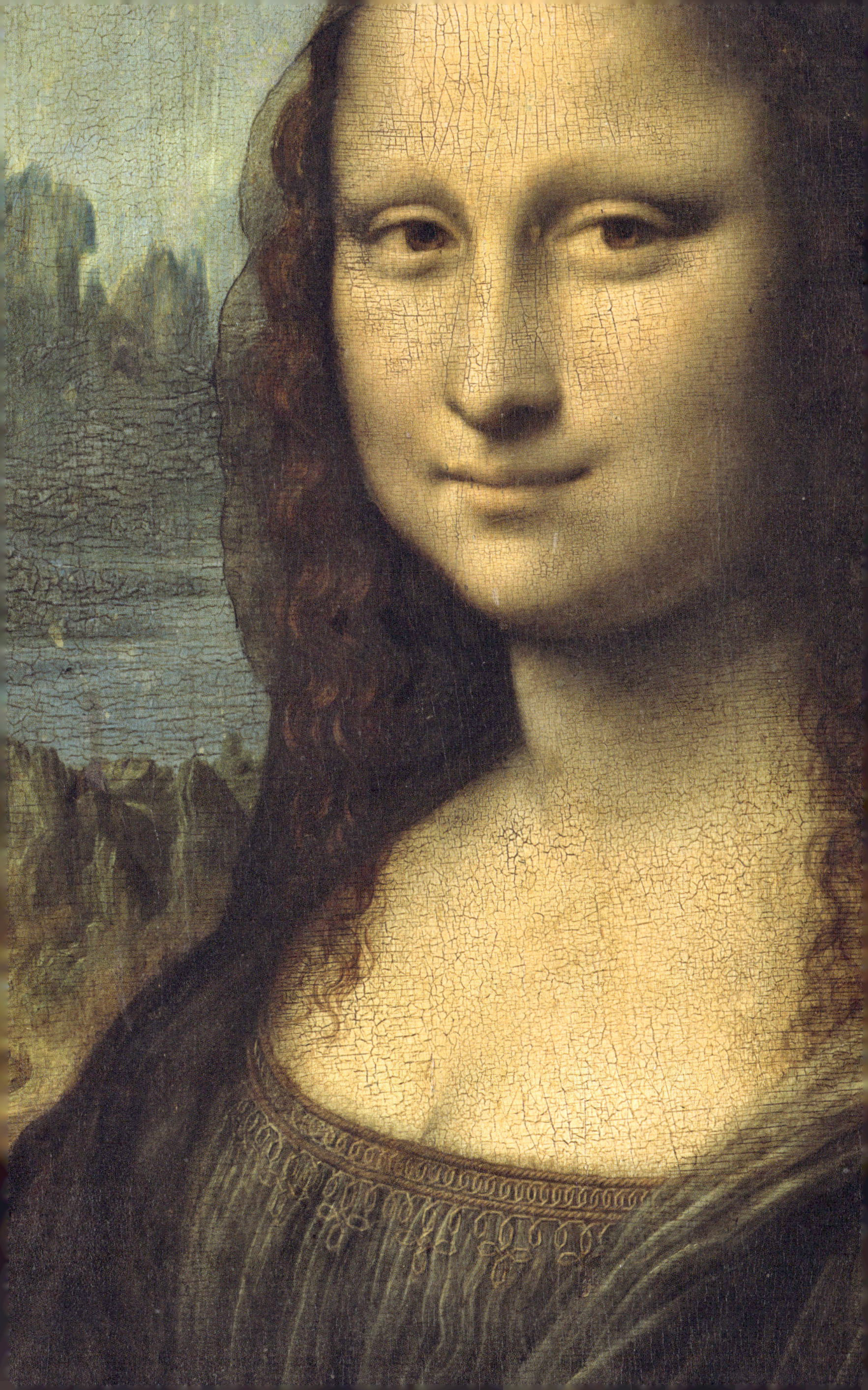

La Belle Jardinière Raphael

On Earth as It Is in Heaven

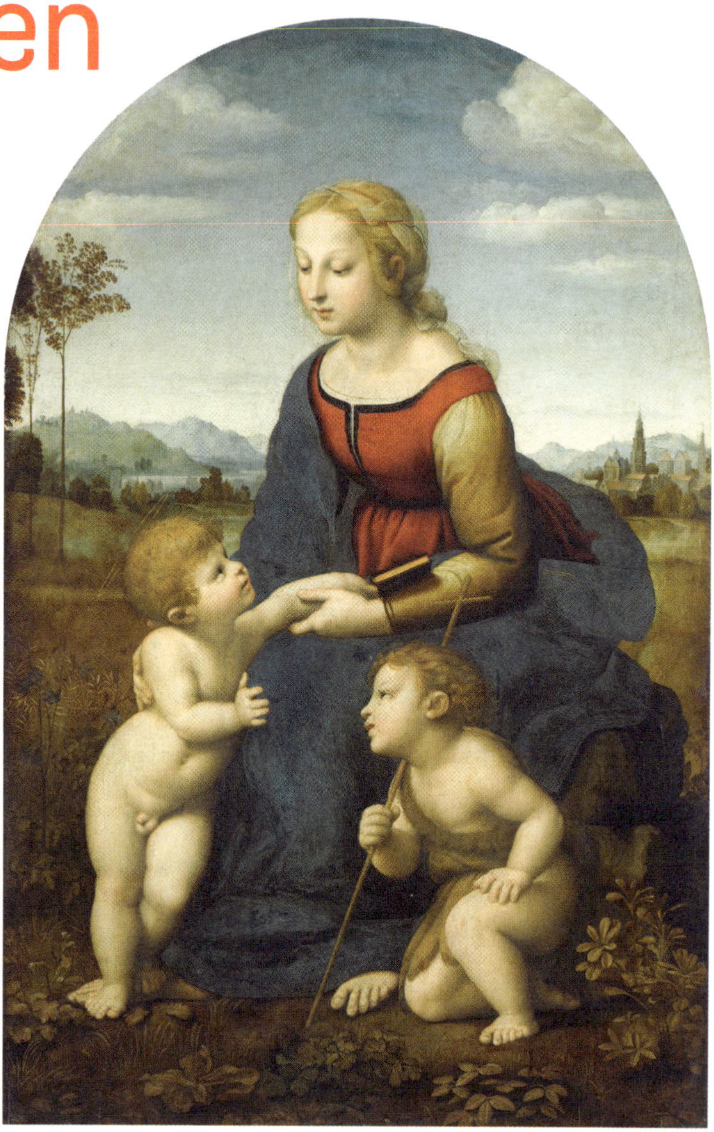

Raffaello Sanzio da Urbino, known as **Raphael**
Madonna and Child with the Young Saint John the Baptist, known as *La Belle Jardinière*, c. 1508, oil on panel, 122 × 80 cm

La Belle Jardinière is one of the most beautiful madonnas ever painted by Raphael. The composite and harmonious work represents the golden age of the Italian Renaissance. Soft like a Perugino, extraordinary like a Michelangelo and above all a da Vinci, *La Belle Jardinière* has often enchanted viewers and sometimes exasperated apprentice artists.

Perfect synthesis

The painting is emblematic of the research and work on synthesis carried out by Raphael in Florence in the early sixteenth century. A graceful young woman and two children are pictured in a pyramidal composition against a verdant backdrop. The painting's strict geometry is softened by the vivid hues and rounded contours of the figures. The brightness of color and light, and the sense of movement in the bodies and eyes are the most characteristic features of that period and can also be found in *The Madonna del Prato* (Vienna) and *The Madonna of the Goldfinch* (Florence). *La Belle Jardinière* crowns the painter's Florentine experiments. The painting's particular harmony, measured gestures, and fine features can be compared to the work of Raphael's master Perugino. The drapery and the toddler's silhouette are reminiscent of Michelangelo's sculpture *Madonna and Child*. The landscape and architecture are evocative of Nordic painting, and Hans Memling in particular. The perfectly smooth brushstrokes, the brown hues in the foreground, the faraway bluish greens and grays create an atmospheric perspective magnified by the sfumato technique. Leonardo da Vinci was highly influential in the Florentine art scene at that time: *The Virgin and Child with Saint Anne* was a model for young painters (see page 92). While the intertwined arms and legs, affectionate looks, and color of the Virgin's garment were depicted in a similar manner by both artists, Raphael's take on landscape and light was peaceful and limpid, whereas da Vinci's was mysterious and hazy.

No time like the past

Raphael's painting exudes a sense of peace and happiness that singled him out among other Renaissance geniuses. Unlike Michelangelo, who was seen as an exuberant and bad-tempered genius, fine arts academies hailed Raphael's flawless drawing, pure lines, and balanced compositions as an essential reference. In the nineteenth century, Raphael's grace was found both delightful and irritating. Eager to emancipate themselves from an academic training they deemed too conformist, young English students sought to create a new painting movement; far from the influence of the Renaissance masters, the Pre-Raphaelite Brotherhood was inspired by Raphael's predecessors, the Primitives.

Cherubs

The Madonna and Child was one of Raphael's favorite themes. Indeed, his madonnas are exhibited in many museums, such as the *Madonna of the Fish* at the Prado Museum in Madrid; the *Esterhazy Madonna* at the Museum of Fine Arts in Budapest; the *Madonna of Foligno* at the Vatican; and the *Sistine Madonna* at the Gemäldegalerie in Dresden, whose cherubs are renowned worldwide. The Madonna is walking on a cloud with her son in her arms while two cherubs seem to be observing the scene. One is holding his chin while the other has his arms crossed. Both look thoughtful and mischievous. They can be seen everywhere now, reproduced on postcards, posters, bed linen, and so on.

Let's Sing from the Same Songbook

The attribution of *The Pastoral Concert* to Titian was often the object of debate. Likewise, the subject of the canvas and its role in the birth of modern painting have inspired many commentators. All this has clearly contributed to the critical fortunes of the small masterpiece.

"Better to be painted by him than to be engendered by nature."

Sperone Speroni

A day in the country

In the nineteenth century, *The Pastoral Concert* was one of the most famous paintings in the Louvre; it was then attributed to Giorgione and widely copied. It inspired several days out in the country, including the famous *Déjeuner sur l'herbe*. Manet had had the opportunity to study it closely and used the subject of the Italian painting, but in his canvas, the presence of unclothed women among clothed men is not justified by any mythological or allegorical pretext. It caused a scandal at the Salon.

The prince of painters

By virtue of his influence and of the commissions he received, Titian was considered one of the first painters on a European scale. His portraits enjoyed the favor of the princely courts of Italy, the pontifical court, and especially the Hapsburg court thanks to the patronage of Charles V then of Philip II of Spain. Titian also took on the role of defender of color against classical draftsmanship. All the masters of color claim to have been influenced by him: Velázquez, and great portraitists such as Rubens and van Dyck.

The legend of the brush

The painter and biographer Carlo Ridolfi relates that, while posing for a portrait, Emperor Charles V bent down to pick up the brush that Titian had just dropped. This episode—probably legendary—was taken up by Alfred de Musset, who has the emperor say these famous words: "Titian is worthy of being served by Caesar."

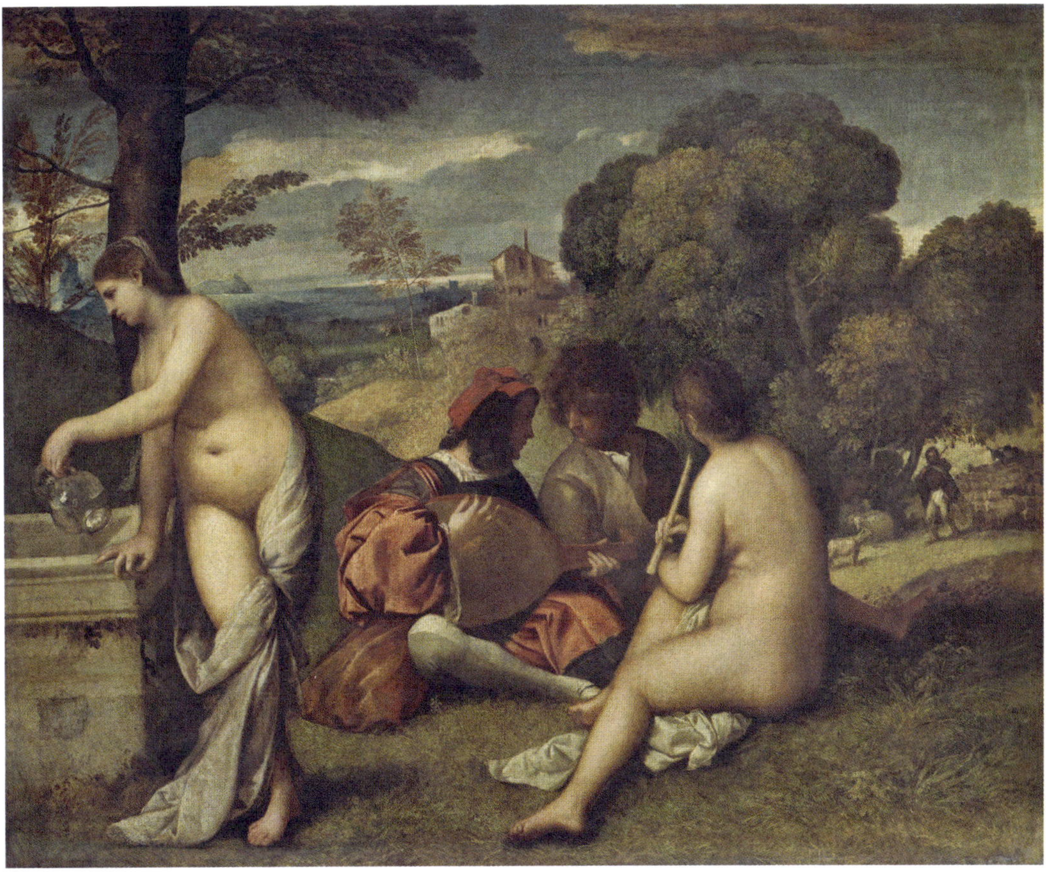

Tiziano Vecellio, known as **Titian**
The Pastoral Concert,
c. 1509,
oil on canvas,
105 × 137 cm

Music in the forefront

Four people on a lawn take part in a concert. A young man holds his lute, a young woman plays the flute while another young woman pours water into a basin. In the background, a shepherd guards his flock. Is it a pastoral scene? An allegory for poetry and music? A simultaneous representation of the visible and the invisible? The naked women, ideal beauties, perhaps spring from the imaginations of the two minstrels. Or is it really a question of the "harmonic" relationship between the figures? Frankly, no hypothesis invalidates any other; on the contrary, they allow us to appreciate refined and witty art as it developed in Cinquecento Venetian humanist circles. The mysterious fluid that connects the figures were long accredited to Giorgione. The fact remains that when Giorgione died of the plague in 1510, Titian, his closest collaborator, had to meet the demands of his master's clientele and imposed himself as his heir. Today, there is a consensus that even if Giorgione initiated the theme of *The Pastoral Concert*, it was Titian who executed it.

Are debates about attribution beneficial?

The Virgin and Child with Saint Anne

The Final Masterpiece

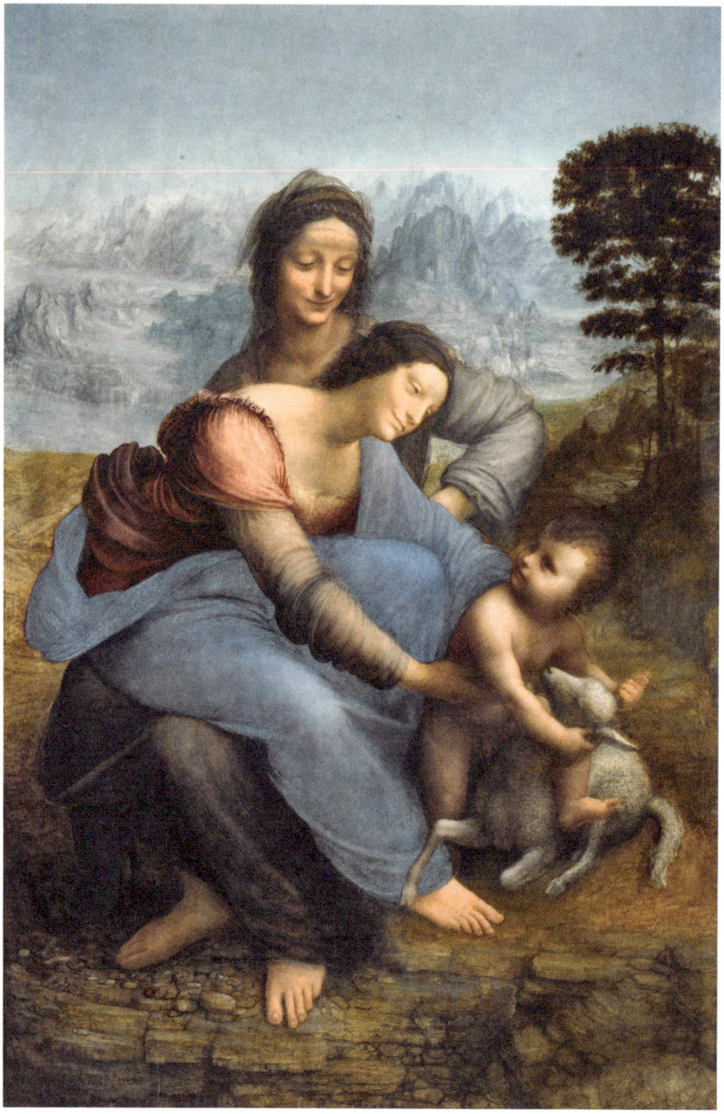

Leonardo da Vinci
The Virgin and Child with Saint Anne,
c. 1501–19,
oil on panel,
168 × 130 cm

One painting crystallizes Leonardo da Vinci's life-long study of anatomy, facial expressions, botany, geology, the movements of water, and perspective. *The Virgin and Child with Saint Anne* is an ambitious composition and one of the most influential Florentine works of its time.

A family resemblance

From the tenth century, rivalries between clerics took the form of a debate that continued to grow between the upholders of the theory of the Immaculate Conception and their opponents. The Immaculists (often Franciscans) thought that Mary could not be stained by sin like other women. She was a virgin, but above all she had not been stained by the original sin. This was the Immaculate Conception. Not everyone agreed on this point. In the fifteen century, the theological argument was accompanied by a wave of piety and the blossoming of the cult of not only Mary, but also her mother, Anne. The Marian Trinity (or the trinitarian Saint Anne) then became a very popular theme greatly appreciated by artists. It allowed them to depict three generations: the grandmother Anne, the mother Mary, and the Infant Jesus.

Leonardo first considered the various configurations possible for treating the subject and the presence, or not, of Saint John the Baptist and the Lamb to embody the sacrifice to come. Beginning in 1503, the artist sketched various versions on preparatory cartoons and undertook the painting of Saint Anne in his Florence studio. In around 1507, during his Milanese years, he took up the composition again and modified certain embellishments. After 1513, he focused on the painting once more, and reworked it until his death in 1519 left the masterpiece unfinished.

The Virgin and Child with Saint Anne was thus the fruit of a very long meditation, which renewed an iconography that was considerably codified at the time.

Influence

"What does Mary see when she holds her arms out to her son here? And does she want to hold him back?"

Viviane Forrester

From the start, Florentine artists and those who visited the master had the pleasure of observing in the studio the large cartoons made by Leonardo. They could admire the fluid gestures and expressiveness of the figures, the both monumental and natural composition, and the complex aspect of the project. It was part of a climate of emulation from which benefited, for example, the young Raphael, who was then apprenticing in the Tuscan capital. Michelangelo perhaps saw in these sketches the possibility of *non finito* that he later applied to sculpture (see page 96). With his experimentation on *The Virgin and Child with Saint Anne*, Leonardo da Vinci provided the impetus and the conditions for a revival of the artistic language during the High Renaissance. Thus, a few decades after his death, the influence of this painting was found in the bold compositions of the mannerists, Pontormo in particular.

After arriving in France as part of the royal collections, *The Virgin and Child with Saint Anne* was the object of new consideration: Raphael painted *The Holy Family*, and Andrea del Sarto, *Charity*. The two compositions are tributes to both Da Vinci and François I, his patron. The Flemish were also inspired by it. *The Virgin and Child with a Lamb* by Quentin Metsys is a striking citation of the painting. Much later, in the middle of the nineteenth century, the panel was selected along with the *Mona Lisa* to join the masterpieces of the Salon Carré in the Louvre. It was then seen by all the great artists of the period and copied by Delacroix, Manet, and Carpeaux.

Makeover

The Virgin and Child with Saint Anne **traversed the centuries, accumulating layers of varnish and retouching. In 2010 it was decided to make an emergency intervention to resolve the serious problems of deterioration of the painting. Two years of work to clean and lighten up the varnish, to remove the retouches that overlapped onto the figures. In the end, to the surprise of the curators then the public, the restoration surpassed expectation, allowing a masterpiece of contrasts and subtility to be discovered: highly modeled figures, a dazzling palette, red lacquers, lapis lazuli blue, cool, powdery tints that create a fascinating atmospheric perspective.**

The interpretation of dreams

Is it necessary to be familiar with the biographical elements and the fantasies of an artist to understand his work? The debate started in 1910 after the publication of an essay by Sigmund Freud entitled "Leonardo da Vinci, A Memory of His Childhood" in which he took a particular interest in *The Virgin and Child with Saint Anne*. The psychanalyst established a parallel between the women bending over the Infant Jesus, who appears to be the same age, and the mother and stepmother of the young Leonardo, apparently greatly marked by the two maternal figures. The artist, moreover, transcribed a dream in which a bird flew toward him when he was still in the cradle and opened his mouth with his tail. Freud thought that the bird was a vulture (a *nibbio*, wrote Leonardo—that is, a kite). He then presented a very convoluted interpretation of the dream based on the symbolism of the vulture in Ancient Egypt and the motif of the bird whose outlines can be made out on the Virgin Mary's blue mantle. The Freudian vision, even though it proved fanciful in the present case, inspired Max Ernst's *The Kiss*.

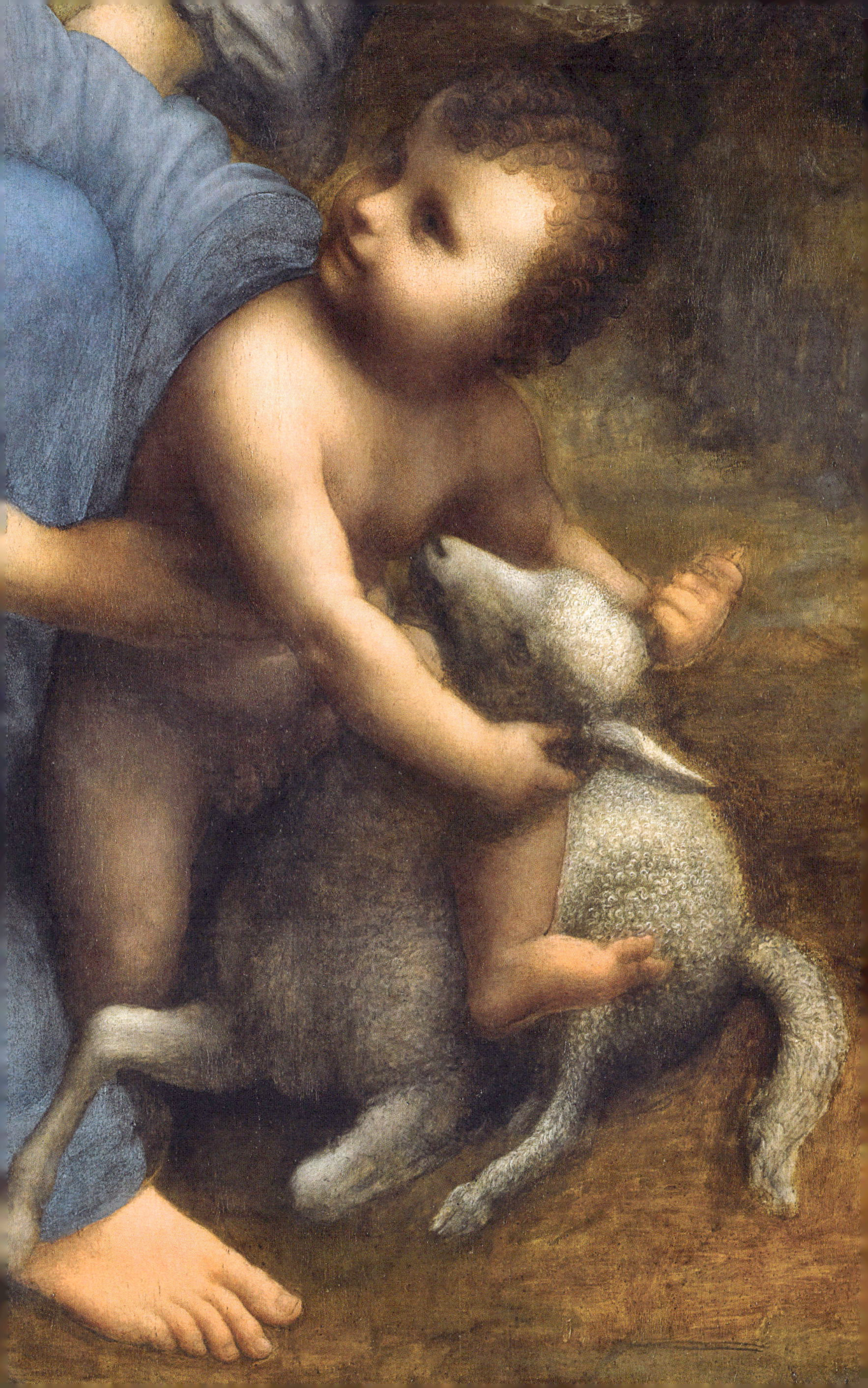

The Dying Slave Michelangelo

La petite mort

In the Galerie Michel-Ange, on the ground floor of the Aile Denon, *The Dying Slave* seems to be stretching voluptuously. The light caresses the marble and highlights the sublime sculpture inspired by classical statuary. Since its creation, *The Dying Slave* has given rise to numerous interpretations and contributed to a new form of subjectivity vis-à-vis works of art.

The enslavement of the arts

Is he experiencing pain or pleasure?

Michelangelo's sculpture *The Dying Slave* was executed at the same time as *The Rebellious Slave* to decorate the colossal tomb of Pope Julius II. But after the pope's death in 1515, plans for the monument became more modest to reduce costs. The two statues left Italy via Roberto Strozzi, to whom Michelangelo had given them, and entered the court of the king of France François I. The initial destination of the slaves (on the lower level of the tomb) suggests, as Vasari wrote, that they may represent the various provinces obedient to the Catholic Church. Michelangelo's biographer Condivi advanced another hypothesis: according to him, the statues represent the enslavement of the arts after the death of a pope who was a great patron. Critics also wondered about the the philosophical meaning of the sculptures. Even so, the presence of such nudes on a pontifical tomb seemed incongruous. The best explication probably came from the Neoplatonic doctrine: the soul is chained to a heavy body from which it must free itself in the hopes of attaining spiritual elevation. The interpretations multiplied over the years. *The Dying Slave* was either seen as the embodiment of abandon, ecstasy, as the image of the man who lets himself be carried along by his destiny or, on the contrary, as the sculptor's effort to liberate the figure from the stone. He was also considered a dreamy adolescent trying to free himself of the chains of sleep (Charles de Tolnay). Marble is a perfect support for these personal interpretations.

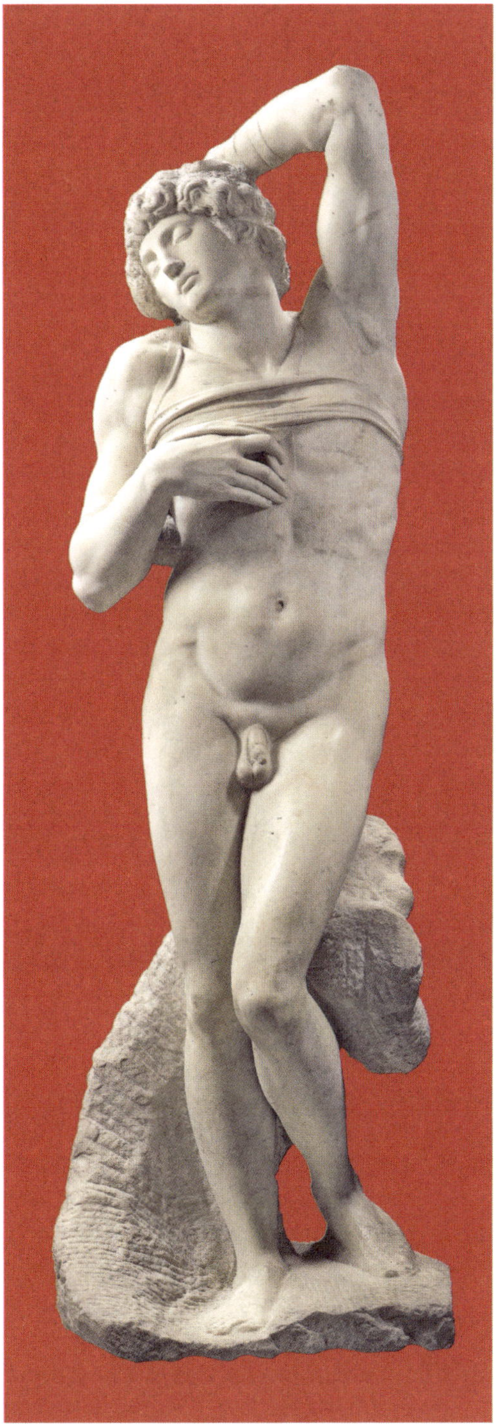

Michelangelo Buonarroti,
known as **Michelangelo**
The Dying Slave, c. 1513–15, marble, 227 cm

Non finito?

It may be thought that the sculptures of the captives are not completely finished, but this was the artist's intention. The principle was called *non finito* by Vasari. When Michelangelo took over the project for the tomb of Julius II in 1531, he executed four other captives (now on display in the Galleria dell'Accademia in Florence). *The Bearded Slave*, *The Awakening Slave*, *The Young Slave*, and *Atlas* appeared to be a little more imprisoned by the marble the two captives in the Louvre. They were deliberately interrupted at an intermediary stage, the marks of the tools—picks, point chisels, rasps—contrasting with the polished stone. Perhaps there were technical reasons for the interruption of the work (the grain of the marble may be seen on certain faces), but the unfinished aspect of this ensemble of sculptures above all gives the impression of effort and struggle.

Dissemination

Today, there are life-size plaster casts of *The Dying Slave* meant for fine art schools and universities, as well as reduced-size terra-cotta or bronze copies appreciated by collectors. The slaves are part of the repertory of sculptural models admired and studied by artists over the ages, but their international fame dates to the nineteenth century. Separated from the definitive version of the pontifical monument and little represented as engravings, they were popularized by photography (Édouard Baldus took a magnificent photograph in 1854) and artists' allusions (*The Bronze Age* by Rodin in 1877; *The Wheel of Fortune* by Edward Burne-Jones in 1885). These tributes are now all in the Musée d'Orsay.

Erasmus Holbein the Younger

A Traveling Portrait

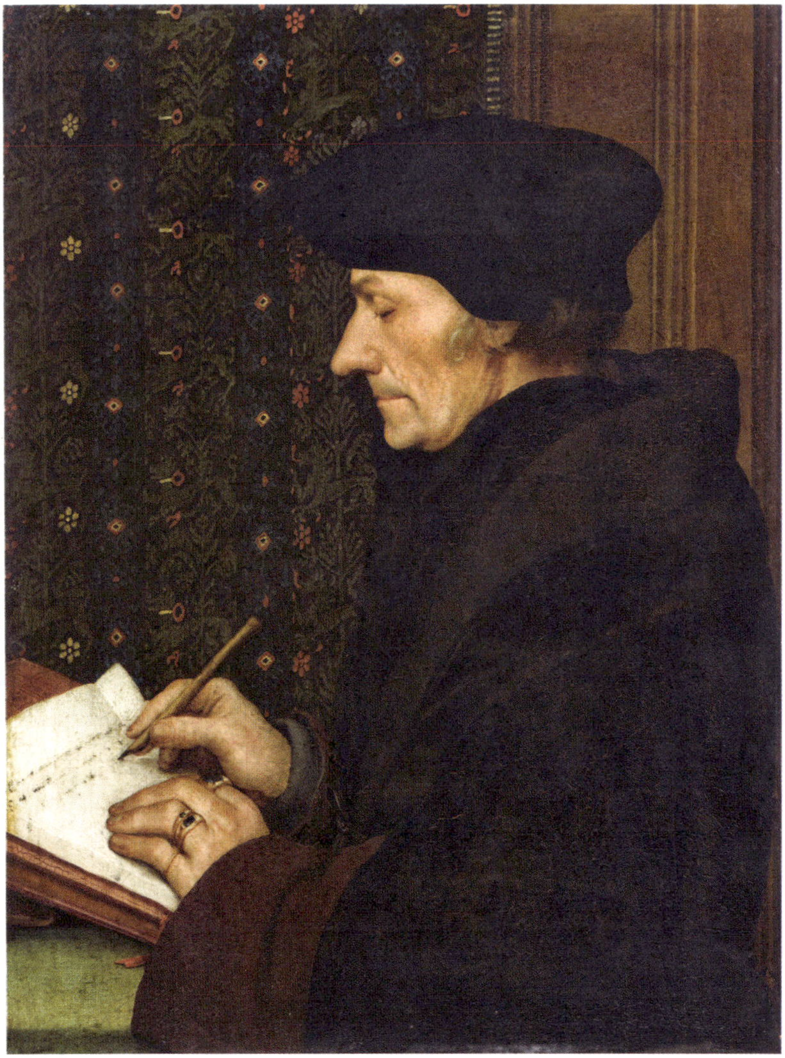

Hans Holbein the Younger
Erasmus, c. 1523, oil on panel, 43 × 33 cm

During the artist's lifetime, the portrait of Erasmus writing constituted a tool for disseminating and promoting humanist thought before merging, over the centuries, with the image that everyone now has of the European philosopher.

Why is Erasmus famous?

The doctor in theology with his encyclopedic knowledge wanted to rid Christianity of all never-ending commentaries by providing readers with accessible translations. Erasmus, who was born in Rotterdam, traveled all over Europe, to Italy, France, and England where he wrote *In Praise of Folly* in a few days. He argued with Martin Luther through an exchange of essays, but advocated peace and reconciliation. He thus put the backs up of both partisans of Reform and of the most traditional Catholicism. As Lucas Cranach disseminated the portrait of Luther all over Europe, Hans Holbein the Younger gave a face to this other great theological figure.

Who is more worthy? He who poses or he who paints?

Changing hands

When he was called to England by Henry VIII, Erasmus asked Holbein to join him and introduced him to cultivated milieus. The philosopher put the painter into contact with Thomas More, another great intellectual figure of the period. Erasmus is said to also have recommended his portrait, which More is thought to have found admirable. Thus, Holbein's reputation grew in England. Another portrait, that of Thomas Cromwell, earned him the admiration of the court. In 1536 he became the official painter to Henry VIII, painting his portrait, that of his son Edward, and those of his successive wives (there is a flattering portrait of Anne of Cleves in the Louvre). Everybody made a beeline for his studio to have their portraits done. The portrait of Erasmus often changed hands, it belonged to Charles I, who gave it to Louis XIII in exchange for the famous *Saint John the Baptist* by Leonardo da Vinci.

"For hours on end one can gaze at this picture, and lend an ear to listen to its all-pervading quietude—for by thus symbolically presenting Erasmus at work, Holbein has immortalized the divine earnestness of every intellectual creator and the invisible patience which is the asset of a genuine artist."

Stefan Zweig, 1935

Holbein is in the details

An outstanding portraitist, Holbein responded to an iconographical program that was tried and tested during the Renaissance: he used posture as well as the symbols of the setting to characterize his figures and indicate their social functions. The shading of the faces is discreet, with no pronounced play of shadows but a magnificent realism. In every one of his paintings shows a taste for exact rendering, that of the clients, their clothing, and familiar objects that compose real still lifes.

The Three Graces Cranach the Elder

In the Spotlight

Over a few months, this small painting went from the intimacy of a private collection to the media fanfare celebrating its entrance into the Louvre. The powers of seduction of Cranach's *The Three Graces*, confined for centuries, were brought to light thanks to a novel fundraising operation.

How does one highlight a national treasure?

Gently

The painting is signed with a winged dragon, which is the mark of Lucas Cranach the Elder, one of the greatest masters of the Germanic Renaissance alongside Dürer and Holbein. Official painter to the prince-electors of Saxony, he was admired for his talents as a portraitist as well as for his allegorical and mythological figures. Many Venuses, Lucretias, and Eves were commissioned, inspiring innumerable variants—including this representative painting that depicts a scene both animated and harmonious with the naked figures that made the artist's name.

All patrons of the arts

The painting remained in a private collection and was only recently show in public for the first time. Things changed when this small masterpiece was given the status of national treasure and the French ministry of culture launched a fundraising campaign with a view to acquiring it. Ten or so companies and over 7,000 donors donated 1 million euros in November 2010 (a quarter of the total amount of the transaction) so that *The Three Graces* could be admired by visitors to the Louvre.

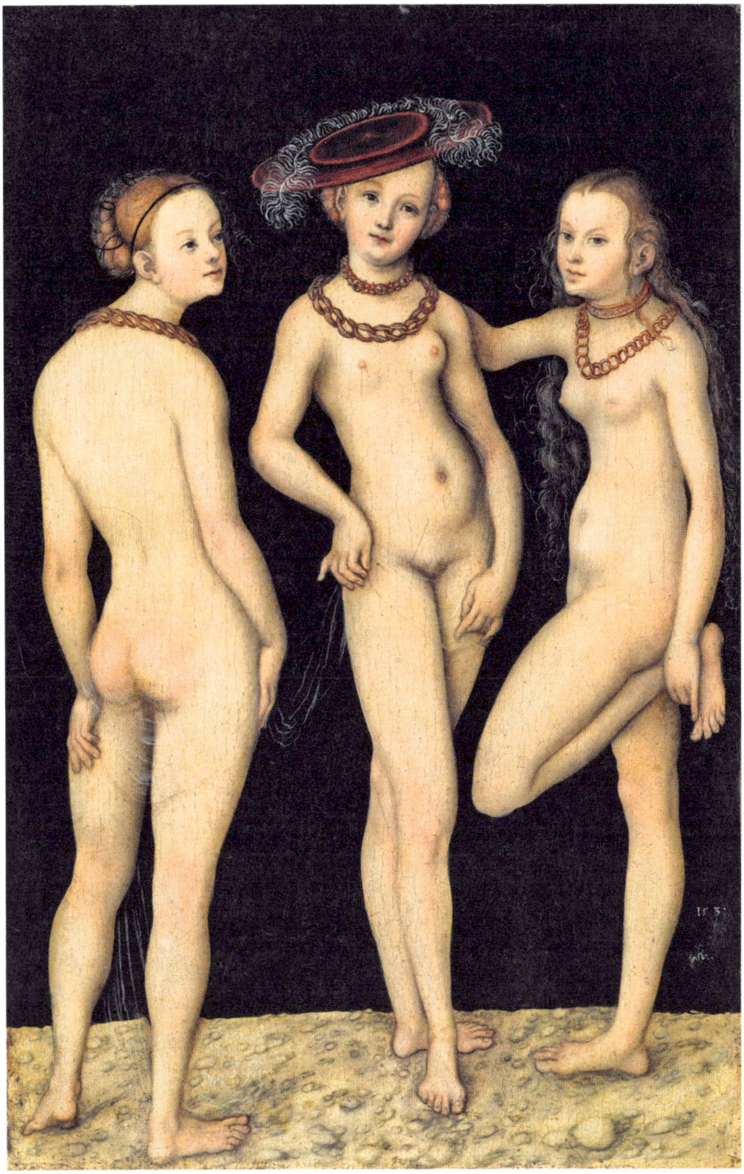

Lucas Cranach the Elder
The Three Graces, 1531,
oil on panel,
36 cm × 24 cm

And other virtues

The Three Graces—Aglaea, Thalia, and Euphrosyne—are the companions of Venus. They incarnate beauty and charm, personifying in turn rejoicing, plenty, and splendor. These figures make prolific appearances in poetry, literature, sculpture, and painting. According to the period, they took on new aesthetics. Those of Botticelli (page 74) and Raphael revived the ideal of classical beauty; those of Rubens became more buxom; those of Jacques Louis-David conformed to the neoclassical canon.

The Wedding Feast at Cana Veronese

You Can Get Lost

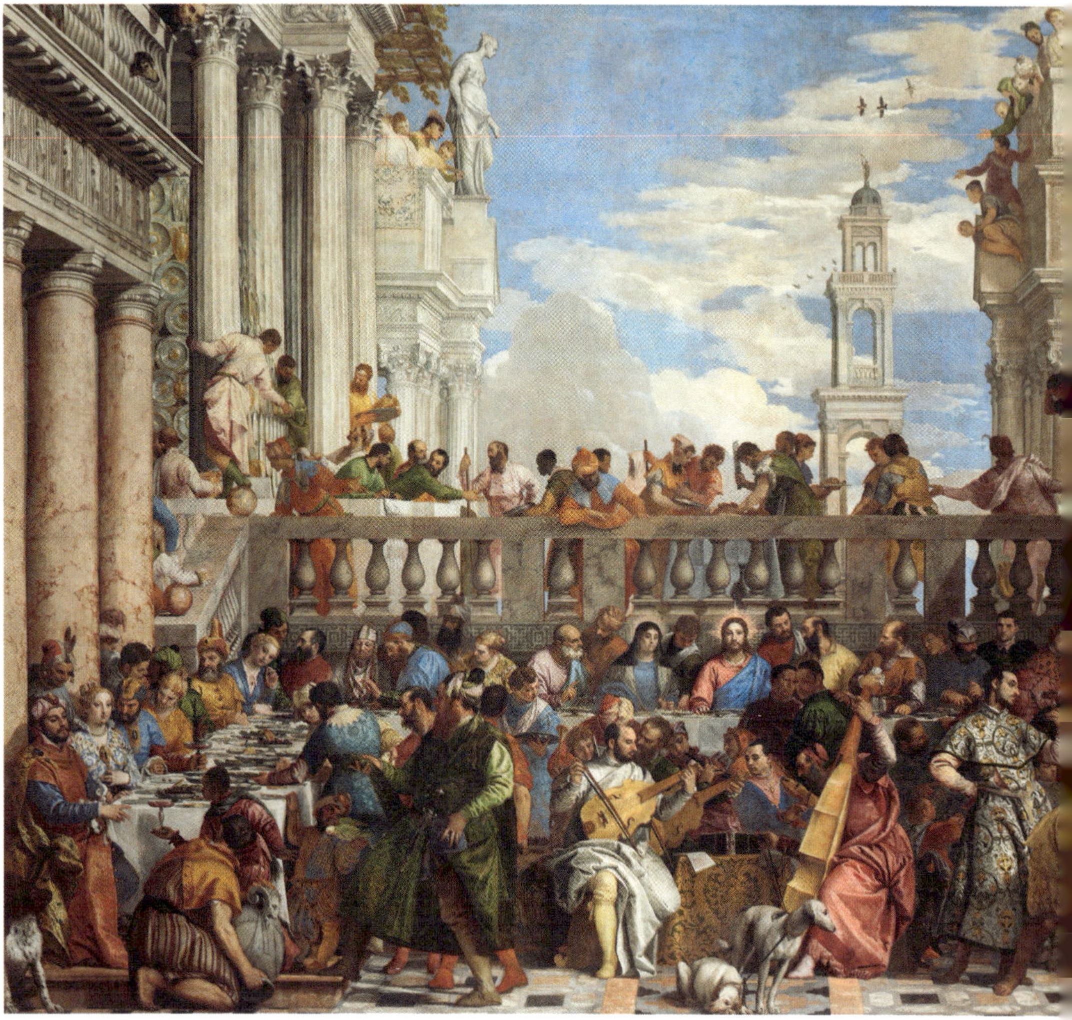

Paolo Caliari, known as **Veronese**
The Wedding Feast at Cana, 1563,
oil on canvas,
677 × 994 cm

The painting had been taken down from the wall of a refectory of a Benedictine convent in Venice; today, it is opposite the *Mona Lisa*. It is the largest painting in the museum and the best-known of the banquet scenes that contributed to the fame of Veronese. Can you find him in the canvas?

in It

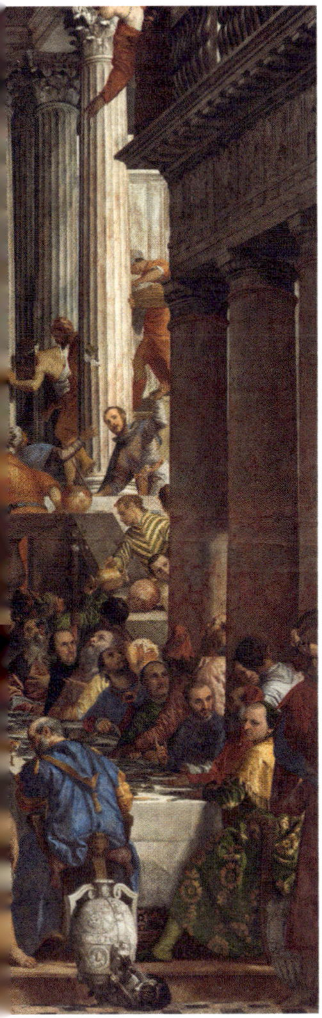

Mingling with the crowd

The Wedding Feast at Cana was requisitioned by France after the Italian campaign, cut into pieces, rolled up, and transported by ship. It entered the Louvre in 1798. After Napoleon's fall—so as not to have to return the work—the French offered to exchange it for Le Brun's *Feast in the House of Simon*, which went to Italy. The largest painting in the Louvre was thus officially and definitively acquired in 1815. The work was regarded with suspicion by a few disconsolate historians who reproached the Venetian school for its anachronisms, eccentricities, and, above all, the lack of sentiment. Charles Blanc, for example, exclaimed: "Ah! No doubt, such a composition cannot satisfy the mind nor touch the heart!" As for the artists, their opinions were mainly positive. Delacroix considered *The Wedding Feast at Cana* a model painting; Baudelaire praised its "paradisiac late-afternoon color"; the painter Taillasson pointed out the implausible details of the painting but invited us to admire the arrangement of the colors and lights; Jean-Jacques Henner confessed that he could not muster any interest in the canvas: "There are too many details, my attention wanders"; while, later, Paul Cézanne was in ecstasies over the color: "*All these* tones *flow* in your *blood*, don't they? You feel reinvigorated by them."

Changing from red to green

Two years and a half were needed to accomplish a technical miracle, which was widely covered in the media. The resurrection of the halftones, the multiplication of small retouche. All this work, carried out in front of the public on scaffolding by six restorers, restored the brilliance of the 67 square meters of painted surface and returned to one of the figures in the foreground (the steward of the festivities) the original color of his garment. The man on the left showing the spouses that the water had been changed into wine saw his coat go from red to green during this restoration.

The mise-en-scène is impressive, full of intelligence and inventiveness, which was characteristic of Veronese's talent. Over a surface of over 6 meters high and nearly 10 meters wide spreads a biblical episode transposed into a Venetian setting itself inspired by antiquity. A dizzying combination. The richness and the luxuriousness of the clothing and buildings echo the opulence of the feast. We are attending a gigantic wedding banquet in which the happy couple is relegated to the left of the painting. The main figure is that of Christ. The composition is reminiscent of Leonardo da Vinci's *The Last Supper*, painted half a century earlier in Milan, but the meal has taken on a gargantuan dimension. Jesus occupies the central place among the hundred or so guests. He watches us, just as Mary on his left watches us. We are asked to witness, in the general melee, the accomplishment of his first miracle, the transformation of water into wine—there was not enough to finish the meal. We then plunge into the colorful bath formed by the crowd, a profusion of figures dressed in ancient traditional costumes, turbans, and outfits or hairstyles such as those sported by Venetian in Veronese's time. The artist combined the sacred and the profane, biblical figures contemporary figures. Certain signs attract the attention—an hourglass placed on the music table, a black veil covering Mary's head, a butcher cutting up a lamb—they announce the Passion of Christ.

Where's Waldo?

There are no testimonies from the periods or writings by the painter giving us the names of the people figuring on the canvas, but a host of suppositions. A few Venetian notables, the satirical writer Aretino, and François I and his wife were no doubt invited to *The Wedding Feast at Cana*. In the eighteenth century, the art theorist A. H. Zanetti put forward a few hypotheses that drew the attention of art lovers to the group of musicians: according to him, the group is made up of the most famous painters in Venice. Tintoretto holding a small violin, Titian playing the violone and leaning over Paolo Veronese all dressed in white, trying to get sounds out of his viola da gamba. These suppositions are no longer current. They make up part of the legends that surround this famous canvas.

"The miracle is within, water changed into wine, the world changed into painting."

Paul Cézanne

After *The Wedding Feast at Cana*, Veronese painted other banquets with the same profusion of figures, fabrics, animals, and food. He was taken to trial over the repeated riots of figures and colors for religious themes. To the Inquisition tribunal that reproached the liberties taken in one of his great Last Suppers and did not appreciate his "jokes," buffoons, parrots, and cherubs, he replied: "I paint as my spirit dictates," adding, undaunted, that "we painters take the same liberties as poets and madmen." The phrase marked generations of painters in Italy.

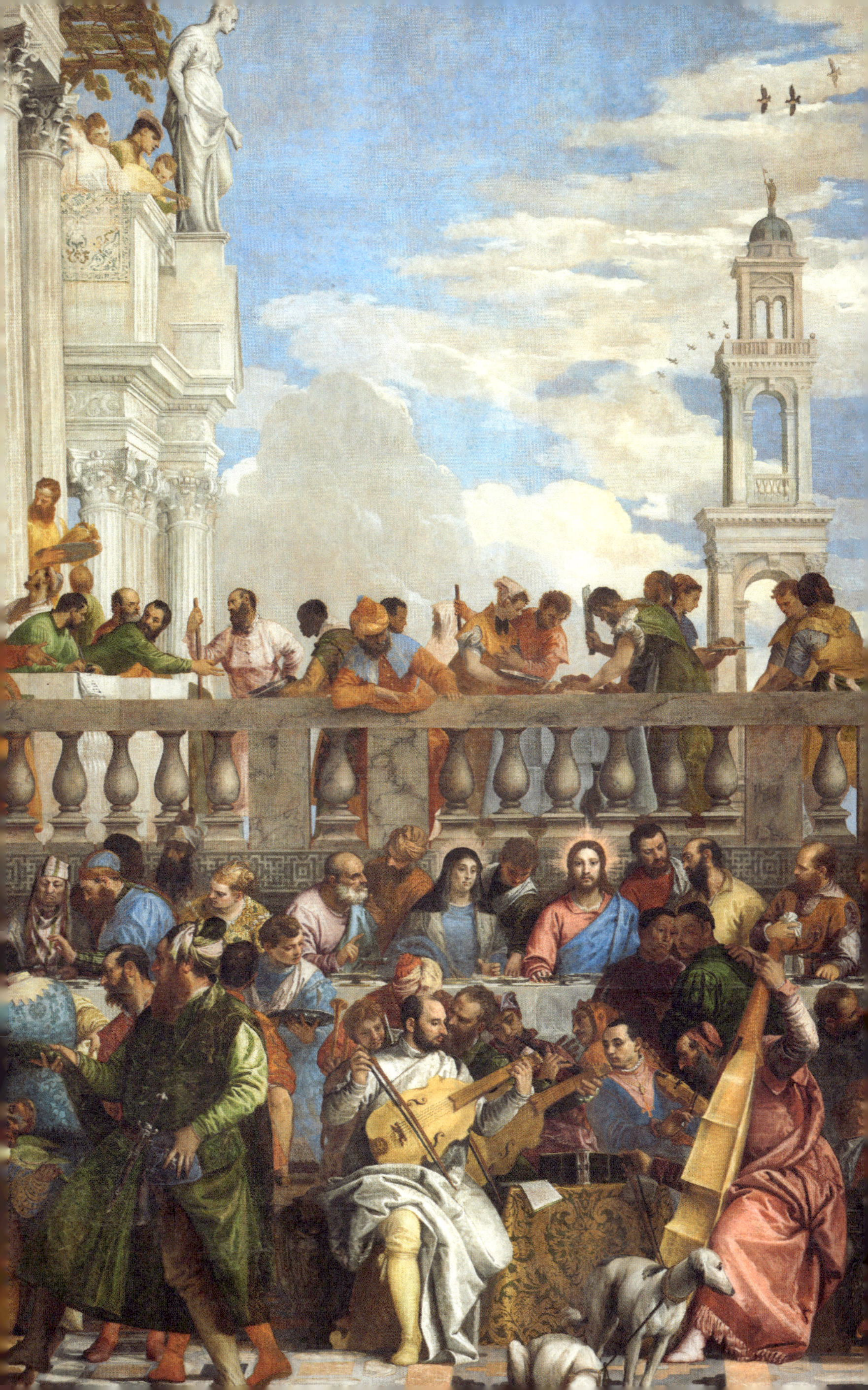

The Beggars

The Farandole of Cripples

The spiritual son of Hieronymus Bosch, Pieter Bruegel the Elder produced an enigmatic oeuvre that immerses us in everyday Flemish life during the Renaissance. His winter landscapes and peasant scenes are well-known yet have started many debates as to how they should be interpreted. *The Beggars* is no exception.

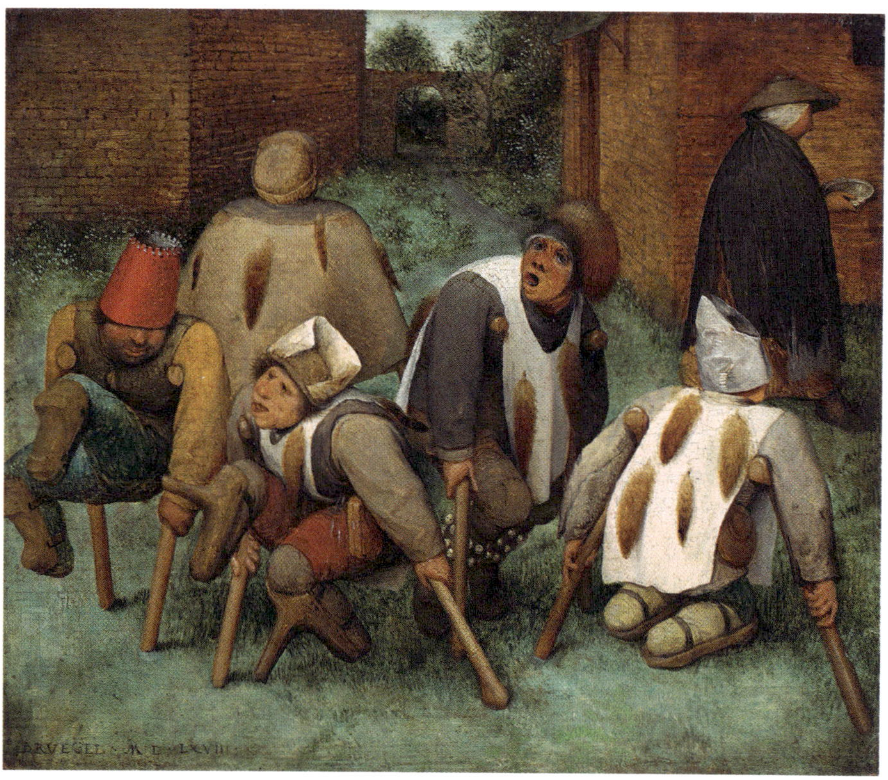

Pieter Bruegel the Elder
The Beggars, 1568,
oil on panel,
185 × 215 cm

Bruegel's painting is both erudite and popular. His first biographer, Carel van Mander, recounts that he frequented village weddings for both the fun and to study them, and that he was nicknamed Peter the Droll or Bruegel the Peasant. His technical training was solid, and he was an educated man. In Antwerp, then Brussels, his friends were scholars and philosophers. He passed on the torch to his children who prolonged his work by producing numerous copies of his genre scenes, whether feasts or parades of beggars. It is for all these reasons that Bruegel has remained famous. His paintings are not numerous but were rather widely disseminated. Their realist quality offers an immediate pleasure and they have been the subject of many scholarly commentaries, academic dissertations, and theological interpretations. Bruegel takes the viewer on a visual and spiritual quest. His works are always anchored in the local tradition and always universal in their meaning and scope. He is also famous for having given a forum of autonomy to the landscape (which became the main subject of a painting) while filling it with humans who seem lost in the space—impotent, insignificant. As in the work of Bosch, Bruegel's vision of the world stuns us.

The beggars' dance

In the Louvre alone, several canvases deal with this subject. The most famous street children are Jusepe de Ribera's *The Clubfoot* and Bartolomé Murillo's *The Young Beggar*. Beggars inspired paintings, particularly representations of Christian charity. Thus, Francis gives his tunic to a beggar in a work by Giotto, and Saint Lawrence distributes alms to the poor in a work by Fra Angelico. In the eighteenth century, the Italian Giacomo Ceruti specialized in "pauperist" art, which earned him the nickname Pitocchetto, the little beggar. Then, in the realist vein, Courbet, Doré, and Manet renewed the theme. Picasso explored the subject from his youth to make, with the acrobats, the finest series of his Blue Period.

Who are these beggars?

People still wonder about the deeper meaning of *The Beggars*: are the fox tails the emblems of the verminous and legless people or the rallying sign used during "Beggars' Revolt" against Spanish domination? Perhaps it is an allusion to the costume worn during the beggars' feast during which cripples sang in the streets. Their headgear is not insignificant either: bishop's mitre, king's crown, soldier's or burgher's beret, peasant's cap—the figures are perhaps representative of the social classes of their period, and their criticism is barely concealed.

Blockbuster

In 2019, numerous events were organized to celebrate the 450th anniversary of the painter's death. On this occasion, Vienna then Brussels hosted the largest monographic exhibition featuring our cripples in the company of pilgrims, blind people, and acrobats in a large composition entitled *The Fight between Carnival and Lent*.

A Man of Four Seasons

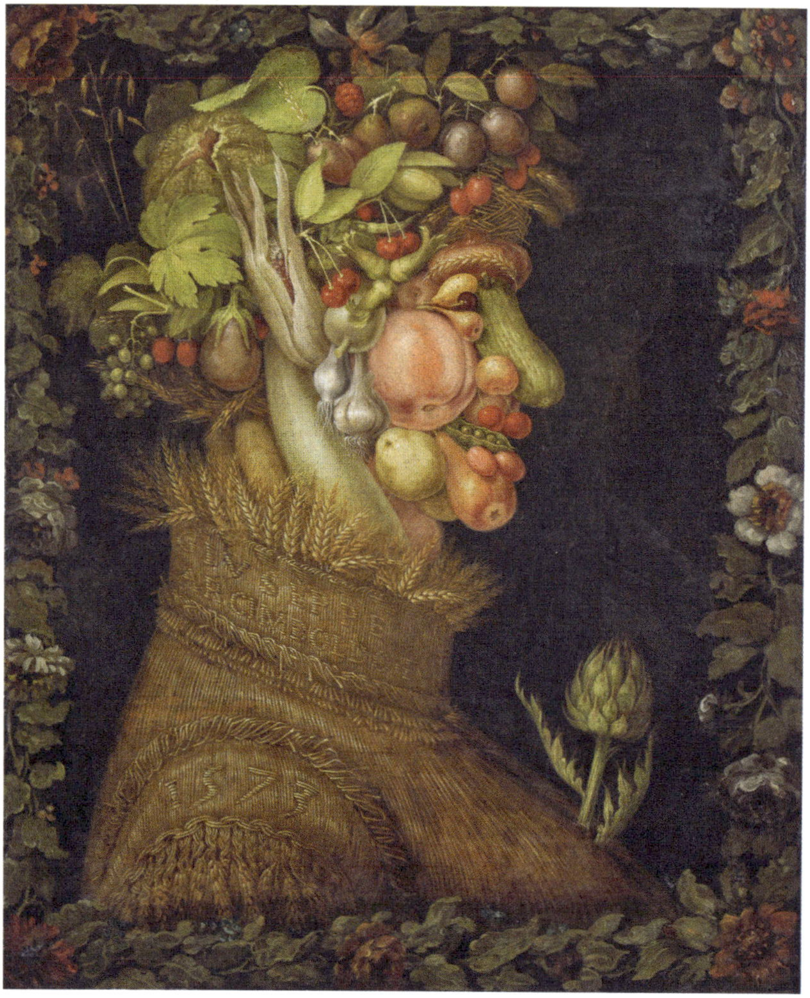

Giuseppe Arcimboldo
Summer, 1573,
oil on panel, 76 × 64 cm

When we think of "the four seasons," the name of Vivaldi pops to mind in terms of music, and that of Arcimboldo in terms of painting. *Summer* was part of an incredible series of heads concocted by Arcimboldo. First rediscovered by the surrealists, these heads became popular the world over in the 1980s.

Somewhat surprisingly, Arcimboldo worked as an event designer. He had a good sense of festivities and a fertile mind, so for a quarter of a century he organized the revels at the Hapsburg court, designing decorations, settings, and fountain displays. Summoned first to Vienna in the service of Ferdinand I, then to Prague where he oversaw Rudolph II's cabinet of curiosities, Arcimboldo kept abreast of the scientific discoveries being made by geographers, explorers, and naturalists. He invented a strange, extravagant form of composition that reflected the intellectual excitement and curiosity of the day. His portraits of the four seasons amused and intrigued Emperor Maximilian II's courtiers.

Is the painting appetizing?

Five a day

Dated 1573 (on the shoulder), the figure of *Summer* is composed of a profusion of fruit and vegetables handled in warm tones. His suit is made of woven wheat, adorned with an artichoke. His eyes are cherries, his nose an eggplant, while his ear is an ear of corn—a plant recently imported from the New World. This painting seems to reflect the Hapsburg empire's golden age. Arcimboldo was well known during his lifetime and appreciated by a knowledgeable, sophisticated audience. After he died, however, he was more or less forgotten.

He was rediscovered—or rather adopted—by the surrealists, who viewed him as their precursor. They appreciated his mastery of collage, sense of illusionism, and startling compositions ("exquisite corpses"). The enormous influence that Arcimboldo's unique way of questioning our relationship to nature had—and continues to have—on artists has been apparent since the late 1980s, when the Palazzo Grassi in Venice hosted an exhibition titled *Effetto Arcimboldo*. A carnivalesque version of the four seasons—fiberglass sculptures some 5 meters high—has been doing the rounds of the United States and Europe since 2012, accompanying shows of Arcimboldo's work in places like Kansas and Arkansas, Milan and Florence, Versailles and Baux-de-Provence. These sculptures by Philipp Haas seem to be extremely effective ways of promoting culture.

Step back

"If you look at the image close up, you see only fruits and vegetables; if you step back, you no longer see anything but a man with a terrible eye, a ribbed doublet, a bristling ruff: distance and proximity are promoters of meaning," wrote Roland Barthes of *Summer*.

Gabrielle d'Estrées

It's the Gesture That Counts

The artist who did this portrait is one of the most famous unknown painters in the history of art. Nothing is known about him, but his masterpiece stimulates eye and mind, a little like the nimble fingers squeezing the delicate nipple here.

"Whatever they tell me about this painting, I'll always see it as a fascinating picture of Sapphic sisterhood. To heck with the truth."
Alain Roger

This enigmatic artist, who belonged to the second school of Fontainebleau, produced a large, colorful canvas whose sensuality and illusionism has appealed to a wide audience. Despite being told that the women in the bath are an allusion to the pregnancy of the beautiful Gabrielle, Henri IV's mistress, as well as to the birth in 1594 of the king's bastard son, César de Vendôme—and despite seeing the ring in the foreground as an offer of marriage and being surprised to make out a naked man on a canvas at the very back of the painting—what really grabs the beholder's attention, etching itself in the mind, is *that* gesture: the gentle pinch of the nipple. The nipple squeezing has become a racy, amusing, conspicuous image—as conspicuous as the fact that Mona Lisa has shaven her moustache.

Bathing beauties

How to arouse the viewer's curiosity

More seriously, this painting comes across as a reminder of a hedonistic era. Indeed, the school of Fontainebleau produced many allegorical works in which idealized figures seem simultaneously remote and available. This genre was highly fashionable in the sixteenth century, when aristocratic art collections contained many "Roman ladies" or "Roman courtesans." The women are inevitably nude and look straight at the beholder, as seen for example in Titian's *Venus of Urbino* and Raphael's *Fornarina*. Their beauty reflects the canons of the day: breasts are high, the nose little and straight, the hair

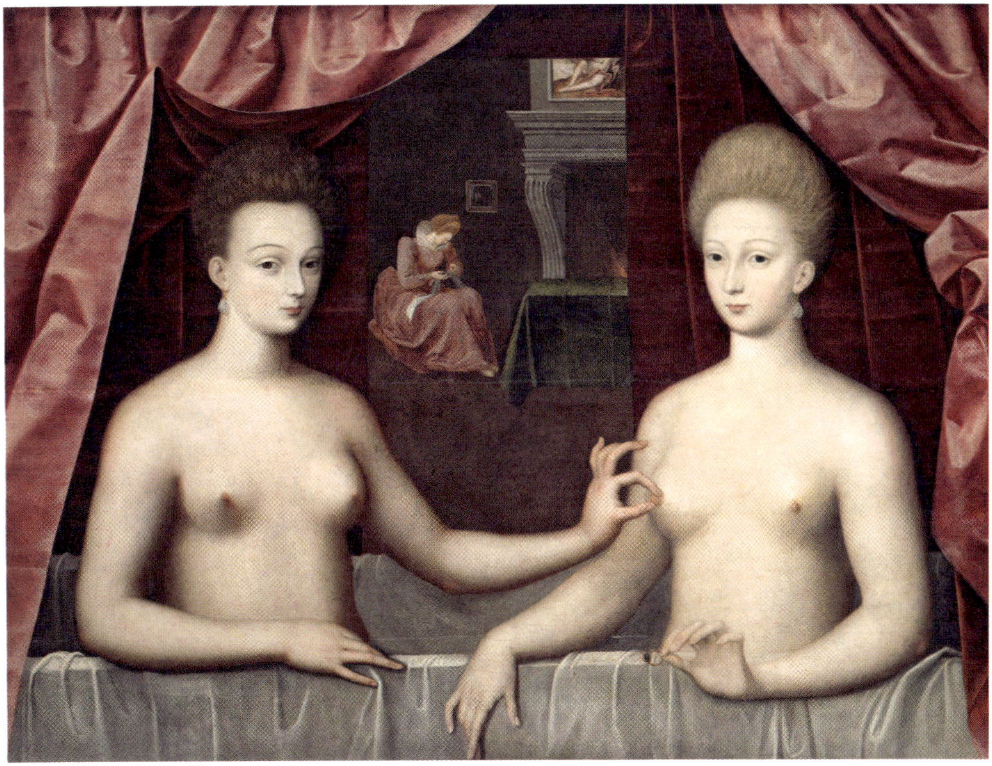

golden, the eyes dark. These ladies with their vacant gazes were sending a message whose ambiguity must have titillated a cultivated beholder in the Renaissance. Nowadays, even though museum-goers are struck by the boldness of this double portrait—supposedly of Gabrielle and Julienne d'Estrées—they also dwell on the quality of the trompe-l'oeil illusionism: the wet cloth that marvelously reveals the copper tub beneath, the two heavy draperies that frame the scene while opening onto another space in the background. Some enthusiastic beholders even pose in front of this large painting, mimicking the two women's gestures.

Gabrielle d'Estrées and her sister, the Duchess of Villars, c. 1594, oil on canvas, 98 × 128 cm

Legacy

The nipple-squeezing gesture always gets a laugh. It has been the object of countless imitations, variations, and pastiches, attesting to its popularity. There have been innumerable tributes to these two sisters, whether in Pop art (Alain Jacquet), performance art (Jacqueline Dauriac), Figuration Libre (Robert Combas), video (Richard Texier), novels (Wolfram Fleischhauer), or photography. A 1998 ad campaign for Yves Saint Laurent Rive Gauche made a splash, with Kate Moss as the Duchess of Villars pinching a male Gabrielle.

Scandalous

Caravaggio's chiaroscuro technique and radical elimination of superfluous details shocked his contemporaries. His art, deemed vulgar, and his uncontrollable personality were the cause of countless controversies right from the seventeenth century. *The Death of the Virgin* incarnates this whiff of heresy even as it conveys a profound spirituality.

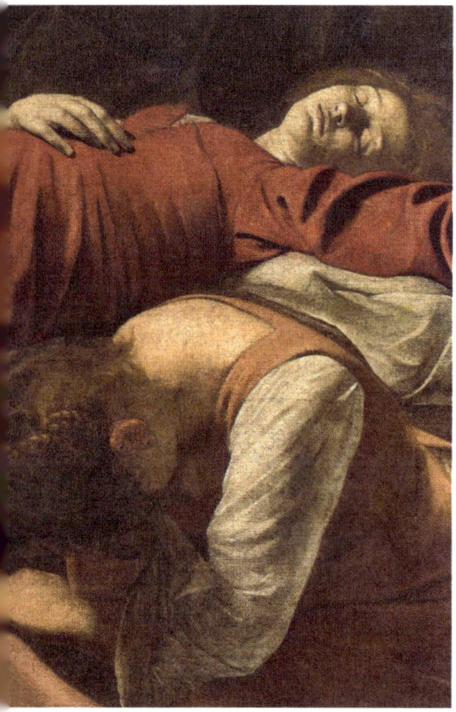

Reputation

A misunderstanding might be behind the fame of this work. Originally, *The Death of the Virgin* was supposed to hang discreetly in the gloom of the church of Santa Maria della Scala in Rome, but the man who commissioned it, a certain Laerzio Cherubini, decided not to leave it hanging in his chapel but rather sold it to the Duke of Mantua in 1606. Biographers of the day wrote that Mary's appearance caused a scandal in the church—her protruding belly, her uncovered feet, the gracelessness of the setting and the protagonists' poses, and the fact the model might have been a prostitute or Caravaggio's mistress. Accounts differed as to why Cherubini parted with this masterpiece, but recent research tends to prove that the monks were *not* shocked by Caravaggio's choice of imagery (bare feet, ancient-style tunics, barely sketched halo). On the contrary, it reflected the image of early Christians and adhered to the precepts of the Catholic Counter-Reformation, which viewed Mary as a human being.

Whatever the case, the *Virgin* soon left the church, having been sold for the tidy sum of 350 ecus. The transaction took place on the advice of the artist Peter Paul Rubens, and the Duke of Mantua exhibited the painting in his own gallery on Via del Corso under the express condition that the work not be copied, thereby increasing its reputation. *The Death of the Virgin* was bought in 1627 by Charles I of England; after the king was executed it was sold first to the director of the East India Company, and then to Louis XIV, who incorporated it into the French royal collection.

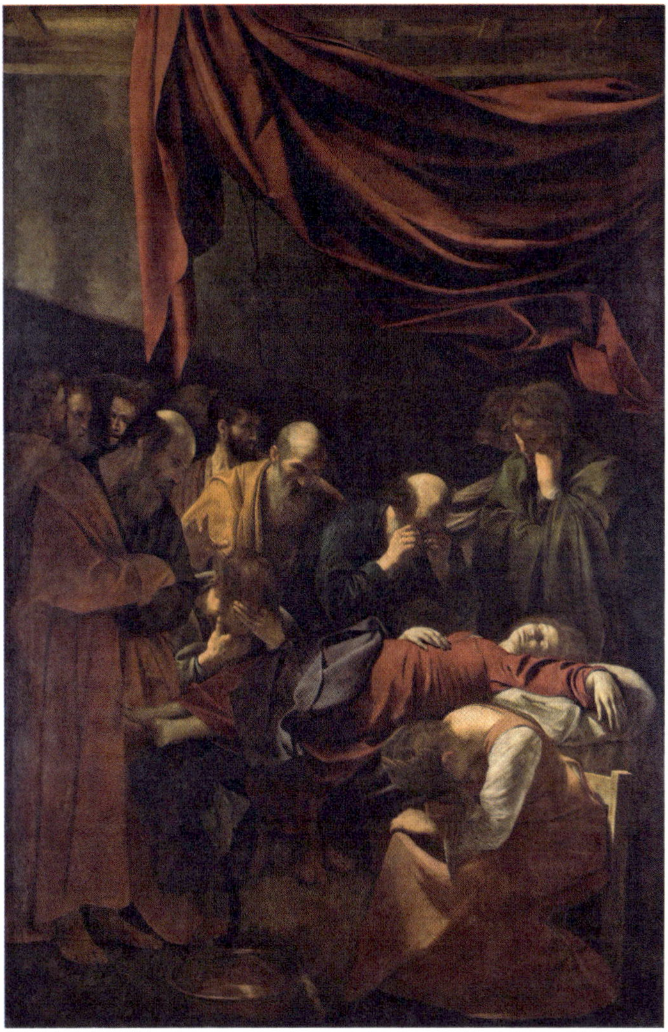

Caravaggesque style

The profound spirituality of Caravaggio's paintings derives from his personal, metaphorical use of light, which strikes people and objects at a raking angle that underscores a specific moment or brief event. This mastery of chiaroscuro was copied by his followers throughout Europe in the seventeenth century.

Michelangelo Merisi da Caravaggio,
known as **Caravaggio**
The Death of the Virgin,
c. 1605–06, oil on canvas,
369 × 245 cm

Controversy

Works by Caravaggio (or Michelangelo Merisi, known by the name of his home town of Caravaggio) immediately made a big impression. The vulgar dimension of his religious scenes could irritate some commentators who—in the middle of the high baroque period—were unsettled by the lack of celestial apparitions, ancient-style settings, nude allegories, reassuring putti, and supernatural effects. Others saw connections with Caravaggio's "dissolute" lifestyle. Indeed, in 1606 the artist had to flee Rome after having killed an adversary in a brawl. His reputation was tarnished by acts of violence, by his allegedly whimsical, outrageous personality, and by his sexual attraction to men. He thus remained in limbo for centuries, until art historians began to stress the avant-garde aspect of his oeuvre. In 1905 Roger Fry argued that Caravaggio was "the first [artist] to proceed not by evolution but by revolution, the first to rely entirely on his own temperamental attitude." But it would take another half century before major exhibitions of his work demonstrated Caravaggio's immense influence on European painting.

Queen Marie de' Medici at Marseille Rubens

Shocking Sea Nymphs

All the baroque power of Flemish artist Peter Paul Rubens is expressed in this scene set in the port of Marseille. As the queen prepares to disembark, her galley is made fast by buxom mythological figures whose nudity took beholders' breaths away.

Everything is lifelike—or almost

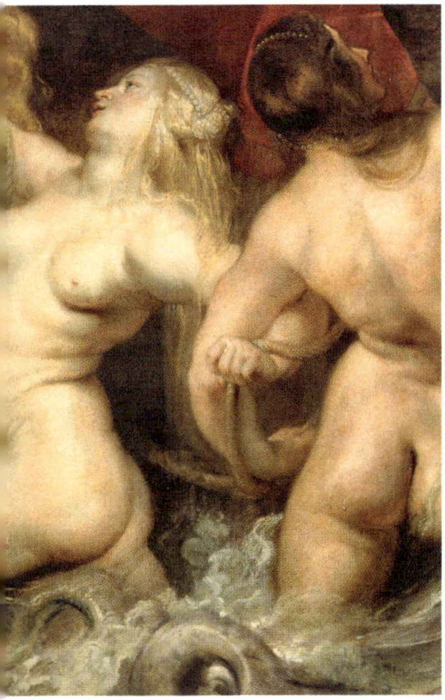

Has Rubens entered everyday language?

The Homeric Rubens (as Delacroix described him)—who painted courtly, religious, and history subjects—enjoyed unprecedented prestige in the seventeenth century, becoming a favorite of the entire European aristocracy for his diplomatic as well as artistic skills. In 1621 he was summoned by the Italian-born queen of France, Marie de' Medici, to execute two large cycles of works (twenty-four canvases each) glorifying her deceased husband Henri IV and herself, designed to decorate the Palais de Luxembourg in Paris. Henri IV, it should be recalled, after having divorced the notorious Queen Margot (Marguerite de Valois) and having nearly married his mistress, Gabrielle d'Estrées (see page 110), sought foreign legitimacy by taking Marie de' Medici as his second wife. The marriage was celebrated by proxy in Florence. Marie then embarked on a magnificent galley and, after having only moderately enjoyed the cruise, landed completely moonstruck at the port of Marseille. She then traveled to the city of Lyon, where her marriage to the lusty Henry could be consummated. In order to build up a legend surrounding the queen and that her authority be recognized, Rubens decided to combine historical reality (the voyage, the galley, the flags, the coats of arms, the dress) with allegorical fantasy.

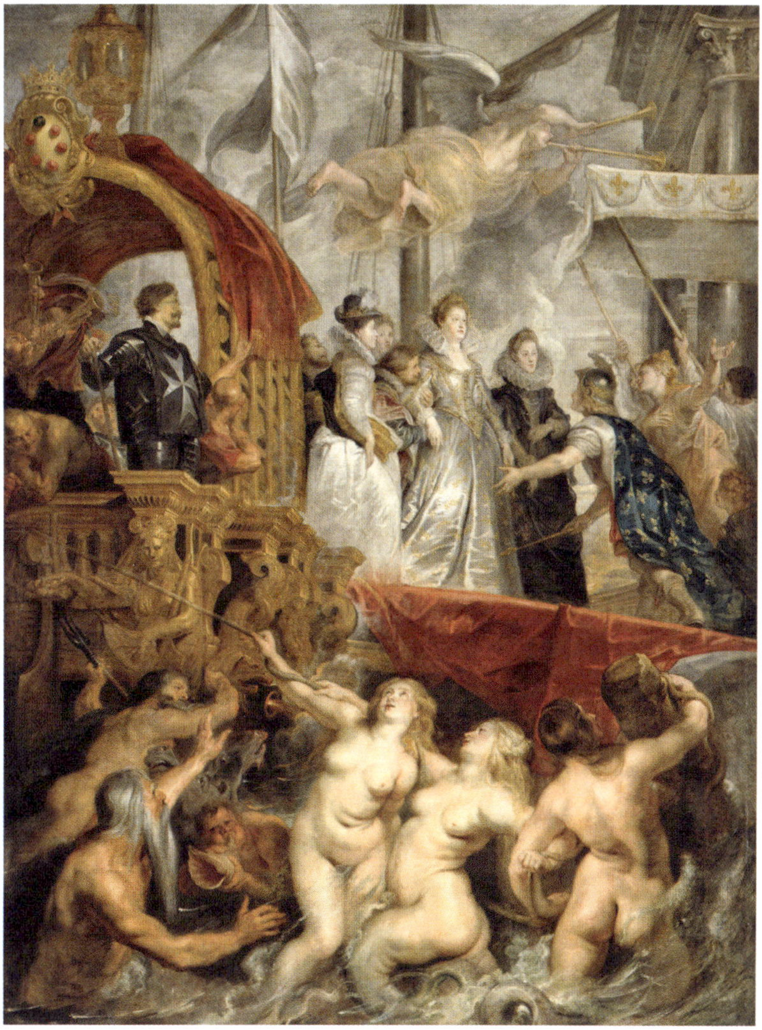

"Every male sensitive to love, every old man with any strength left, will joyfully let himself be caught up in this splendid net."

Alfred Michiels

"Never has painting gone further in the depiction of flesh, the texture of skin, and the watery shiver of light."

Théophile Gautier

Peter Paul Rubens
Queen Marie de' Medici Landing at Marseille, November 3, 1600,
c. 1622, oil on canvas,
394 × 295 cm

Rubenesque

When critics mocked Courbet's realistic nudes in the nineteenth century, they described them as "Rubenesque." Rubenesque meant "buxom," ample, plump. The artist's name thus became an epithet, a trademark, a sign of plumpness. In *Claudine in Paris*, the novelist Colette has her protagonist, Claudine, examine her body in a bathtub of warm water, part by part, from her nipples to her long legs to the dimples in her back, finally exclaiming, "I wasn't a Rubens, far from it, but I'm not keen on the 'beautiful butcher's wife' type."

The Cheat with the Ace of Diamonds

La Tour

Nasty Trick

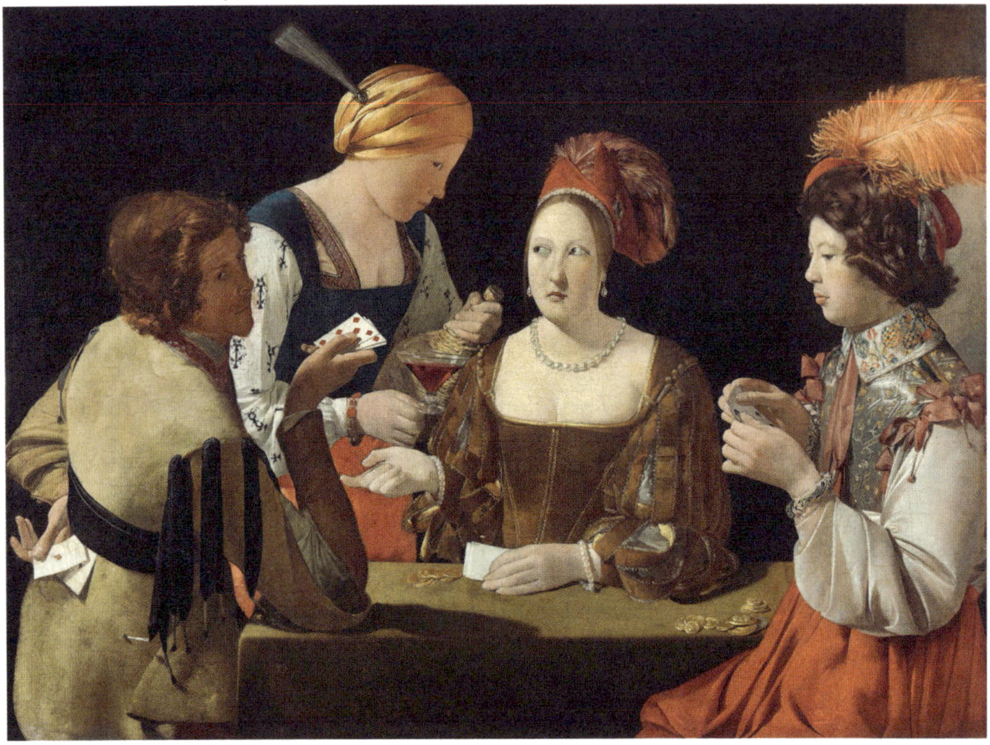

Well-known during his lifetime, later totally forgotten, Georges de La Tour recovered his proper place in the history of French painting thanks to *The Cheat with the Ace of Diamonds*. The very clever composition of this painting may well make the beholder complicit in a nasty trick.

Georges de La Tour
The Cheat with the Ace of Diamonds,
c. 1635–38,
oil on canvas,
106 × 146 cm

Game, set, and match

A French tennis player of Russian stock, Pierre-Henri Landry, was behind the discovery of this classic picture. The young sportsman bought *The Cheat with the Ace of Diamonds* in 1926 (or 1931) from an antique shop on Île Saint-Louis in Paris.

Landry not only wanted to win the Davis Cup, but also to collect old masters. Georges de La Tour, an artist from Lorraine, had been sidelined for centuries. Only Hermann Voss, a German art historian keen on little-known artists, had noticed paintings bearing La Tour's signature in Rennes and Nantes. Landry and Voss came into contact in the early 1930s, and the historian published an article that paved the way for La Tour's rehabilitation. In 1934 the canvas was sent to London for an exhibition of French art, and was later displayed at the Orangerie in Paris as part of a legendary show on "painters of reality": *Les peintres de la réalité en France au XVIIe siècle* (see Le Nain, p. 120). From that point onward, enthusiasm for La Tour grew. As several public-registry documents and brief mentions of his work began making it possible to piece the puzzle together, the corpus of La Tour's work increased. A 1972 retrospective, again hosted by the Orangerie, was a big hit and provided an opportunity for the French ministry of culture to score points by buying the masterpiece. "[The rediscovery of] La Tour is a triumph of art history, and its justification," exclaimed specialist Jacques Thuillier in the exhibition catalog.

We now know that La Tour had a brilliant career during the reign of Henri II of Lorraine (a great admirer of Caravaggio). Later, he became an official painter to Louis XIII of France and was granted lodging in the Louvre. Information gleaned during the twentieth century made it possible to distinguish two periods in La Tour's career. The first is nocturnal, where pictures are lit simply by a flame, in the tradition of Caravaggio, as wonderfully exemplified by his many scenes of the penitent Magdalen with a candle. The second period, called diurnal, involves a more personal realism with life-size figures and pale colors. *The Cheat* belongs to this period of intense maturity. It is not only highly refined, but also includes the beholder in a moral tale—the rich young man with orange feather is apparently caught up in everything the seventeenth century considered worst: gambling, wine, and lust. How can he get out of it? Everything hangs in the balance. The beholder, in trying to decide, can take the time to study every detail and gesture in this luminous work. The two women are complicit: the servant extends a glass to her mistress—probably a courtesan, given the string of pearls she is wearing. Their glances are sidelong. The lateral lighting reveals the back of the card sharp, whose head is bare and coat fairly ordinary. From his belt he draws the ace that will enable him to win the hand. The theme of the card sharp was handled by Caravaggio, then often imitated throughout Europe. La Tour here adds intriguing elements, such as a falsely archaic handling and an exchange of glances that seems to perturb the action. The right hands of the three figures on the left execute a startling ballet. The contrast of mat and glossy hues, shadow and light, and simplified volumes all render the physical gestures very abstract. Who is being fooled? Who is complicit? The young man, meanwhile, concentrates hard, even if everything in this painting suggests that he will soon lose his shirt.

Italian scam

The theme of the card sharp or the fortune teller who steals the onlooker's purse was highly fashionable from the mid sixteenth century onward. Certainly inspired by stock characters from the commedia dell'arte, this genre spread from Italy into Flanders, France, and Spain. Caravaggio, La Tour, the Le Nain brothers, Theodoor Rombouts, and Pieter de Hooch all caught the gambling bug. Cézanne's famous *Card Players* was a remote descendent of this transalpine fever.

The Arcadian Shepherds Poussin

Open Sesame!

Although Nicolas Poussin spent most of his life in Italy, his works epitomized the aesthetics of French classicism. *The Arcadian Shepherds* intrigued the great European thinkers of the Enlightenment movement before becoming a case study for art historians and a "household" chromolithograph.

Warning

Who is the woman in the foreground?

Arcadia, the land of green pastures described by Virgil, the kingdom of innocent shepherds and sprightly nymphs where spring is eternal, where humans and nature rejoice in peace and harmony, Arcadia can be melancholic at times. Unsettled, even. Sometimes, while out on a walk, something beneath a grove or elsewhere reminds the shepherds of their mortal condition. *The Arcadian Shepherds* were first painted by Guercino: his small baroque canvas depicts two shepherds contemplating an engraved stone topped with a decomposing skull. Initially inspired by this scene, Poussin produced another version of the vanity thirteen years later, in which the skull was replaced with the words "Et in Arcadia ego" inscribed on a tomb in capital letters. One of the three shepherds turns to a woman draped in yellow and blue and shows her the engraved words that could be translated as "I exist, even in Arcadia." The work has given rise to a multitude of interpretations, especially during the eighteenth century. The engraved sentence in particular has sparked much debate, for its meaning changes according to who pronounces it: the deceased or Death itself. *Et in Arcadia ego* can be interpreted as a simple warning (I too lived in Arcadia . . . and I died), a hedonistic motto (I too lived in Arcadia . . . and I was as happy there as you can be now), or the magic formula to a newfound paradise. Such was Goethe's use of *Et in Arcadia ego* in his *Italian Journey*, as a direct reference to Poussin's work. To the Enlightenment thinkers, the Arcadian myth was inherent to the painting. For example, Diderot drew on it for his theory of dramatic poetry.

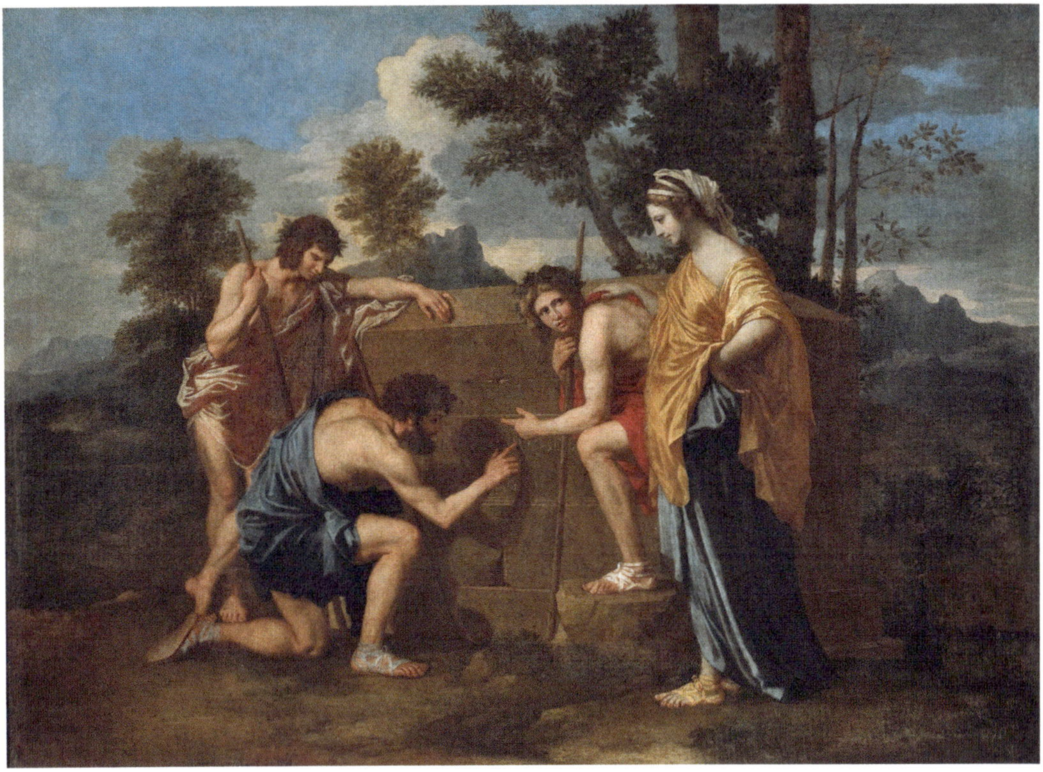

The Arcadian Shepherds were turning into a reference. Erwin Panofsky's compelling writings on the subject shed light on the Arcadian myth according to Poussin and provide valuable insights as to why it should be interpreted and why the roles of the figures are important, such as that of the female figure in the foreground.

Nicolas Poussin
The Arcadian Shepherds, also known as *Et in Arcadia ego*, c. 1638–40, oil on canvas, 85 × 121 cm

The mysterious woman

Who is this woman? Among the many people who have sought to answer that question, the anthropologist Claude Lévi-Strauss puts forward a convincing theory: she replaced the skull in the previous versions of the myth. He suggests that the draped apparition represents Death or Destiny. Furthermore, he wrote that the renown of Poussin's work, "the most popular, reproduced in chromo and displayed in households," according to him, was largely due to that mysterious and impressive woman. Death was present in the painting, unbeknownst to us.

Peasant Family in an Interior

Le Nain

People of Little Means

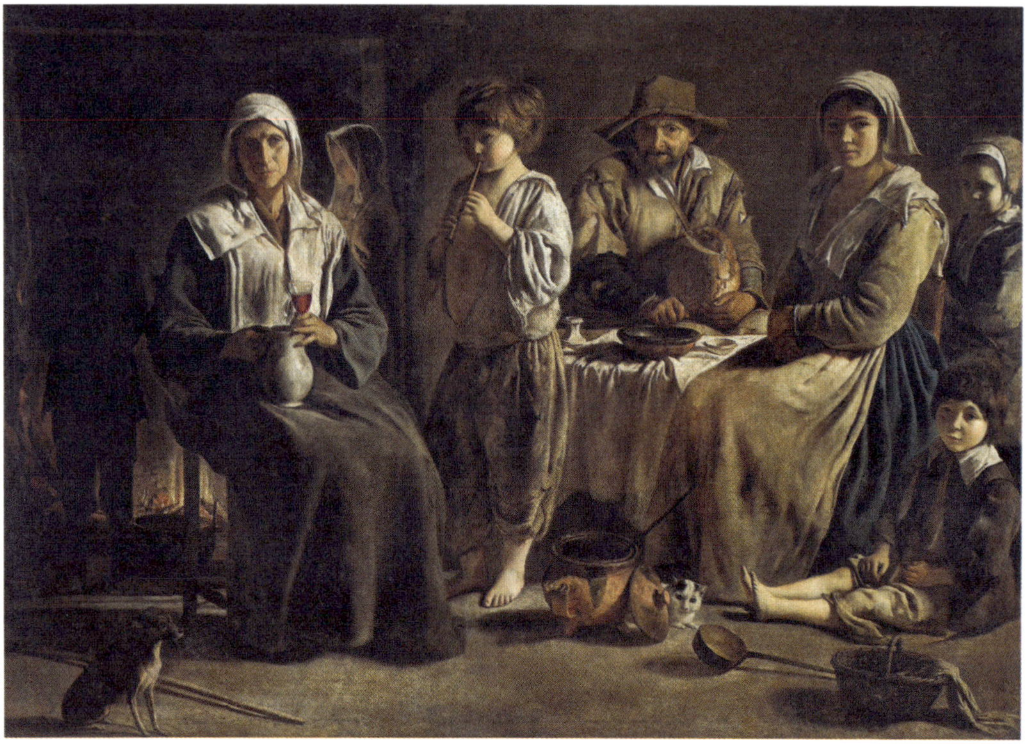

Louis Le Nain (?)
Peasant Family in an Interior,
c. 1642,
oil on canvas,
113 × 159 cm

Peasant Family in an Interior is one of the Louvre icons and a masterpiece of French art. This is partly due to historians who contributed to turning the Le Nain brothers into major seventeenth-century painters. Without them, the painters would have remained anonymous like so many thatched cottage paintings adorning the walls of provincial mansions.

A long rehabilitation period

The Le Nain brothers (Antoine, Louis and Mathieu) became members of the Académie Royale de Peinture et de Sculpture in the year of its creation (1648), as "painters of *bambochades*" of a minor genre. To the great theorist Félibien, their manner was "not very noble" and their subjects were of "low and often ridiculous action." Although they were commissioned many works and were recognized during their lifetime, they were not always appreciated for their true worth. In the nineteenth century, Champfleury the champion of realism, the admirer of Balzac and Courbet, took an interest in their work. After many years spent perusing the academy's catalogs and archives, the art critic wrote several books on what he called the "painters of reality." He forged their legend by claiming that their relative anonymity was due to their modesty, and that their love of the countryside made them flee the capital city's honor and riches. Champ fleury's work was well received by art historians but left the public rather indifferent. At the turn of the twentieth century, Anthony Valabrègue noted a change in sensitivity: "Today, we find that these painters are closer to us than the noble and pompous masters." The time had come to reinstate the "painters of the people." Along with providing biographical details to show that the Le Nain brothers were far from poor and actually quite enjoyed the limelight, Valabrègue looked into the profound meaning of their works, rooted in hospitality and contemplation. This moral dimension was starting to draw in a wider audience.

Back into the limelight

Peasant Family in an Interior appeared in a Drouot sale in 1914. There was no trace of a reproduction, engraving, or description before that. The painting then belonged to the Marquis de Marmier, who had probably inherited it from his ancestors. It was acquired for 12,000 francs by the merchant Demotte who sold it again the following year. Then, the Louvre acquired it for 100,000 francs. The painting was well-received and immediately hailed by art historians as a major work despite the lack of a signature. Everyone was captivated by the everyday life scene when farmers unwind from a hard day's work by listening to a sweet piece of music played by a young boy.

Since when has this type of painting been appreciated?

Popular Front

A few years later, a major event was held in France during the interwar period. Called *Les peintres de la réalité en France au XVIIe siècle*, the exhibition that showcased the work of Georges de La Tour gave new prominence to seventeenth-century French art, allowing it to be compared with paintings by Maurice Denis, Balthus, Matisse, Picasso, and Léger, and thus show the extent and power of realism in art. As the Popular Front was emerging, the Le Nain brothers' painting matched the ideal vision of a France that sought to stand firm in its beliefs and social structure. The popular solidarity evoked by the Le Nain brothers was much appreciated by critics and audiences alike.

Portrait of the Artist at his Easel Rembrandt

Self-Promotion

Although self-portraiture had become a common practice among artists during the Renaissance, it took on a special dimension with Rembrandt. His career was punctuated by roughly one hundred painted or engraved self-portraits, making his face familiar to us.

Business card

Narcissism, introspection, or obsession with aging? Starting in his youth, Rembrandt did many self-portraits and sold them as his career progressed. The paintings and prints of him were initially straightforward studies of heads (called *tronies*) that displayed various expressions: beaming smile, eyes wide, and so on. They served as samples for clients who visited his studio, demonstrating his talent as a portraitist and the good likeness of the sitter. The initial reason for Rembrandt's numerous self-portraits was therefore practical and economical. In his youthful paintings, Rembrandt depicted himself largely plunged in shadow—his face can barely be made out. His mouth is half-open, as though he is trying to describe some particular phenomenon. He is examining himself. From his very first *Anatomy Lesson*, Rembrandt earned a reputation for his perfect rendering of human skin, which earned many commissions. With his own self-portraits, he was handing out the equivalent of business cards.

What was Rembrandt's first name?

The painter who signed his canvases Rembrandt perhaps hoped to join Raphael, Titian, and Michelangelo in the pantheon of artistic geniuses. Like them, Rembrandt Haarmenzoon van Rijn achieved such fame that his first name became his only name.

At work

The Louvre's portrait by Rembrandt of himself is a mature work, the first in a series where the artist shows himself at his easel, holding his tools. This type of composition had been popular in the preceding century, then became rarer in the seventeenth century, although it might be noted that during the same period Vermeer completed

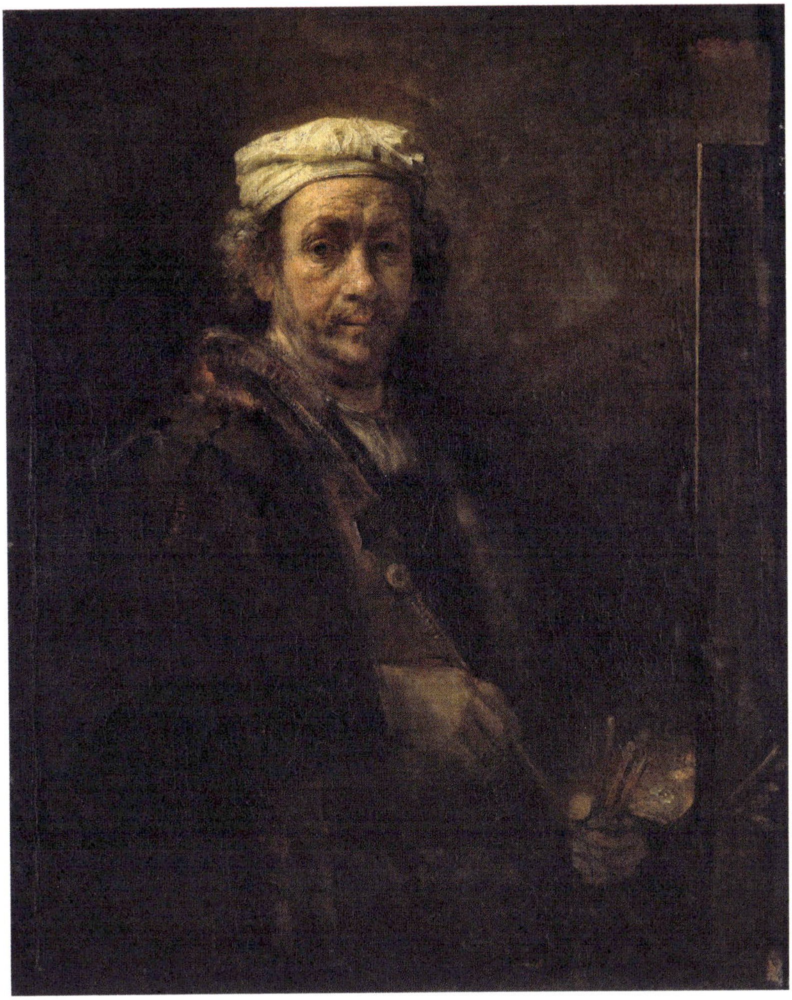

Rembrandt Harmenszoon van Rijn
Portrait of the Artist at his Easel,
1660, oil on canvas,
111 × 85 cm

"Rembrandt goes so deep into the mysterious that he says things for which there are no words in any language."

Vincent van Gogh

an extraordinary *Allegory of Painting* that showed himself from the back, facing his easel and model. Here Rembrandt was in his fifties, and his career had taken a grim turn: after having achieved fame, he was stripped of his property. We see a discredited painter who barely escaped humiliating bankruptcy and who had to sell his house, furniture, and collection of prints and drawings. Wearing a threadbare coat and work cap, unshaven, and with bags beneath his eyes, he seems marked by life's trials. But his brushwork remains energetic and his pose conveys the noble simplicity of an artist able to depict himself with the authenticity of an aging man. The artist continues to examine himself. Rembrandt never explained why he did so many self-portraits, nor what he felt when he painted them, which is maybe why they fascinate us so much.

Life's Rich Tapestry

Vermeer's paintings are intriguing. They call for contemplation and careful observation, and sometimes even arouse covetousness and obsession. Their rarity has attracted counterfeiters and their beauty has charmed many visitors.

The Sphinx of Delft

Vermeer's life is an enigma to art lovers. Renamed the Sphinx of Delft, he came into the limelight during the second half of the nineteenth century when a series of three articles were published in *La Gazette des beaux-arts*. The Dutch master had been relatively unknown until then, producing works for wealthy clients in a small but prosperous town. Slowly but surely, he composed small interior scenes that entered private collections and were sold according to successions. His sudden rise to fame placed Vermeer between Rembrandt and Frans Hals. He was acclaimed as one of the major Dutch Golden Age artists, and his reputation has never ceased to grow since. Théophile Thoré, the author of the three articles known under the pseudonym William Bürger, was quite fascinating, too. A pamphleteer under the July Monarchy and a defender of the 1848 Revolution, he developed a political approach to art and saw the little Dutch masters as heroes who resisted Italian domination. He was forced into exile and fell victim to censorship (hence his pseudonym). He took advantage of his travels to compile a listing of Dutch paintings. In *La Gazette des beaux-arts*, he put forth Vermeer's extraordinary ability to depict natural light and subtle use of color. After Thoré supplied eleven paintings for the painter's first "retrospective exhibition," the first Vermeer entered the Louvre.

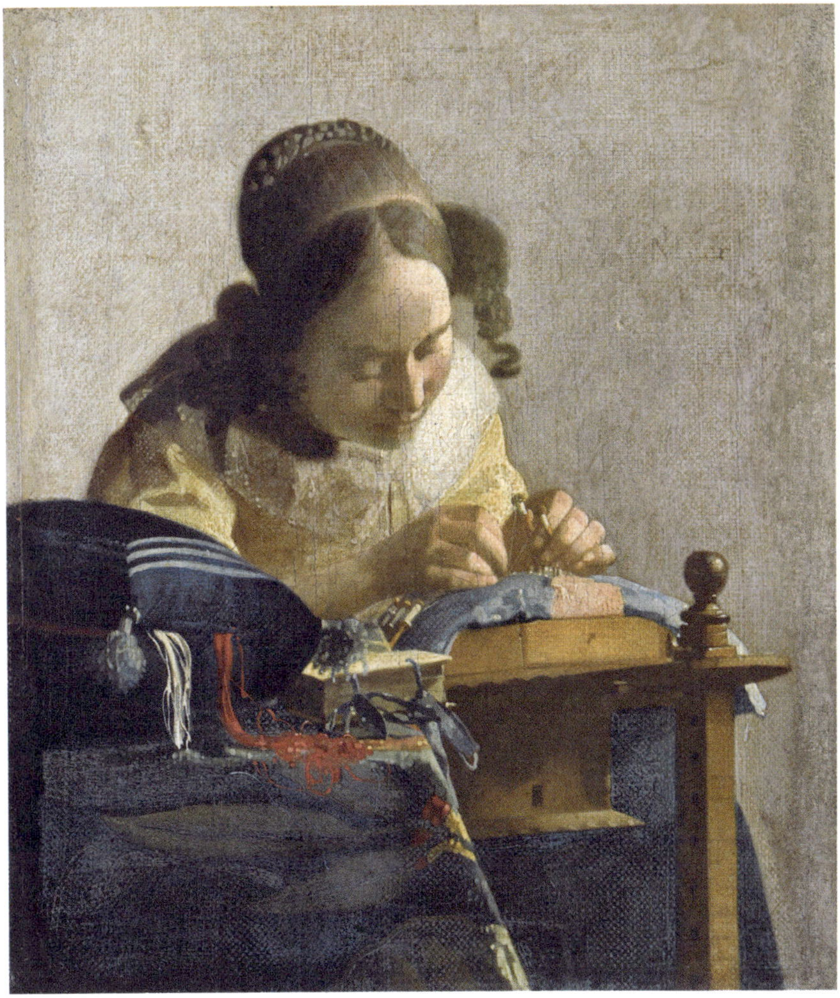

Johannes Vermeer
The Lacemaker,
c. 1669–70,
oil on canvas glued to panel,
24 × 21 cm

Through the magnifying glass

The Lacemaker was acquired in 1870 at an auction. Vermeer's smallest painting instantly connects with the viewer and draws him into observing the young woman's focused gestures as well as the finesse of the elements in the interior scene. Against the bare wall, a dark-blue cushion with pale-blue pompoms catches the eye. As more details come into focus, we are drawn to the thread pulled by the lacemaker while the colorful strands spill out of the white and red bobbins and flood the lower part of the

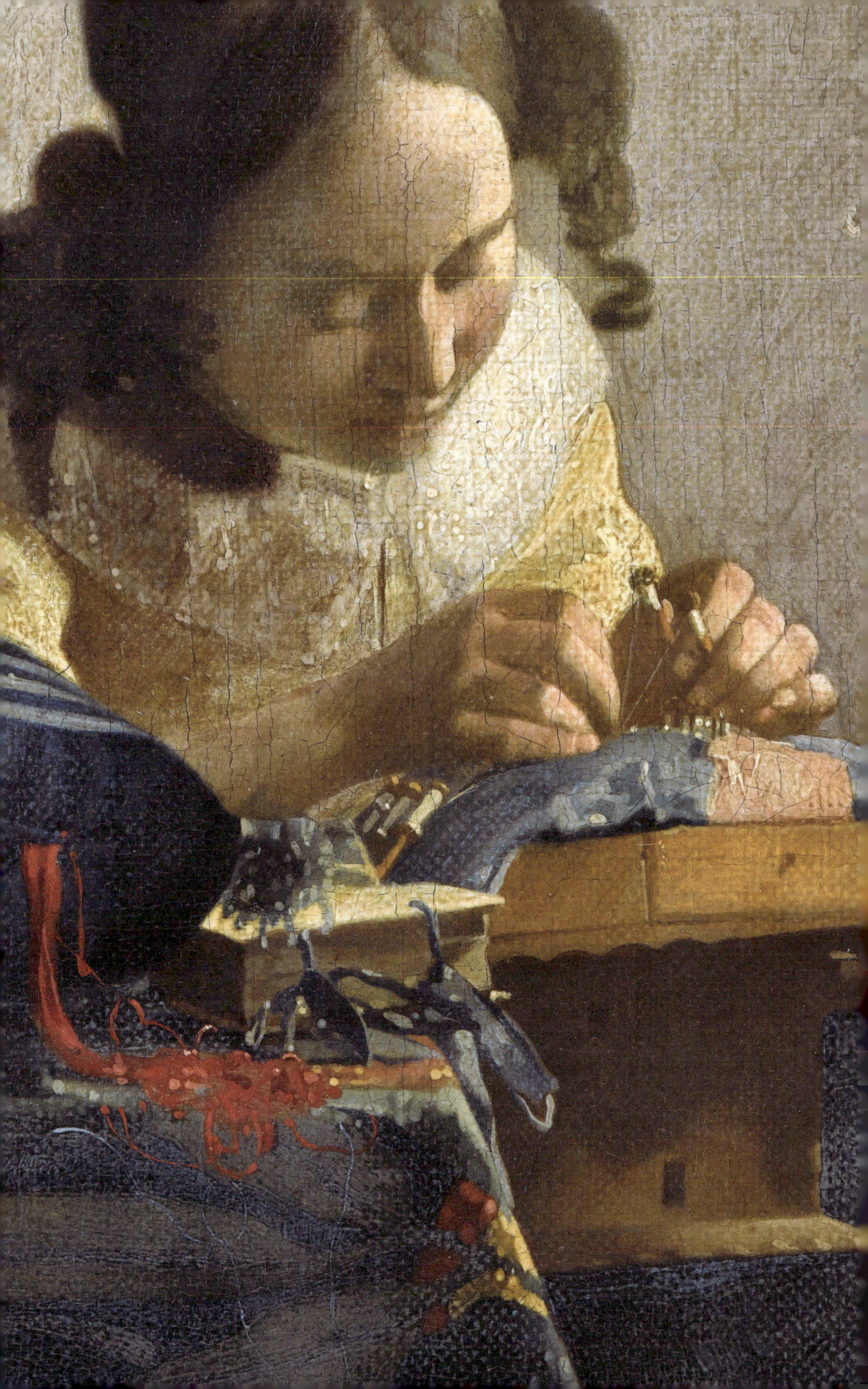

painting. We step closer and see tiny white, yellow, and blue dots like specks of light that contribute to the overall effect. Vermeer experts believe that the artist painted *The Lacemaker* in a dark room. This would explain the canvas' perfect composition and unique effect, but the theory remains unproven to this day. Needle holes visible through a magnifying glass could have been the result of strings pulled across the canvas to draw convergence lines and better apprehend perspective. The small work has generated much interest and attention over the decades, and the theories are still going strong.

How to pin it down

A particular light

Vermeer's painting has been admired countless times for more than a century by art lovers whose attraction for the penetrating representations of Dutch interiors turned these genre paintings into the most precious of objects. Due to the rarity of the paintings, searches were launched in the attics of the Netherlands and disputes arose over attribution. Great art forgers have sought to reproduce the particular light and tone. The most gifted among them, Han van Meegeren, even became a national hero for managing to fool the Nazi officer Göring. *The Milkmaid* became one of the most famous paintings in the world, followed by *Girl with a Pearl Earring* (Scarlett Johansson starred in the movie adaptation), now known as the Northern Mona Lisa.

The Reign of Soft Power

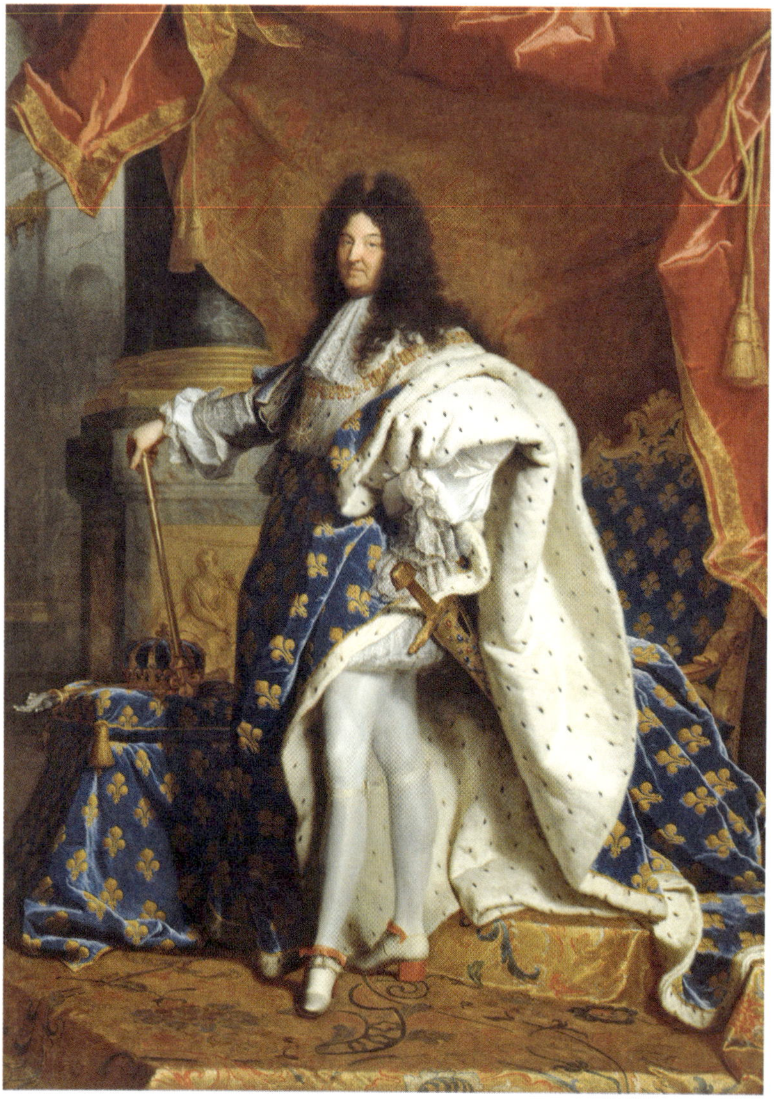

Hyacinthe Rigaud
Louis XIV (1638–1715),
1701, oil on canvas,
277 × 194 cm

Presented in Louis XIV's grand apartment in Versailles before an audience of loyal courtiers in January 1702, this ceremonial painting became the archetype of official portraits. Even now, presidents are often pictured in a posture similar to that of the Sun King.

The Petite Académie

It is the story of a king who wanted to be a god. In addition to unlimited means, he had the support of his government to reach his goal and become an absolute monarch. But the clothes alone were not enough for the king to achieve a divine stature; the very mention of his name had to be evocative of a sublime and wonderful being. The "Petite Académie" was thus formed to "reinvent" the king's public image. Supervised by Colbert, it was in charge of controlling the manufacture of the sovereign's representations. A wide variety of supports such as tapestries, engravings, medals, poems, ballets, and operas served the glory of the Sun King (in reference to Jupiter, a Greek god depicted in majesty). The many decorations, engravings, and medals were dispatched to the six provincial academies as well as in the Jesuit colleges with the motto "*Nec pluribus impar*" (meaning "None his equal," "Above all," or "Everything is possible for him"). They circulated among the ruling classes in the kingdom's various cities. The form of "soft power" thus exercised by Colbert culminated after his death with Hyacinthe Rigaud's extraordinary *portrait d'apparat* (state portrait).

"I am the image"

Louis XIV had initially commissioned the large painting as a gift for his grandson the Duke of Anjou, the new king of Spain (better known as Philip V). The Sun King was so pleased with the result that he kept the original canvas and asked Hyacinthe Rigaud to make a copy for his grandson.

The king's two bodies

The canvas measures 2.77 meters in height. The king is depicted in a majestic three-quarter view, full-length pose. Dominating his subjects from atop a raised platform, he is wearing a blue mantle decorated with golden fleur-de-lis and lined with ermine. He is surrounded by the regalia given to the young Louis by the Archbishop of Reims half a century earlier at the coronation: the scepter; the crown placed on a stool matching the royal habit, next to the Hand of Justice; Charlemagne's sword Joyeuse, hanging from the belt. Although every detail signifies absolute power, there is a discrepancy between the king's head and his legs. It brings to mind the phrase coined by the historian Ernst Kantorowicz, "The King's Two Bodies," representing the sovereign as both an immortal figure of power and a mere mortal. While the face is that of a sixty-three-year-old man with sagging cheeks, his feet in fourth position and encased in red heels adorned with ribbons belong to the young Louis performing in the court ballets.

Rococo and Jeers

Even though it was not featured in the first compendium of Watteau's engravings nor in the early nineteenth-century Louvre catalog, *Pilgrimage to the Isle of Cythera* was already famous. Praised by the academy or mocked by the student painters, it embodied *fêtes galantes* and an expression of happiness and pastoral innocence in a conventional world—a theme favored by the great poets.

Reception piece

In the eighteenth century, the aristocratic society reveled in the freedom of morals that replaced the pious rigor of the Sun King. It was in this context that Watteau painted *Pilgrimage to the Isle of Cythera*. The artist submitted the canvas as his reception piece at the Académie Royale de Peinture et de Sculpture. A new genre of painting was born: the *fête galante*. In art history textbooks, the work marks the transition from triumphant classicism to rococo.

A target

The painting entered the Louvre's collections in 1795 but did not appear in the royal museum's catalog until 1816. The painter Pierre Nolasque Bergeret recalled that when he was a student, Watteau's rococo style was considered "decadent." David's students, including Bergeret, swore only by the Greek and Roman. The painting depicting a *fête galante* was hung in a study room and used as a target by art students who threw pellets of bread or earth at it. One day, a student painter reportedly punched it with such force that it fell to the ground. *Pilgrimage to the Isle of Cythera* was relegated to the attic, and remained there until the Restoration.

Young fools

Watteau returned to favor at the same time as Rubens. Color was back in fashion and the decorative arts were having a field day. During the Second Empire, poetry drew on similar imagery to express nostalgia for graceful, frivolous, and easy love affairs. Gérard de Nerval even sailed to Cythera: "I imagined those untamed pilgrims of love in coats of shimmering satin." In 1869, Paul Verlaine published a collection of startling and enthralling poems entitled *Fêtes galantes* in homage to the painter's frolicsome work.

The critical fortune of the painting owed much to the poets turning Watteau's figures into familiar, "playful and elegant princesses" frolicking in "unreal landscapes" (Baudelaire).

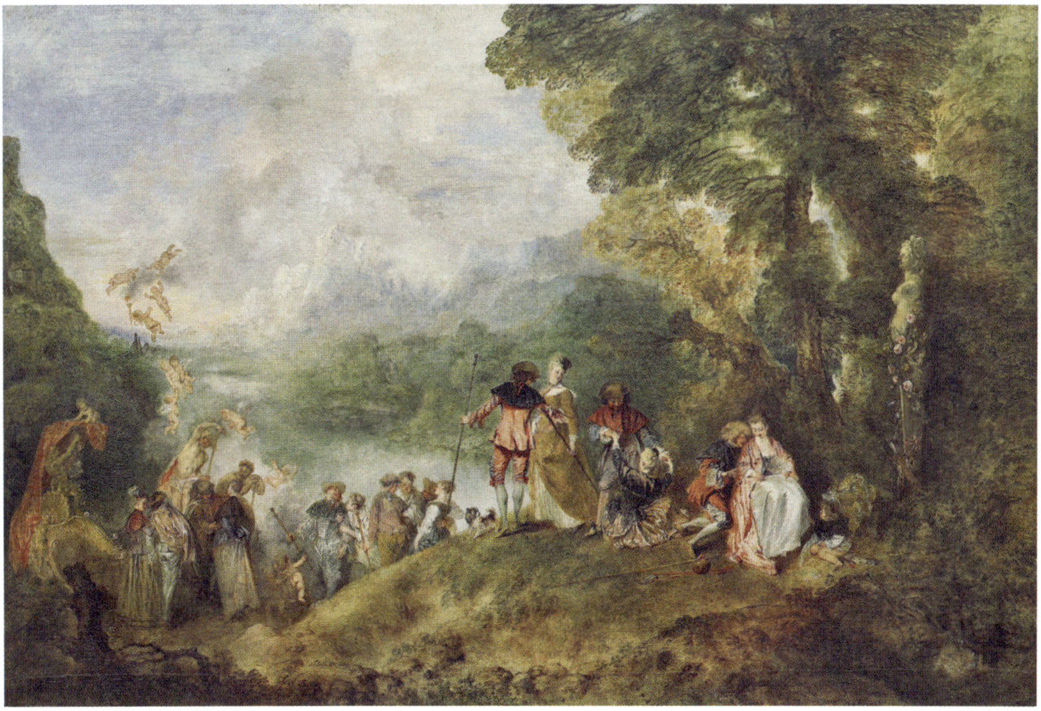

Jean Antoine Watteau
Pilgrimage to the Isle of Cythera, also known as *Embarkation to the Isle of Cythera*, 1717, oil on canvas, 129 × 194 cm

"High-heels were struggling with a full-length dress So that, between the wind and the terrain, At times a shining stocking would be seen, And gone too soon. We liked that foolishness."

Verlaine, "The Young Fools"

Auguste Rodin's descriptive interpretation of *Pilgrimage to the Isle of Cythera* in 1911 also made a lasting impression. Like a medieval painting where different actions are in the same plane or like sequential scenes in a storyboard, Rodin saw the painting as a representation of the successive stages of love. According to him, to begin with, the young woman is (or pretends to be) indifferent towards her suitor; then, she takes the hand he proffers to help her stand up. *Embarkation* or *Pilgrimage to the Isle of Cythera*? The former director of the National Gallery Michael Levey wondered about the title: the movement of the pilgrims from right to left suggests that they may be regretfully leaving the island instead of happily embarking for Cythera. His 1961 article caused a stir among the art critics of the time and opened the way for a whole series of interpretations. The painting was henceforth seen as an allegory for the passing of time and the transient nature of passion. Cythera had become but an illusion, a distant dream in the wake of a *fête galante*.

131

The Lock Fragonard

Debauched

Fragonard's *The Lock* illustrates the cover of the paperback edition of *Les Liaisons dangereuses*. The small rococo masterpiece is a symbol of the libertine ancien régime, erotic passion, lust, and rape, as well as one of the Louvre's most popular acquisitions.

A libertine marvel

As of 1784, *The Lock* was made famous by the many prints in circulation. And even though it only recently entered the Louvre's collections, the public was already familiar with the work from having studied it at school or seen it in commercials. It epitomizes debauchery in our collective imagination and perfectly illustrates the works of Sade and Choderlos de Laclos.

During his lifetime, Fragonard was acknowledged the master of risqué subjects and alluring twists. His paintings mirror the rather free morals of the century. Wealthy clients infatuated with erotic paintings commissioned rather salacious depictions from him such as *The Happy Accidents of the Swing*. The painter excelled in the art of depicting *fêtes galantes* and intimate scenes (*Match to Powderkeg*, *La Gimblette*) that invariably involved scantily dressed women. His vibrant use of color and light enlivens his compositions, and his signature brushwork is a fascinating blend of mastery and spontaneity.

"The scene takes place near a bed whose disorder reveals the full scope of the subject."

A. J. Paillet

The philanderer and the sinner

A man and a woman are locked in a passionate wrestle amid a clutter of rich fabrics, he standing on tiptoe, reaching for the lock, she with her dress undone, head tilted to the side, about to faint (or give in). Her right arm is pushing a kiss away, her left hand is up in a slight gesture of resistance. The apple on the table is a clear symbol of sin and the bouquet on the ground represents a defloration scene. But as the historian Daniel Arasse pointed out, the theatrical void of the central and disproportionate bed swathed in sheets and curtains

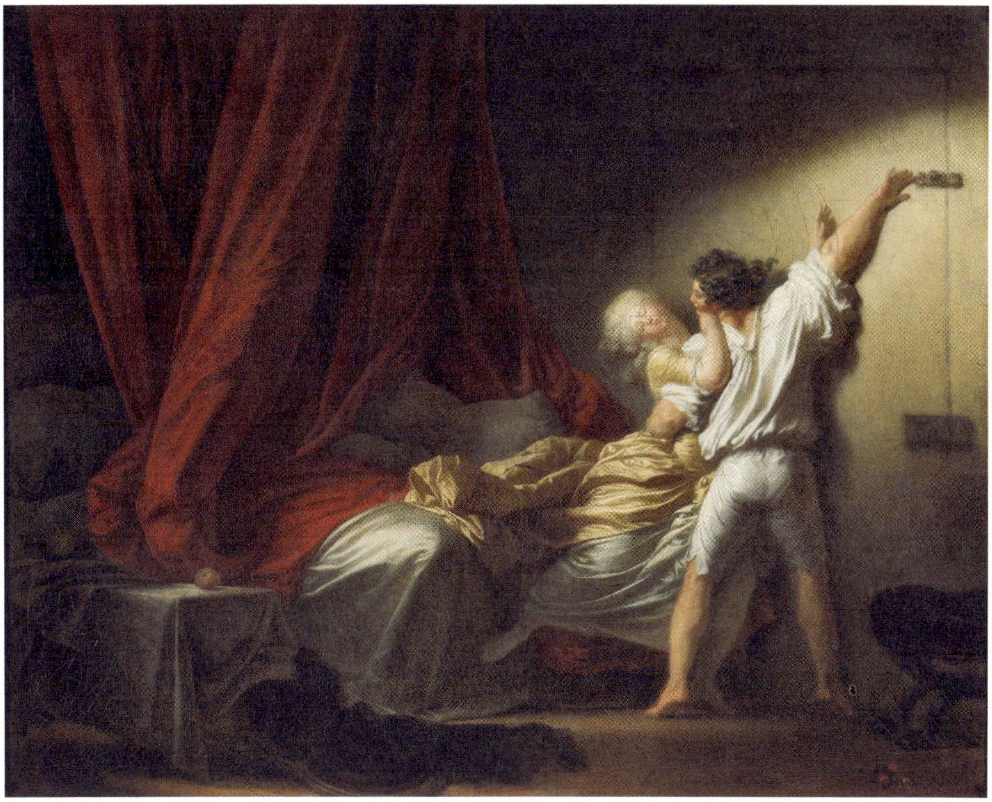

can also be interpreted as the painting's main subject. The intrigue lies in the fabric's erotic folds: the breasts outlined by the pillows, the penis enwrapped in the curtain, the knee beneath the sheet.

Jean Honoré Fragonard
The Lock
c. 1777, oil on canvas,
74 × 94 cm

Too famous to be true

Are they fighting or frolicking?

The painting was commissioned by a marquis whose collection had quite a reputation. Upon his death, *The Lock* was sold. The work passed from hand to hand and vanished after the Revolution, but engravings had been made of it whose dissemination ensured the fame of Fragonard's libertine painting. Innumerable pastiches and pornographic versions ensued. The canvas reappeared in the twentieth century and was put up for sale with the words "attributed to" and "school of" Fragonard—the auctioneers had reservations about the name of the painter. Thanks to a French ministry of finance grant, *The Lock* was bought for a little over 5 million francs. It entered the Louvre in 1974 and passed a series of tests that confirmed its authenticity: characteristic of Fragonard's late works, *The Lock* had indeed been painted by him.

Psyche Revived by Cupid's Kiss

Canova

The Most Beautiful Bibelot

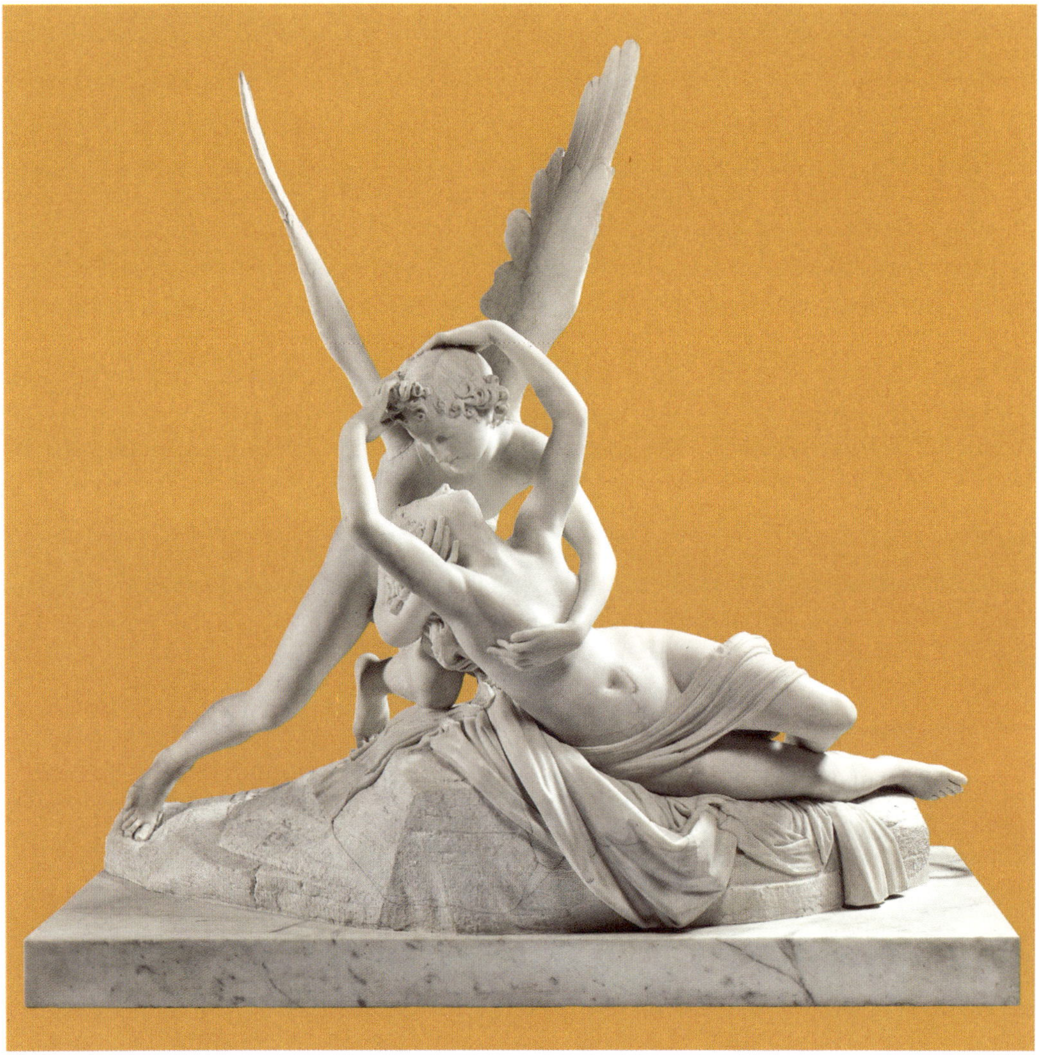

Psyche Revived by Cupid's Kiss is a perfectly executed marble sculpture. Some critics have deemed it too complex, too baroque, not neoclassical enough, lacking in perspective, and so on. The viewer must walk around it to fully appreciate it, and that is precisely what makes it so interesting.

Château life

The theme of Cupid and Psyche gained prominence during the neoclassical period. The god and his young lover were the object of countless adaptations in literature, music, painting, and sculpture. One marble in particular stands out, so graceful and delicate in its realistic rendering of skin, veil, and feather textures. It was first officially shown in 1802 at the Château de Villiers-la-Garenne. Its owner Joachim Murat had acquired it with another group on the same theme and by the same sculptor. The work was due to be shipped from Rome to the home of its commissioner, Colonel John Campbell in England, but it had to remain in Canova's studio, where it was admired by many passing artists, collectors, and writers. By the time *Psyche Revived by Cupid's Kiss* arrived in France eleven years later, art lovers had already seen it or heard about it. When Murat was named King of Naples in 1808, he gave the sculpture to Napoleon I who exhibited it in the Château de Compiègne.

The winged Cupid holds a beautiful young woman who is lying unconscious on a rock. She plunged into a deep sleep after opening a flask. Based on the myth developed in Apuleius' *Metamorphoses*, Cupid makes sure that Psyche is still alive. He holds her in his arms and kisses her tenderly. She comes to her senses and lovingly reaches up for him. Canova based his composition both on the myth and on his own recollection of a painting he saw in Herculaneum. The man's kneeling pose and the woman's arm movements were inspired by Roman iconography. The marble reveals the full scope of the sculptor's virtuosity. In particular, the translucent wings are perfectly integrated to the back.

Antonio Canova
Psyche Revived by Cupid's Kiss,
c. 1793,
marble,
155 × 168 cm

By-products

Canova received new commissions. Prince Yusupov wanted to acquire the same sculpture, only in a more modest version: Psyche's legs were consequently covered with a muslin drape. The plaster cast was later offered to Canova's student Adamo Tadolini, who in turn produced a marble. At least five slightly different versions appeared; tiny butterfly wings grew on Psyche's back, and smaller marble and bronze versions were disseminated throughout Europe like so many winged messengers spreading the Italian sculptor's fame. *Psyche Revived by Cupid's Kiss* was soon featured on cameo medallions, decorative boxes, and tobacco pouches.

Seen and approved

"Canova had the courage not to copy the Greeks, but to invent a beauty of his own as the Greeks had done. What a humiliation for the pedants! And so, they'll still be insulting him fifty years after his death, and for that reason his glory will increase all the faster."
Stendhal, 1816

Small and big kisses

Winged figures and deep sleep are recurrent themes in folk tales, Shakespeare's *A Midsummer Night's Dream*, and *Sleeping Beauty*—whose most famous versions were written by Charles Perrault (1697) and the Grimm Brothers (1812). Bouguereau's paintings perpetuate the myth of Psyche and Cupid, or Flora and Zephyr. Auguste Rodin's sculptures represent Psyche with other figures: the gestures in *Eternal Springtime* are reminiscent of Canova's work; the kiss uniting the *Divine Comedy* lovers Paolo and Francesca was a great success. The sculptural group was renamed *The Kiss*, and the French government ordered a larger marble version of it. It took Rodin ten years to sculpt, and finally deliver, what he called his "big bibelot."

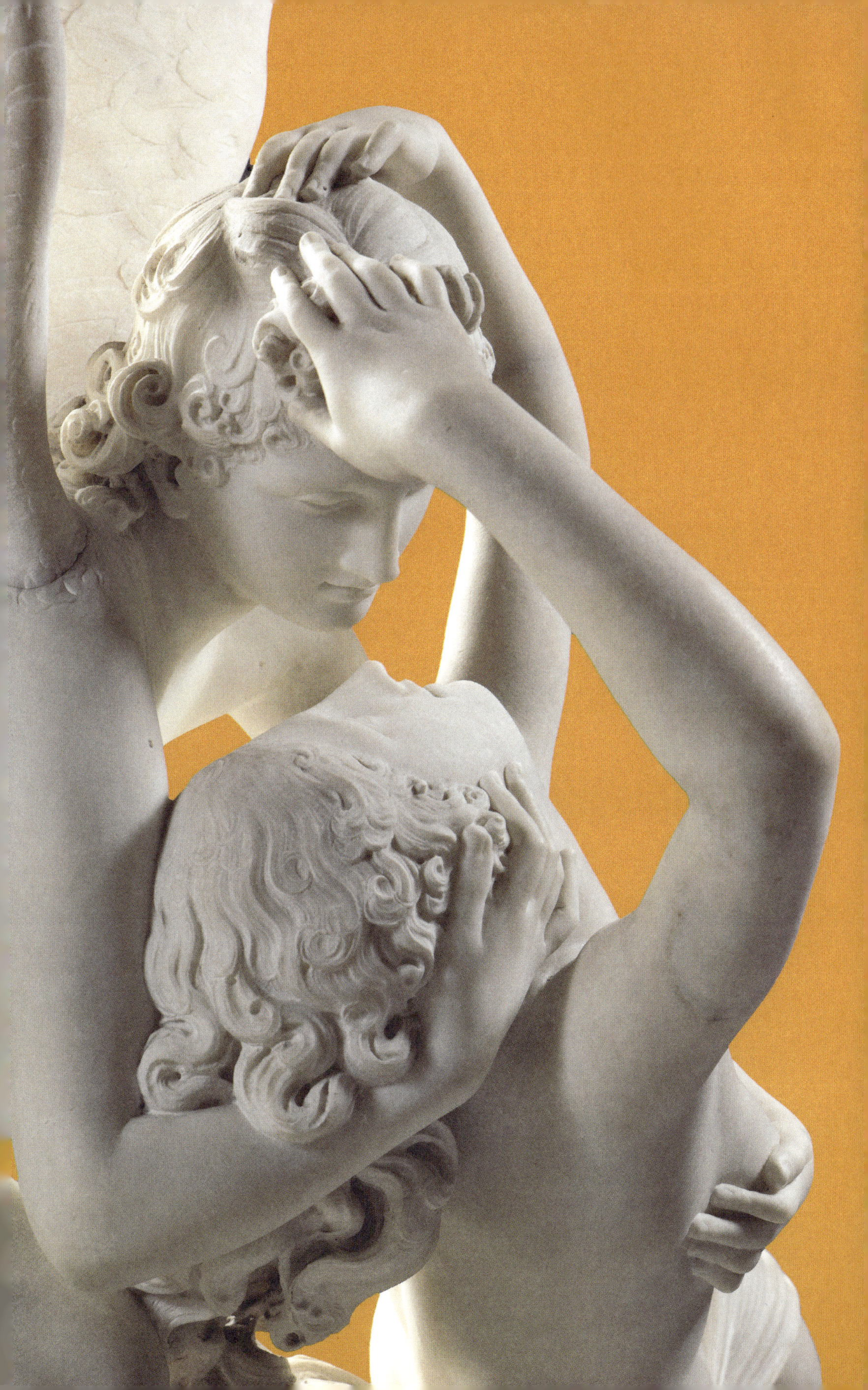

The Coronation of Napoleon

David

One Walked

Fifteen years after the French Revolution, fifteen thousand people were invited to Notre-Dame to celebrate Napoleon's coronation—or perhaps that of his wife, as represented in the immense painting by the master of neoclassicism.

In the service of majesty

On December 2, 1804, the First Consul Napoleon Bonaparte—proclaimed Emperor of the French by the *sénatus-consulte* of May 18 that same year—and his wife, Josephine de Beauharnais, were crowned in Notre-Dame Cathedral in Paris. The ceremony was held in the presence of Pope Pius VII, the diplomatic corps, and the emperor's family. The royal attributes on show (scepter, sword, crown) testified to the sacred nature of the event. Large velvet and silk hangings festooned with fringes, braids, and coats of arms covered the walls of the cathedral and concealed the stigmata of the Revolution. A great painter had to immortalize this scene.
Appointed first painter to the emperor, Jacques Louis David set up his studio in the former church of Cluny and spent the following three years portraying personalities, as well as their garments and accessories, as realistically as possible. The painting depicting the emperor crowning his wife was first shown to the empress and Napoleon in the painter's studio in December 1807, then at the Louvre, and finally at the Salon d'Automne the following year. The challenge consisted in identifying the people represented—a special brochure was even published to this end. The delighted emperor exclaimed: "How great, how beautiful! All the objects have such relief! What truth! This is not a painting; one walks into this picture." Napoleon, who was very pleased, added: "I am

Jacques Louis David
The Coronation of Napoleon,
1806–08,
oil on canvas,
621 × 979 cm

into this Picture

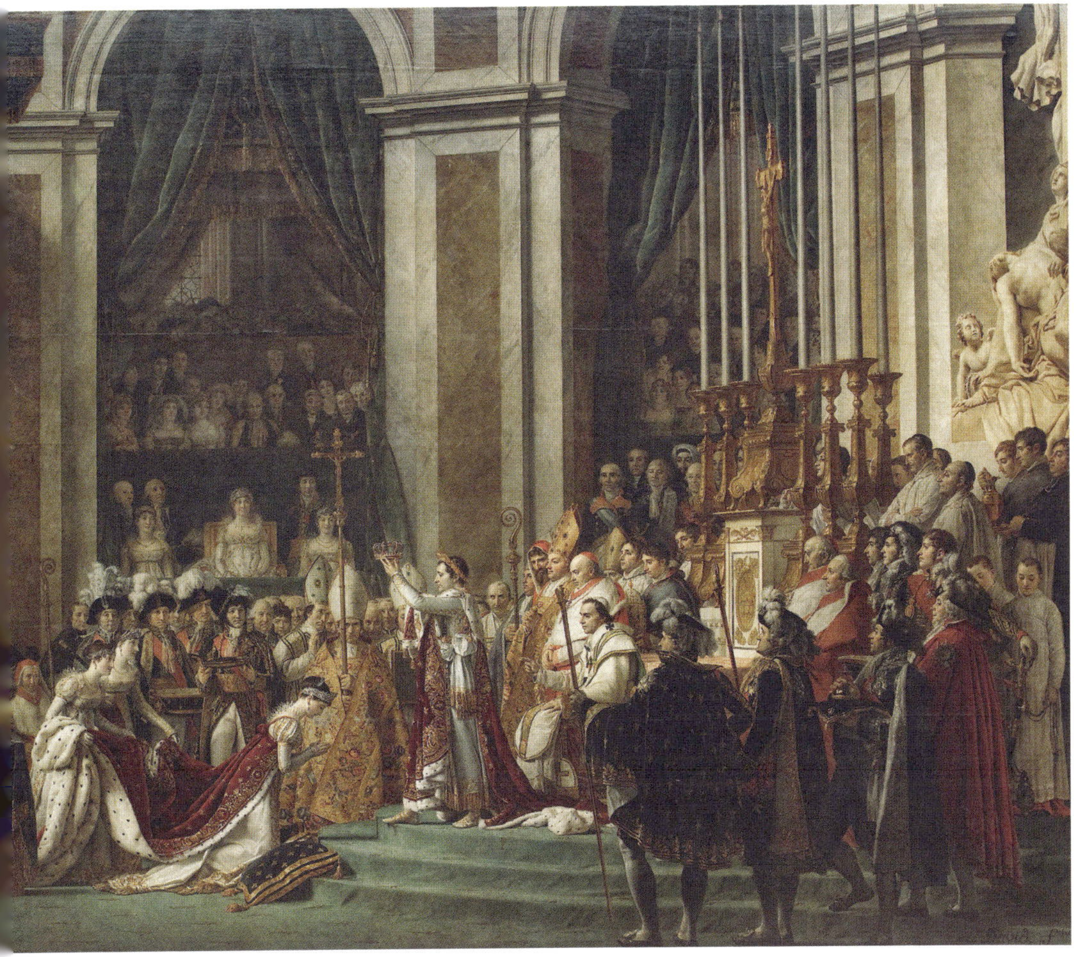

"David is a singular composite of realism and ideal."

Delacroix

grateful to you for conveying for centuries to come the proof of affection that I wanted to give to the woman who shares with me the pains of government."

Name-dropping

Josephine de Beauharnais is kneeling in the center of this startling gallery of 191 figures, receiving the crown from her husband's hands. The great dignitaries of the Empire are pictured in the foreground, on the right: Archchancellor Cambacérès, Archtreasurer Lebrun, Grand Chamberlain Talleyrand, Marshall Marrat, and War Minister Berthier. In the assembly, on the left, Napoleon Bonaparte's family: his sisters Pauline, Elisa, and Caroline, and his brothers Joseph and Louis, as well as Hortense Beauharnais. Pope Pius VII is represented as a simple witness blessing the scene. And David himself is portrayed sitting rather inconspicuously with his family and friends behind a stately Letizia Bonaparte, who did not actually attend the ceremony, in the central box.

Light and shade

Who is the center of attention? The painter, the emperor, his spouse, or his mother?

This immense canvas crowned two decades of artistic glory. The painter's first success dates to 1785, when he sent *The Oath of the Horatii* to the Salon. His monumental painting that favored lines over color and movement was hailed as the manifesto of neoclassicism. Students came from all over Europe to train in his Louvre studios. During the Revolution, he served the nation as a member of the Convention. He voted for the king's death, hosted republican celebrations, and created controversy with a paying exhibition of *The Intervention of the Sabine Women*: although the male nudes shocked, they attracted 50,000 visitors. David produced his famous equestrian portrait (*Napoleon Crossing the Alps*, 1801) and became first painter to the emperor. "I will slip into posterity in the shadow of my hero," said the painter of Napoleon, thus linking his glory with *The Coronation of Napoleon*.

The most famous painting of the Empire was on public display for six months before it vanished out of sight: when Napoleon remarried with Marie-Louise in 1810, the canvas glorifying Josephine became a burden. But David was commissioned a same-size replica from a group of American businessmen. The copy was begun in Paris and completed in 1822 while the artist was exiled in Brussels. It was subsequently sent on a tour across the Channel and the Atlantic. Rehabilitated in 1838 by Louis-Philippe, the original *Coronation of Napoleon* finally found its place in the Louvre, where it became a reference for the many visitors drawn by its neoclassical style and by the figure of the emperor.

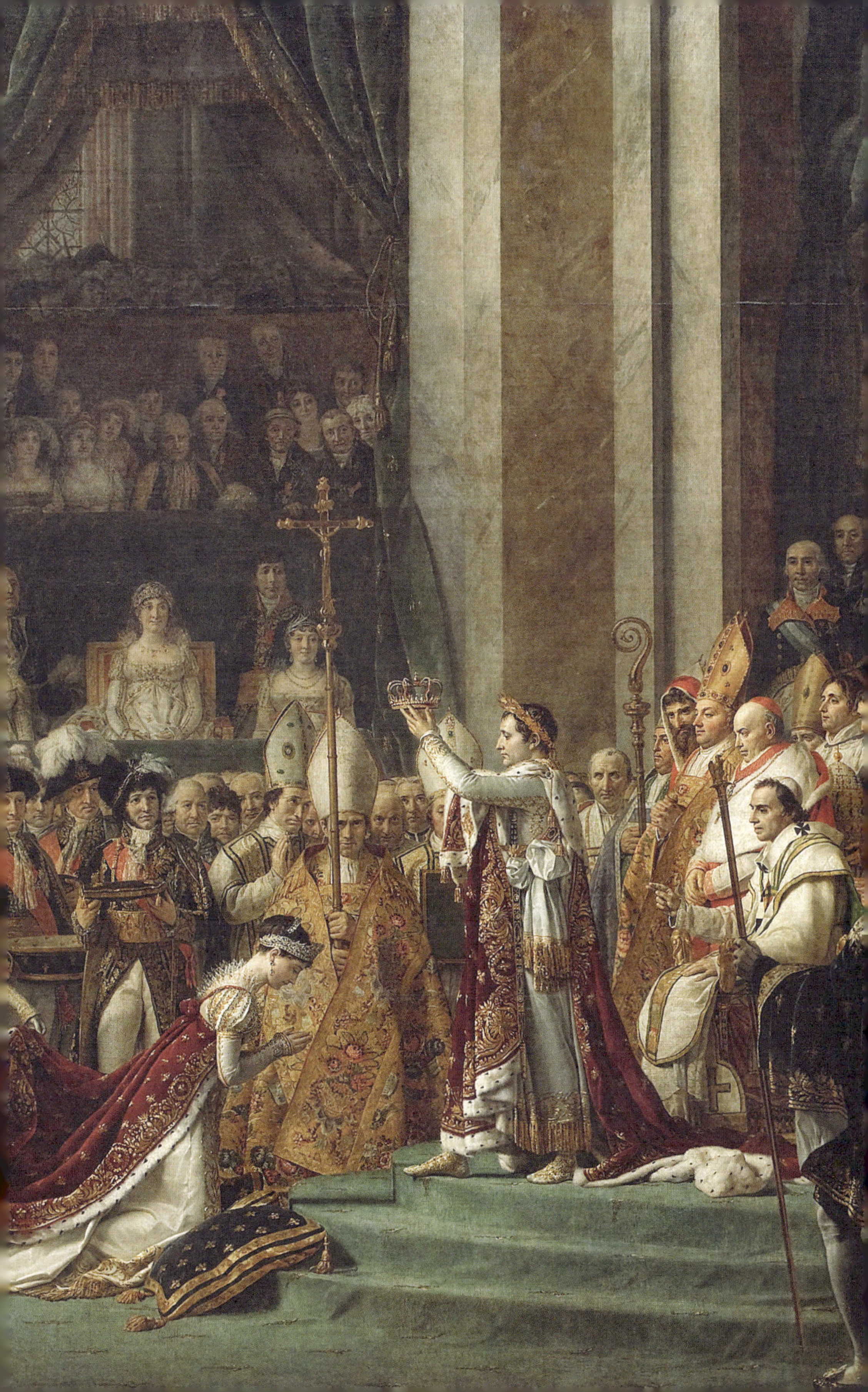

The Grande Odalisque   Ingres

Vertebrale

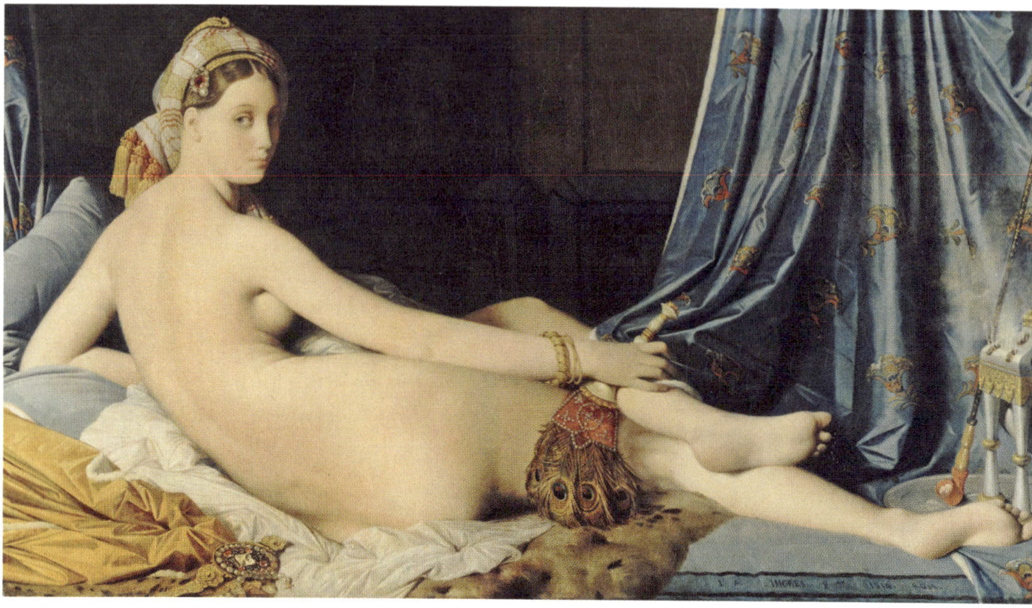

This woman does not exist, yet she is one of the best-known figures in the Louvre. Famous for her erotic presence, the directness of her gaze, and the audacity of her anatomical distortion, *The Grande Odalisque* has become a genre in its own right.

Jean Auguste Dominique Ingres
The Grande Odalisque,
1814,
oil on canvas,
91 × 162 cm

Ordeal

Why would one want to slate such a beautiful back?

Ingres frowned when he saw Géricault's *The Raft of the Medusa*, which caused a sensation at the 1819 Salon (see page 144). He found the painting hideous, no less. Perhaps he was upset by the simultaneous poor reception of his *Odalisque*, deemed a "systematic distortion." The figure's monotonous skin tone and unsightly folds were mocked, as well as the absence of bones, muscles, blood, life, relief, and so on: "The unrealistic proportions are clearly deliberate on the artist's part," critic Charles Paul Landon said. People were trying to find excuses for a promising painter who had won the Prix de Rome a few years earlier, but who had seemingly made a mistake this time: "He thought he was resurrecting a pure and primitive style of painting dating back from antiquity, but he was completely misled by a later and more degenerate execution of that style." Étienne Jean Delécluze, who was as confused as his fellow critics, half-heartedly tried to link the subject to mythology by comparing the elongated figure to a nymph. Everyone felt uneasy. No one understoodo.

The sleeper

A naked woman in a languid pose is looking at you from behind. She is leaning on her left arm and holding her calf with her right hand. The accessories around her evoke a harem. Initially a private commission, the work unsettled visitors at the Salon. The queen of Naples, Caroline Murat (wife of Joachim and sister of Napoleon), who already owned *The Sleeper*, had asked Ingres—who lived in Rome—to produce another nude. But the fall of the Empire in 1814 meant that the young painter could not be paid the agreed price and ended up stuck with his *Grande Odalisque*. The work was eventually sold, not during the Salon but shortly afterwards to Count de Pourtales-Gorgier, chamberlain to the king of Prussia.
By the time *The Grande Odalisque* entered the Louvre in 1899, Ingres had become an acclaimed portraitist and artist. According to Édouard Manet, he was the master of the masters; Edgar Degas owned more than ten of the painter's works; Ingres inspired young painters who advocated drawing and color; and Matisse developed a keen interest in the theme of the odalisque. The series he produced in Nice in the 1920s was both a vibrant tribute and an opportune pretext to "paint nudes" by integrating Islamic decorative art into his compositions; Picasso even created a curvaceous woman with raw, clean lines. *The Grande Odalisque* continued to inspire other twentieth-century artists into producing their own version of it.

Extra vertebrae

"His Odalisque has three vertebrae too many," the critic Auguste Hilarion de Kératry said to Amaury-Duval, one of Ingres' pupils. We now know that the Odalisque has five extra vertebrae in her back instead of three. Doctors and historians published the results of their research in the *Journal of the Royal Society of Medicine* in 2004.

Guerrilla Girl

The Grande Odalisque became a popular reference in many domains. The author's name and the figure's sex slave status were sometimes disregarded. The odalisque's languid attitude was often seen in the harem scenes of movies and series. It was on the cover of books on psychology, personal development, and even design. In advertising, it was the archetype of woman either objectified or magnified. A symbol of artistic quality and refined painting, the nude was represented in school textbooks and stationery without anyone raising an eyebrow. The odalisque thus became a genre in itself, a commonplace, until the day when the activist artists Guerrilla Girls posted a photographic montage of *The Grande Odalisque*'s face covered with a gorilla mask in front of the Metropolitan Museum. Their slogan "*Do Women Have to be Naked to Get into the Met. Museum?*" denounced the fact that many more women have succeeded in entering the museum as naked models than as artists in their own right.

The Raft of the Medusa

Géricault

Adrift

It was a rude shock when Parisians first saw this scene of a shipwreck at the Salon of 1819. The pile of corpses on a canvas some 5 meters high by 7 meters wide made a big impression. Which is still the case today, for that matter. This depiction of disaster, hung in the Salle Mollien next to Géricault's colossal *Wounded Cuirassier* (1814), leaves no beholder unmoved. *The Raft of the Medusa* has become a figurehead of romanticism—and as a political statement that resonates with today's migrant crisis.

Accursed artist?

"Mr. Géricault appears to be mistaken. The goal of painting is to speak to the eyes and soul, not to repulse."
Pierre Alexandre Coupin

The less you know about people, the more you talk about them. This pithy comment could apply to Géricault. Compared to Jacques Louis David before him, or to Ingres and Delacroix after him, little is known about the life of Géricault. His career was brief, his death early. Legend has replaced documentation. In our minds, Géricault was a marginal artist dazzled by the strength of horses and intrigued by contemporary mental illnesses ("monomania"). He was a painter of powerful bodies that were wounded, amputated, or dead. He comes across as a dark genius. Some details of his life might support that legend—in 1812, when he was training under Guérin, he was banned from entering the Louvre after having insulted and hit a student. Upon returning from Rome, he was a young dandy more drawn to human interest stories than academic subjects. *The Raft of the Medusa*, painted when he was twenty-seven, ultimately reinforced that reputation.

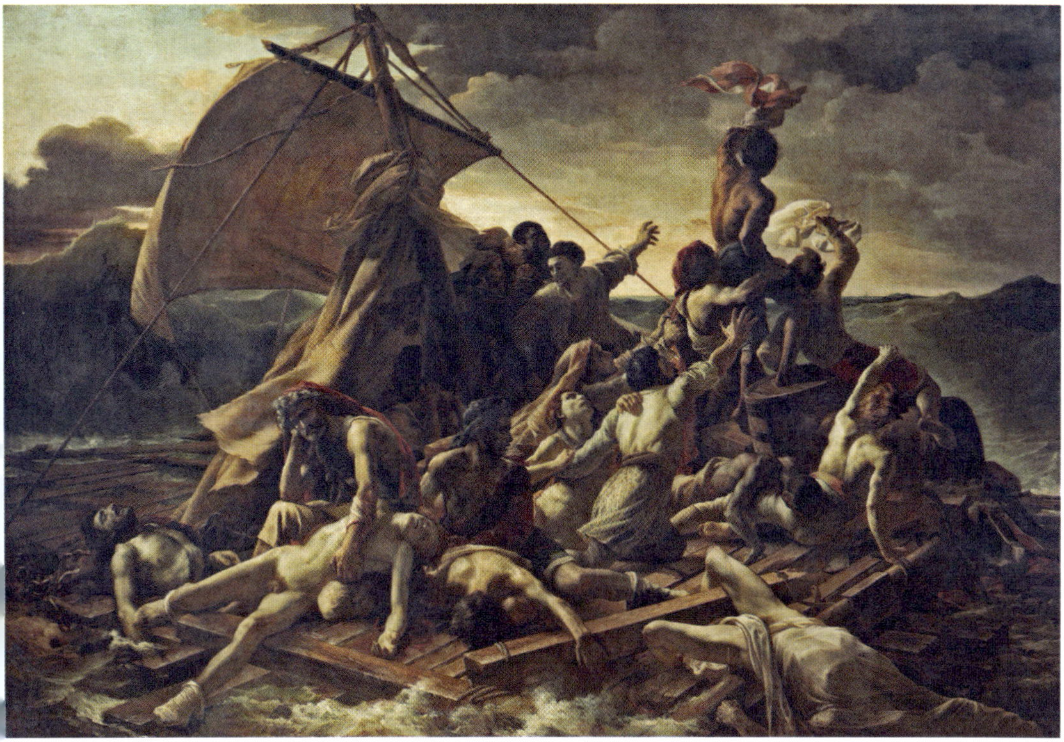

Théodore Géricault
The Raft of the Medusa,
1818–19,
oil on canvas,
491 × 716 cm

The story behind *The Raft*

In 1816 a French royal frigate sank off the coast of what is now Mauritania. The incompetence of the captain (an aristocrat) hastened the shipwreck. One hundred and fifty men crammed onto a raft 20 meters long. The makeshift crew endured mutinies, brawls, drownings, and even acts of cannibalism. After two weeks, only fifteen people were still alive. The survivors saw a ship on the horizon and waved rags to summon help—but the ship sailed on. Géricault decided to paint this moment of dashed hopes. He researched the tragedy and the sensational trial that followed. He met two of the survivors and had them pose. He purchased a large canvas and specially fitted out a studio near the Beaujon hospital, where he studied the faces of dying patients and the flesh of cadavers. It took Géricault a whole year to complete this masterpiece. He built a raft on which to place his models and traveled as far as Le Havre to paint the sky and sea from life. All these efforts at reconstruction, based on an incident that became a national scandal, indicate a concern for historical reality and a modern vision of painting.

Censure and outcry

The director of the Musées Royaux accepted Géricault's submission for the Salon but tried to avoid a polemic. He chose a neutral title (*Scene of a Shipwreck*) and hung the painting very high, making the dark, shiny mass hard to decipher.

On opening night, supporters of neoclassicism, ideal beauty, and antiquity gagged at the sight. They felt it was a painting that someone had "forgotten to paint" and they interpreted this view of disorder as morally degrading. In contrast, other voices defended the commitment of a humanist, liberal artist who managed to suggest how people governed by a reactionary king could backslide. Some thirty press stories thus slid from artistic debate to political clash.

Should art only teach us beauty?

"I won't have this Medusa and these other theater paintings, which show us nothing of men except corpses, which depict only ugliness and hideousness. No, I won't have them! Art should be only beauty, should teach us only beauty."

Jean Auguste Dominique Ingres,
Notes et pensées

In London the following year, the painting was a truly popular and critical success. In the space of a month, twenty thousand visitors went to admire the spirited artwork that boldly depicted a debacle by the French royal navy. Even if political issues have evolved over the years, *The Raft of the Medusa* continues to be employed as an image of the various failings of government. Thus in 2015 the street artist Banksy did a mural in Calais that copied the motif, showing shipwrecked migrants in the foreground as a car ferry in the distance quietly sails toward England.

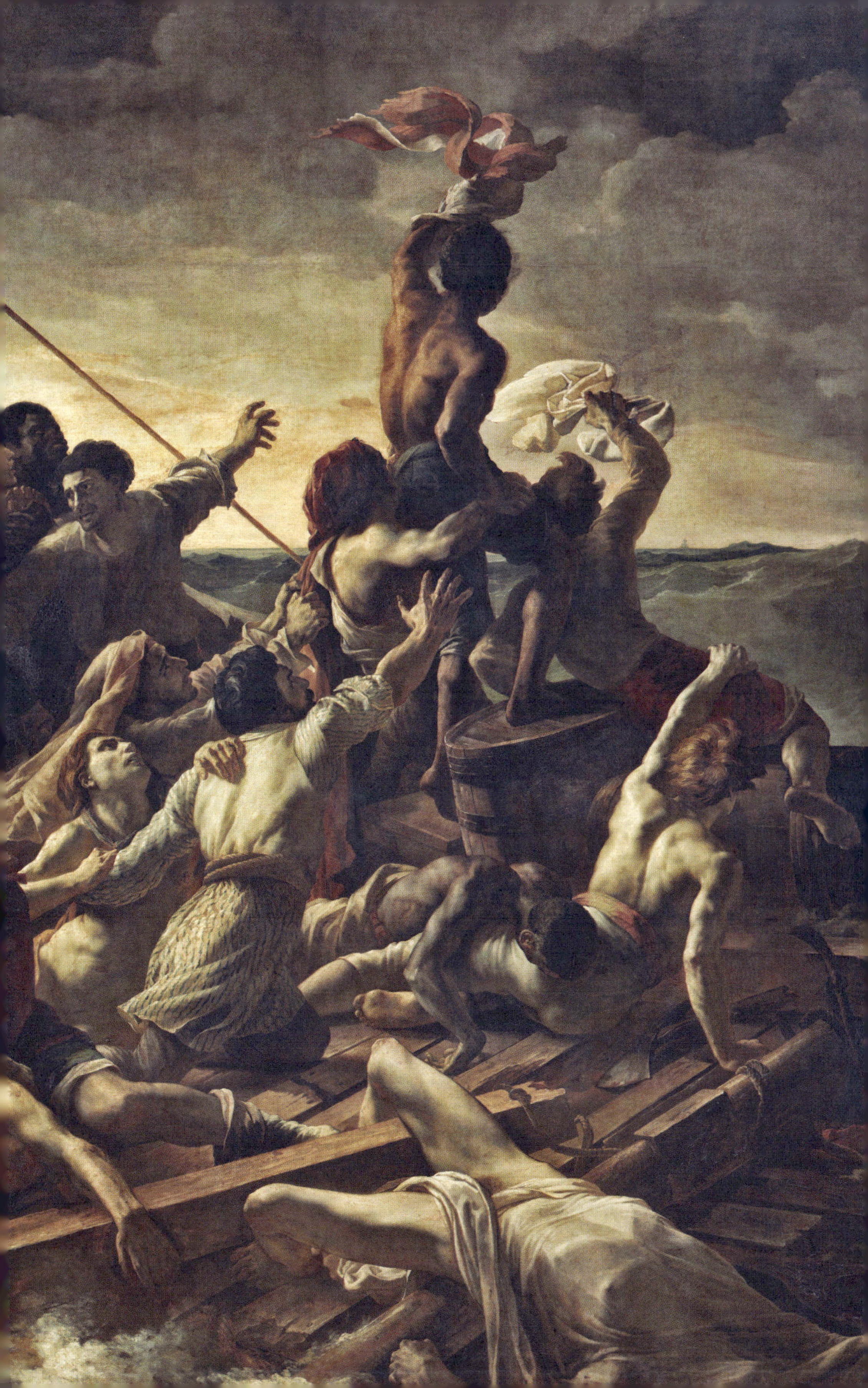

Liberty Leading the People Delacroix

Glorious

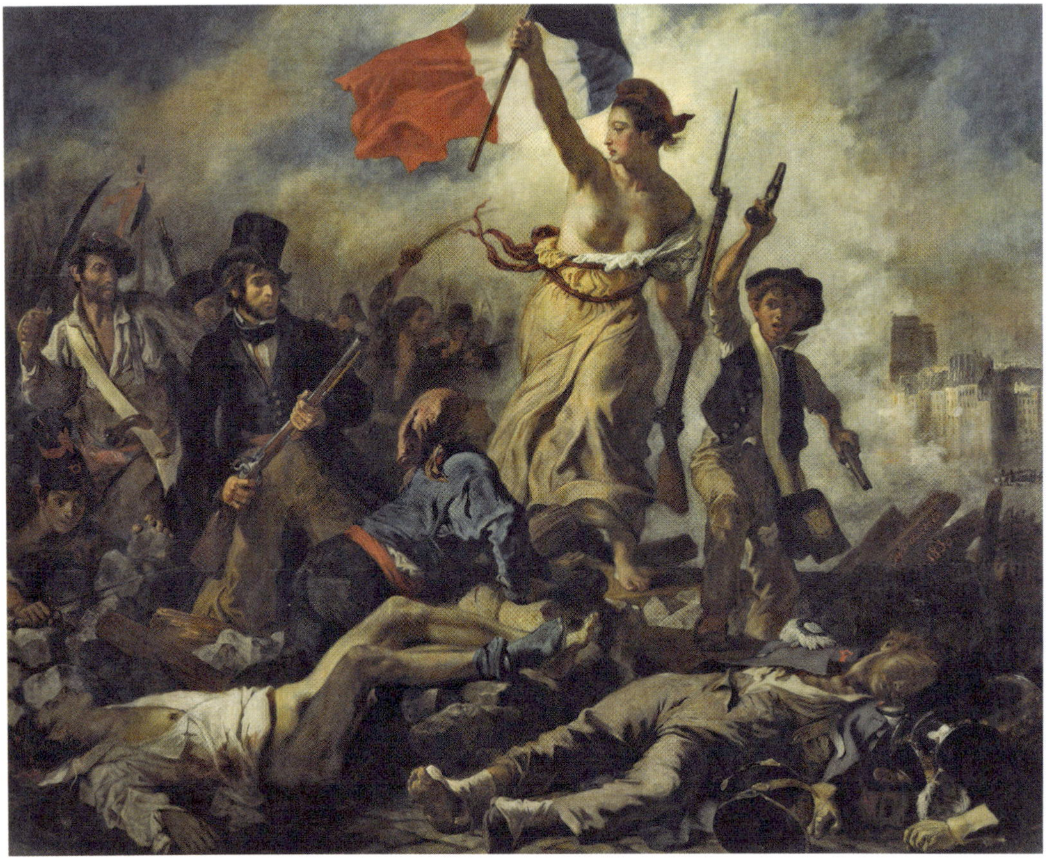

Eugène Delacroix
Liberty Leading the People,
1830,
oil on canvas,
260 × 325

Where does the insurrection come from?

Exhibited at the Salon of 1831, *Liberty Leading the People* was bought by the French government, which soon found it to be a liability and thus prudently withdrew it from sight. Delacroix had produced an allegory so powerful and original that it threatened to become a new call to popular uprising. Even today, Liberty's bare breasts can trigger strong reactions.

Mixed reception

"I've undertaken a modern subject—a barricade—and if I haven't brought victory to the nation, at least I'm painting for it."

Eugène Delacroix

Every Salon was an event at which artists sought to gain wider recognition. A week before the opening, the German poet Heinrich Heine published an article in the magazine *L'Artiste* in which he said he believed Delacroix would exhibit a depiction of a barricade. He never doubted that the painting would be widely noticed. Today we might say Heine was helping to create a buzz. Not far from two tigers and a scene depicting the young Raphael meditating in his studio was *A Barricade: Liberty Leading the People*. It stood out from paintings by other artists that glorified the new regime, known as the July Monarchy. It was striking for its intense colors, bold execution, and revolutionary message. Crowds clustered in front the picture, never quite knowing where they stood. The reception was generally enthusiastic, even if critics did not understand the real meaning of the work. Delacroix's painting depicts one of the "three glorious days" of popular uprising that led to the overthrow of the Bourbon Monarchy—but why show a cabaret heroine flanked by dirty figures? Was the heap of corpses in the foreground a way of denigrating the victory by evoking the numerous victims? Some thirty opinions were published in the press, all revealing the same incomprehension: the composition was magnificent, recalling Géricault's *The Raft of the Medusa* (see page 144) in its pyramidal design, its base strewn with corpses, but people did not know whether the work was a tribute or ironic. So what did the German poet think? Heine liked the female figure's impetuous gestures, even if he thought she was a "bizarre mixture of Phryne [an Athenian courtesan], fishwife, and goddess of liberty."

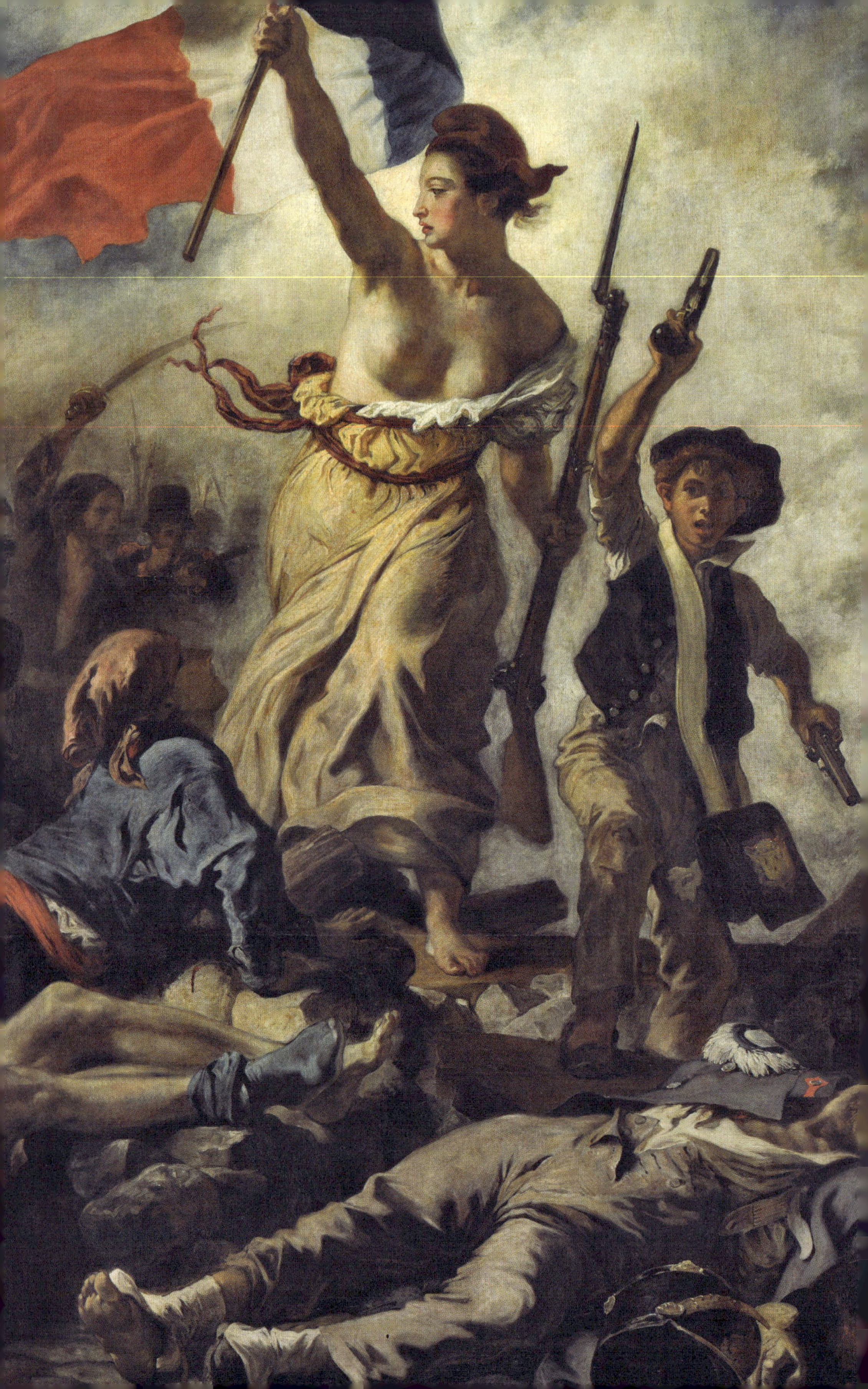

Reunited

Liberty is a daughter of the people. With her Grecian profile, she is neither classical nor realistic. The government bought the painting for 3,000 francs and placed it in storage. In 1855 Napoleon III's permission was required before it was shown in that year's Universal Exposition. At that time, Delacroix was considered a socially aware artist, one who thrilled when the rebels raised the tricolor flag over the towers of Notre Dame. His paintings of the *Death of Sardanapalus* and *Liberty Leading the People* were considered masterpieces of romanticism. In 1831 *Liberty* entered the Musée du Luxembourg, where it was intermittently displayed, then went to the Louvre in 1874. It had become an icon in less than half a century.

Gavroche

The famous Paris street urchin sports the black velvet beret worn by university students as he advances, pistols in hand, urging the rebels to fight. A symbol of rebellious youth, idealism, and just causes, the figure is now associated with Gavroche, the fictional character in Victor Hugo's *Les Misérables*. Indeed, the great French writer based his character on the kid painted by Delacroix, even if the events recounted in the novel took place two years later.

"Beauty is run of the mill—it is so depressing. Painting—or rather the drive to paint—seems a total folly."

Eugène Delacroix

The figure of Liberty, wearing the Phrygian cap, more broadly evokes the French Revolution and the dress of the revolutionary masses. The red, white, and blue flag was henceforth a symbol of the struggle to defend democracy. The work had not only become an emblem, it also inspired Auguste Bartholdi's Statue of Liberty. In the twentieth century it could be seen more or less everywhere, in school textbooks, in theaters, and in the press—it became part of French heritage and symbolized the nation reunited around its core values. It was also appropriated, subverted, and caricatured in art, the press, and advertising. From 1978 to 1995, Liberty adorned the hundred-franc banknote. Since 1982 her face has been used for a series of postage stamps. Nowadays, artists and activists tend to stress the political significance of a personification of the nation on top of a barricade. Whenever they need a powerful image, whenever they want to express the struggle for freedom, free speech, and national unity, the French are apt to turn to this woman with her arm raised and her breasts bare. The Femen flaunt the same attributes.

Dead Loves

Delaroche is not as famous now as he once was. Painted as a tribute to his late wife, *The Young Martyr* addresses the theme of Ophelia's death, so dear to the romantics and Pre-Raphaelites' hearts.

"It may be the saddest and holiest of all my compositions."
Paul Delaroche

Ophelia-ization

The Young Martyr is a favorite among visitors at the Louvre. It calls for contemplation. Sentenced to death for refusing to recant, a Roman woman is thrown hands tied into the Tiber River. The last rays of the setting sun are glistening beyond the riverbanks. In the darkness, two Christians glimpse the dead martyr being carried away by the waters. Her head is cushioned by her mane of blond hair. A hagiographic halo illuminates the young beauty. The scene is reminiscent of *Ophelia* painted by Millais in 1852, and of Shakespeare's Ophelia who loses her mind and commits suicide after Hamlet abandons her. One can also be touched by the way the artist evokes the death of his wife Louise Vernet. Grief is expressed in the painting through the encroaching darkness, and the innocent girl's martyrdom through the simplicity of the composition.

The happy medium

"With wise concessions, cautious boldness, and a form of bourgeois romanticism, he compromised and diverted the great movement led by Victor Hugo and Eugène Delacroix. His flawlessly executed paintings arranged like denouements drew large crowds." In two sentences, Théophile Gautier exposed Delaroche's renown as well as his discredit since his death. Delaroche was an established artist from a well-off family who married fine art professor Horace Vernet's daughter. He was an artist of the "happy medium"—a movement that developed during the July Monarchy. Although his moderate style was

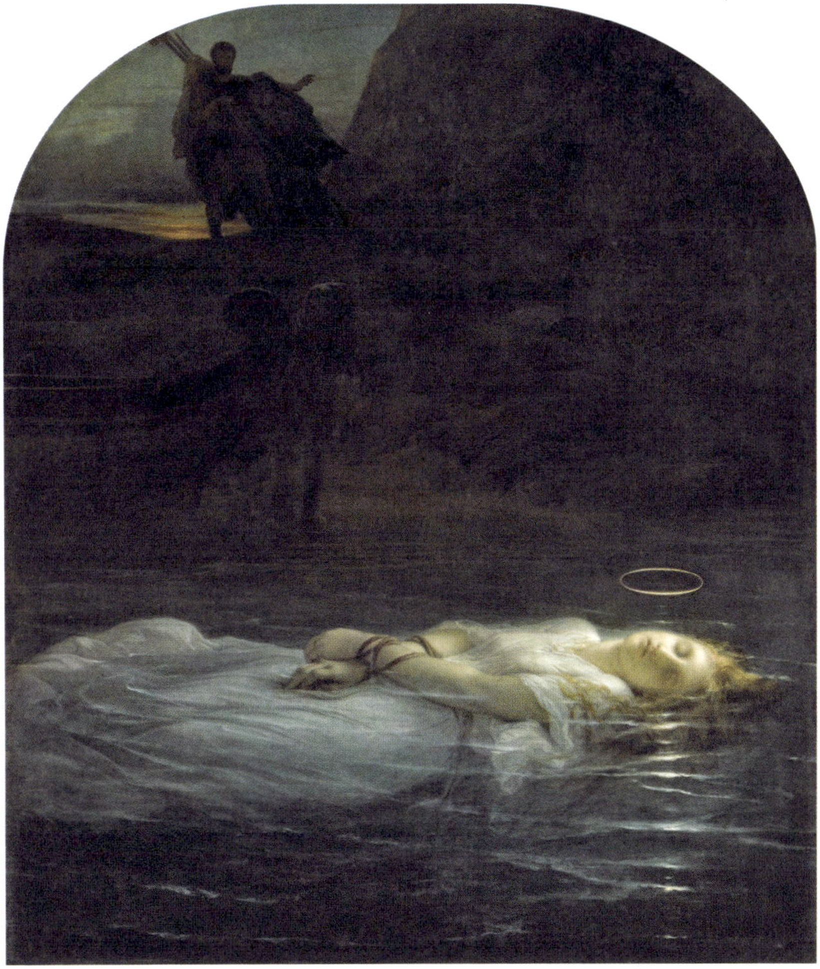

Paul Delaroche
The Young Martyr,
1865,
oil on canvas,
171 × 148 cm

shunned by the romantics and inconsistent with Ingresque neoclassicism, it attracted many visitors. Delaroche was extremely gifted and excelled in the "historical anecdote" genre, such as in *Joan of Arc is Being Interrogated* and *The Execution of Lady Jane Grey*. *The Children of Edward* was his most popular work in the nineteenth century. In a style described as "troubadour," it depicts Edward IV's two sons imprisoned in the Tower of London, huddled against each other on a canopy bed.

Such highly dramatic mise-en-scènes were systematically engraved and widely disseminated. Postcards of *The Young Martyr* sold well, alongside the Winged Victory of Samothrace and the *Mona Lisa*.

Pharaonic

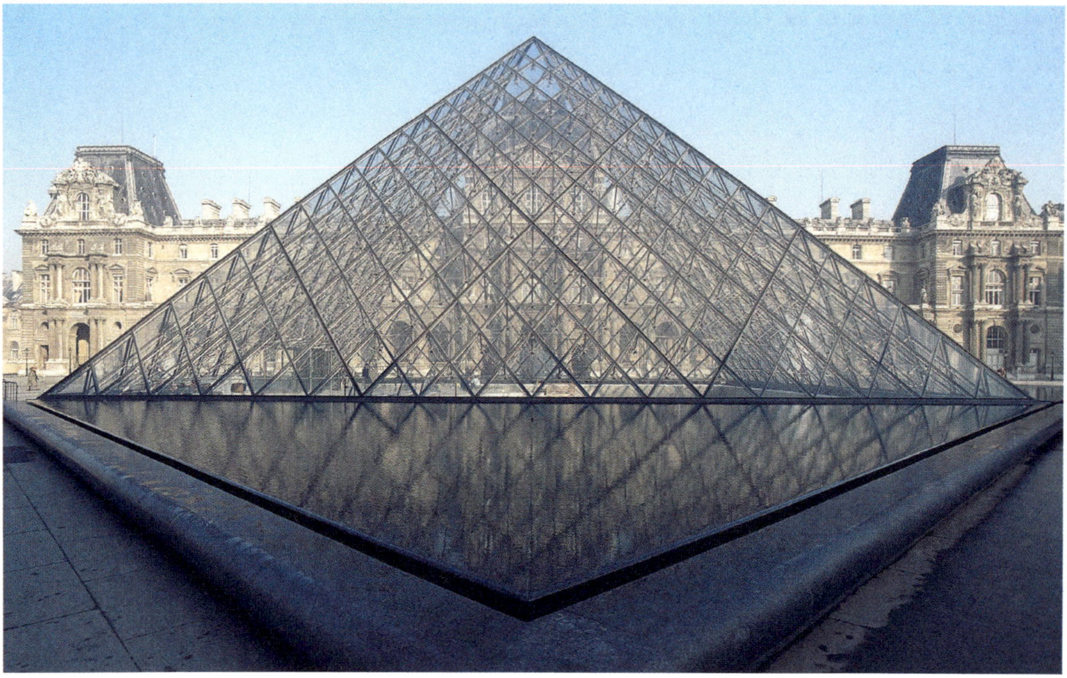

We nearly forgot about it. This work is as renowned today as the paintings in the Salle des États or the sculptures in the Galerie Michel-Ange. The world-famous structure has been photographed from every angle. Tourists flock from everywhere to take selfies with it. We nearly forgot about the Louvre Pyramid.

Ieoh Ming Pei
Louvre Pyramid,
1985–89, 216 cm,
base surface area: 1,000 m2

Prestige

Rising over 21 meters, the Louvre Pyramid consists of 675 glass diamonds encased in a metallic structure. The impressive work was commissioned by President François Mitterrand from the Chinese-American architect Ieoh Ming Pei in 1984 and inaugurated in 1989—the year of the

French Revolution bicentennial. Pei's use of geometry, perspective, landscape, and water mirrors was inspired by André Le Nôtre, Louis XIV's gardener at Les Tuileries and then Versailles. The pyramid's transparency, design, and technological prowess marked a profound shift into modernity. A vast hall connects the museum's different departments. From Egyptian antiquities to nineteenth-century paintings, the pyramid sits atop forty centuries of history. The exhibition space was increased twofold; the medieval enclosure was made visible; an auditorium and a reception area were created. The pyramid is the tip of the iceberg, it symbolizes light, space, accessibility to the public, as well as the museum's new layout and international prestige.

A foreign body?

Under the pyramid, forty centuries of history

It was no walk in the park for the architect. Even before his project was selected, the idea of a transparent pyramid was deemed incongruous by the Commission Supérieure des Monuments Historiques (CSMH), whose members feared that the architectural structure would mar the majesty and harmony of the site. When the project was approved, the press turned the matter into an affair of state. "Poor France!" headlined the daily newspaper *France-Soir*, while *Le Figaro* denounced a "lowest level of architecture." The age-old quarrel between Ancients and Moderns had been revived. People had to take a stand, and those in favor became complicit of a "creeping commodification" to the detriment of culture. Contemporary art does not mix easily with heritage. Some concerns were legitimate; the people were entitled to wonder about a project of such pharaonic scale, but a number of critics used it as a pretext to target the president himself. The project's detractors were against a socialist placing a foreign body in the courtyard of the palace of kings.
The CSMH and the Mairie de Paris asked for a full-scale simulation of the pyramid. In April and May 1985, over two weekends, a 35-meter-per-side pyramidal structure of wire ropes lifted by a crane was shown to thousands of visitors. The event was a success: the shape, the transparency, the angle seemed just right. The time had come to do away with the vast parking lot and wasteland garden. The pyramid had won the battle. It has since celebrated its thirtieth anniversary, and 10 million visitors come from all over the world every year to be reflected in its myriad of diamonds.

PHOTOGRAPHIC CREDITS

Paris, Réunion des musées nationaux-Grand Palais (RMN - GP):
RMN-Grand Palais (musée du Louvre) / Jean-Gilles Berizzi: pp. 59, 64, 67, 114; RMN-Grand Palais (musée du Louvre) / Gérard Blot: pp. 10 (left), 125, 126, 128; RMN-Grand Palais (musée du Louvre) / Gérard Blot / Christian Jean: p. 25; RMN-Grand Palais (musée du Louvre) / Adrien Didierjean: Cover (top), p. 116; RMN-Grand Palais (musée du Louvre) / Hervé Lewandowski: pp. 20, 35, 37, 115; RMN-Grand Palais (musée du Louvre) / Thierry Le Mage: pp. 6–7 (top), 142; RMN-Grand Palais (musée du Louvre) / René-Gabriel Ojéda: pp. 4 (bottom), 6–7 (botton), 9 (right), 24, 71–73, 92, 95, 153; RMN-Grand Palais (musée du Louvre) / Tony Querrec: pp. 8 (top), 19 (bottom), 81, 106, 111, 123; RMN-Grand Palais (musée du Louvre) / Mathieu Rabeau: pp. 112–113; RMN-Grand Palais (musée du Louvre) / Franck Raux: pp. 8 (bottom), 28, 29, 77–79, 88; RMN-Grand Palais (musée du Louvre) / Michel Urtado: Cover (bottom), pp. 4 (top), 9 (left), 10 (right), 12–13 (bottom), 16 (left), 54, 74, 75, 82, 87, 91, 98, 102–103, 105, 108, 145, 147–148, 150; Musée du Louvre, Dist. RMN-Grand Palais / Martine Beck-Coppola: p. 101; Musée du Louvre, Dist. RMN-Grand Palais / Raphaël Chipault: pp. 2 (left), 13 (h), 27, 97, 134, 137; Musée du Louvre, Dist. RMN-Grand Palais / Christian Decamps : pp. 2 (right), 23, 31; Musée du Louvre, Dist. RMN-Grand Palais / Angèle Dequier: pp. 5 (top), 12 (top), 16 (right), 53, 61–62, 69, 119–120, 131, 133, 138–139, 141; Musée du Louvre, Dist. RMN-Grand Palais / Hughes Dubois: pp. 50–51, 56–57; Musée du Louvre, Dist. RMN-Grand Palais / Philippe Fuzeau: pp. 19 (top), 32; Musée du Louvre, Dist. RMN-Grand Palais / Daniel Lebée / Carine Déambrosis: pp. 11 (top), 49; Musée du Louvre, Dist. RMN-Grand Palais / Thierry Ollivier: pp. 5 (bottom), 11 (bottom), 38–39, 41, 43–44, 47

RÉUNION DES MUSÉES NATIONAUX – GRAND PALAIS

Director of publishing
Sophie Laporte

Head of publications
Muriel Rausch

Editorial coordinator
Julien Vandenbroucque
assisted by Clothilde Bollard-Duval

Translators
Susan Brown
Deke Dusinberre (pages 110-17, 122-23 and 144-51)
Chrisoula Petridis (pages 90-07)

Copy editor
Chrisoula Petridis

Picture researcher
Marianne Lemarignier

RMN–GP photo agency researcher
Philippe Couton

Graphic designer
Brice Tourneux

Layout
Hervé Delemotte

Production manager
Hugues Charreyron

MUSÉE DU LOUVRE

Head of outreach and cultural events
Dominique de Font-Réaulx

Assistant director of publications and production
Laurence Castany

Director of publications
Violaine Bouvet-Lanselle
assisted by Colette Confortès

Photoengraving
Fotimprim, Paris, France

Printed in May 2019 by Ingoprint, Barcelona, Spain

Dépôt légal: June 2019

ISBN: 978-2-7118-7414-9
GB 10 7414

COVER, FROM TOP TO BOTTOM

Georges de La Tour, *The Cheat with the Ace of Diamonds*, detail. See p. 116.

Leonardo da Vinci, *Portrait of Lisa Gherardini*, known as *The Gioconda* or *Monna Lisa*, detail. See p. 82.

PAGE 2, FROM LEFT TO RIGHT

Michelangelo Buonarroti, known as Michelangelo, *The Dying Slave*, detail. See p. 97.

The Seated Scribe, detail. See p. 23.

PAGES 4–5, FROM LEFT TO RIGHT AND FROM TOP TO BOTTOM

Giotto di Bondone, *Saint Francis of Assisi Receiving the Stigmata*, detail. See p. 53.

Leonardo da Vinci, *The Virgin and Child with Saint Anne*, detail. See p. 92.

Jan van Eyck, *The Madonna of Chancellor Rolin*, detail. See p. 61.

The Winged Victory of Samothrace, detail. See p. 41.

PAGES 6–7, FROM TOP TO BOTTOM

Jean Auguste Dominique Ingres, *The Grande Odalisque*, detail. See p. 142.

Paul Delaroche, *The Young Martyr*, detail. See p. 153.

PAGES 8–9, FROM TOP TO BOTTOM AND FROM LEFT TO RIGHT

Albrecht Dürer, *Portrait of the Artist Holding a Thistle*, detail. See p. 81.

Raffaello Sanzio da Urbino, known as Raphael, *Madonna and Child with the Young Saint John the Baptist*, known as *La Belle Jardinière*, detail. See p. 88.

Alessandro Filipepi, known as Botticelli, *Venus and the Three Graces Presenting Gifts to a Young Woman*, detail. See p. 74.

Andrea Mantegna, *Saint Sebastian*, detail. See p. 73.

PAGES 10–1, FROM LEFT TO RIGHT AND FROM TOP TO BOTTOM

Hyacinthe Rigaud, *Louis XIV (1638-1715)*, detail. See p. 128.

Eugène Delacroix, *Liberty Leading the People*, detail. See p. 148.

Agasias of Ephesus, son of Dositheus, *The Borghese Gladiator*, detail. See p. 49.

Sleeping Hermaphroditos, detail. See p. 38.

PAGES 12–3, FROM TOP TO BOTTOM AND FROM LEFT TO RIGHT

Jean Honoré Fragonard, *The Lock*, detail. See p. 133.

Théodore Géricault, *The Raft of the Medusa*, detail. See p. 145.

Antonio Canova, *Psyche Revived by Cupid's Kiss*, detail. See p. 134.

PAGE 16, FROM LEFT TO RIGHT

Giuseppe Arcimboldo, *Summer*, detail. See p. 108.

Jean Antoine Watteau, *Pilgrimage to the Isle of Cythera*, also known as *Embarkation to the Isle of Cythera*, detail. See p. 131.

PAGE 19, FROM TOP TO BOTTOM

The Sarcophagus of the Spouses, detail. See p. 32.

Gabrielle d'Estrées and her sister, the Duchess of Villars, detail. See p. 111.